RACIAL
IDENTITY
IN CONTEXT

RACIAL IDENTITY IN CONTEXT

THE LEGACY OF
KENNETH B. CLARK

EDITED BY
GINA PHILOGÈNE

2000-2010
DECADE
of BEHAVIOR

American Psychological Association
Washington, DC

Published by
American Psychological Association
750 First Street, NE
Washington, DC 20002
www.apa.org

To order
APA Order Department
P.O. Box 92984
Washington, DC 20090-2984
Tel: (800) 374-2721; Direct: (202) 336-5510
Fax: (202) 336-5502; TDD/TTY: (202) 336-6123
Online: www.apa.org/books/
E-mail: order@apa.org

In the U.K., Europe, Africa,
and the Middle East,
copies may be ordered from
American Psychological Association
3 Henrietta Street
Covent Garden, London
WC2E 8LU England

Typeset in Century Schoolbook by World Composition Services, Inc., Sterling, VA

Printer: Data Reproductions, Auburn Hills, MI
Cover Designer: Naylor Design, Washington, DC
Technical/Production Editor: Dan Brachtesende

The opinions and statements published are the responsibility of the authors, and such opinions and statements do not necessarily represent the policies of the American Psychological Association.

Library of Congress Cataloging-in-Publication Data

Racial identity in context : the legacy of Kenneth B. Clark / edited by Gina Philogène.
    p. cm. — (Decade of behavior)
  Includes bibliographical references and index.
  ISBN 1-59147-122-2
    1. African Americans—Race identity. 2. African Americans—Psychology. 3. Group identity—United States. 4. African Americans—Civil rights. 5. United States—Race relations. 6. Racism—United States. 7. Clark, Kenneth Bancroft, 1914—-Influence. 8. Social psychology—United States. I. Clark, Kenneth Bancroft, 1914- II. Philogène, Gina. III. Series.

E185.625.R33 2004
305.896'073—dc22   2003027333

British Library Cataloguing-in-Publication Data
A CIP record is available from the British Library.

Printed in the United States of America
First Edition

APA Science Volumes

Attribution and Social Interaction: The Legacy of Edward E. Jones

Best Methods for the Analysis of Change: Recent Advances, Unanswered Questions, Future Directions

Cardiovascular Reactivity to Psychological Stress and Disease

The Challenge in Mathematics and Science Education: Psychology's Response

Changing Employment Relations: Behavioral and Social Perspectives

Children Exposed to Marital Violence: Theory, Research, and Applied Issues

Cognition: Conceptual and Methodological Issues

Cognitive Bases of Musical Communication

Cognitive Dissonance: Progress on a Pivotal Theory in Social Psychology

Conceptualization and Measurement of Organism–Environment Interaction

Converging Operations in the Study of Visual Selective Attention

Creative Thought: An Investigation of Conceptual Structures and Processes

Developmental Psychoacoustics

Diversity in Work Teams: Research Paradigms for a Changing Workplace

Emotion and Culture: Empirical Studies of Mutual Influence

Emotion, Disclosure, and Health

Evolving Explanations of Development: Ecological Approaches to Organism–Environment Systems

Examining Lives in Context: Perspectives on the Ecology of Human Development

Global Prospects for Education: Development, Culture, and Schooling

Hostility, Coping, and Health

Measuring Patient Changes in Mood, Anxiety, and Personality Disorders: Toward a Core Battery

Occasion Setting: Associative Learning and Cognition in Animals

Organ Donation and Transplantation: Psychological and Behavioral Factors

Origins and Development of Schizophrenia: Advances in Experimental Psychopathology

The Perception of Structure

Perspectives on Socially Shared Cognition

Psychological Testing of Hispanics

Psychology of Women's Health: Progress and Challenges in Research and Application

Researching Community Psychology: Issues of Theory and Methods

The Rising Curve: Long-Term Gains in IQ and Related Measures

Sexism and Stereotypes in Modern Society: The Gender Science of Janet Taylor Spence

APA Decade of Behavior Volumes

Contents

Contributors

Ludy T. Benjamin Jr., Department of Psychology, Texas A&M University, College Station

Kendrick T. Brown, Department of Psychology, Macalester College, St. Paul, MN

Frances Cherry, Department of Psychology, Carleton University, Ottawa, Ontario, Canada

Ellen M. Crouse, Department of Psychology, University of Montana, Missoula

Kay Deaux, Graduate Center, City University of New York, New York

Sandra Graham, Department of Education, University of California, Los Angeles

Hillary Haley, Department of Psychology, University of California, Los Angeles

Ferdinand Jones, Department of Psychology, Brown University, Providence, RI

James M. Jones, Department of Psychology, University of Delaware, Newark

Linwood J. Lewis, Department of Psychology, Sarah Lawrence College, Bronxville, NY

Brian Lowery, Graduate School of Business, Stanford University, Stanford, CA

Neil Malamuth, Department of Psychology, University of California, Los Angeles

Fathali M. Moghaddam, Department of Psychology, Georgetown University, Washington, DC

Enrique W. Neblett Jr., Department of Psychology, University of Michigan, Ann Arbor

Thomas F. Pettigrew, Department of Psychology, University of California, Santa Cruz

Gina Philogène, Department of Psychology, Sarah Lawrence College, Bronxville, NY

Barbara Schechter, Department of Psychology, Sarah Lawrence College, Bronxville, NY

Robert M. Sellers, Department of Psychology, University of Michigan, Ann Arbor

J. Nicole Shelton, Department of Psychology, Princeton University, Princeton, NJ

Jim Sidanius, Department of Psychology, University of California, Los Angeles

Claude M. Steele, Department of Psychology, Stanford University, Stanford, CA

Foreword

In early 1988, the American Psychological Association (APA) Science Directorate began its sponsorship of what would become an exceptionally successful activity in support of psychological science—the APA Scientific Conferences program. This program has showcased some of the most important topics in psychological science and has provided a forum for collaboration among many leading figures in the field.

The program has inspired a series of books that have presented cutting-edge work in all areas of psychology. At the turn of the millennium, the series was renamed the Decade of Behavior Series to help advance the goals of this important initiative. The Decade of Behavior is a major interdisciplinary campaign designed to promote the contributions of the behavioral and social sciences to our most important societal challenges in the decade leading up to 2010. Although a key goal has been to inform the public about these scientific contributions, other activities have been designed to encourage and further collaboration among scientists. Hence, the series that was the "APA Science Series" has continued as the "Decade of Behavior Series." This represents one element in APA's efforts to promote the Decade of Behavior initiative as one of its endorsing organizations. For additional information about the Decade of Behavior, please visit http://www.decadeofbehavior.org.

Over the course of the past years, the Science Conference and Decade of Behavior Series has allowed psychological scientists to share and explore cutting-edge findings in psychology. The APA Science Directorate looks forward to continuing this successful program and to sponsoring other conferences and books in the years ahead. This series has been so successful that we have chosen to extend it to include books that, although they do not arise from conferences, report with the same high quality of scholarship on the latest research.

We are pleased that this important contribution to the literature was supported in part by the Decade of Behavior program. Congratulations to the editors and contributors of this volume on their sterling effort.

Steven J. Breckler, PhD　　　Virginia E. Holt
Executive Director for Science　　*Assistant Executive Director for Science*

Acknowledgments

I would like to give a special thanks to Kate Harris and Hilton Clark, the children of Kenneth and Mamie Clark, for supporting my project—both conference and book—and facilitating access to information about their father. My gratitude also extends to President Michele Myers, Dean Barbara Kaplan, and the staff at Sarah Lawrence College. Without their support neither conference nor book would have seen the light of day. My colleagues in the Department of Psychology of Sarah Lawrence College deserve a special mention for their sustained support. I would also like to thank the Science Directorate of the American Psychological Association (APA) for giving me the opportunity to present this work. Two outside referees provided most helpful comments on the first draft and suggestions for revision. Last but not least, I wish to thank Ed Meidenbauer, the APA's development editor on that project, for his patience, good humor, and excellent advice.

RACIAL IDENTITY IN CONTEXT

1

Introduction: Race as a Defining Feature of American Culture

Gina Philogène

The beginning of a new millennium is a good time for reflection, prompting us to assess the state of affairs and our progress with a look back into our past. When reflecting on the evolution of American society, we realize that race has always played a central role in shaping so many of its dimensions—above all politics, the law, and intergroup relations.

The issue of race, a dominant cultural marker guiding people's thinking and actions, tells us a lot about America. The extent to which it continues to define this culture and keeps its citizens from developing a common vision for their society can be seen in many instances. Recent improvements notwithstanding, race-based biases are still manifest everywhere. The country's judicial system, for instance, has condemned a disproportionately large number of Black American males to prison and on death row. Our education system, in which segregation and unequal treatment prevail, remains as a result largely made up of two unequal tiers. In the housing market, access to mortgage financing continues to be subjected to race-based discrimination. The same can be said for access to health care through affordable insurance.

One of the major reasons for the persistence of race as a determining factor of social relations has been the failure of the civil rights movement to prevent a very large number of Black Americans from being arguably worse off today than before. Urban ghettos, never rebuilt after the widespread riots of the 1960s (Watts, Newark, Detroit, etc.), have faced decades of sustained decline and neglect. This situation has left their populations in desperate living conditions. It seems difficult for the country even today to shake its legacy of racism (Bell, 1992) and its "obsession" with race (Terkel, 1992).

Of course, race relations have undergone dramatic changes in recent decades. Analyses of those changes in racial dynamics during the last century allow us to comprehend more clearly how our society has been transformed as a whole. Reflecting the deep embeddedness of race among Americans, the social sciences—and in particular psychology—have spent a lot of time focusing on this issue and its impact on the culture at large.

Early on, mainstream American psychologists, in the tradition of Bache (1895) and Ferguson (1916), lent implicit support to the segregation of the two races on the basis of measurable differences in ability and personality traits. This helped reify the issue of race to the point at which it came to have a concrete existence in social practices and public discourse. However, ever since the contribution of Kenneth and Mamie Clark, whose research contributed to shaping the landmark Supreme Court decision *Brown v. Board of Education* (1954) ending segregation in public schools, American psychology has evolved along a more dialectical path reflecting significant changes in race relations. By making race an issue of ongoing debate within the profession (see, for instance, the debates in the *American Psychologist* in Yee, Fairchild, Weizman, & Wyatt 1993; Yee, Fairchild, Wyatt, & Weizman, 1995), psychologists have gradually moved into a position in which they can provide broader society some guidance in its difficult struggle with the legacy of race.

Even though race is a societal construction, the reality it helps to shape as a collectively elaborated thought construct has an immense impact on individuals as well as groups—the point made precisely by the findings of Kenneth and Mamie Clark's famous "doll study" (Clark & Clark, 1947). Thus the issue is a highly relevant one for psychologists to consider. Efforts to suppress the issue or ignore the category, as may still linger among some European psychology journals whose editorial boards refuse to publish articles using "race" as a historical category with psychological consequences, are misdirected and perhaps even naïve. In a country that has for the most part defined its evolution with this issue at its center, it seems nowadays unthinkable to ignore race. The legacy of racism can only be overcome through objective analysis and dialogue.

This book serves the purpose by acknowledging the contributions made by Black social psychologists to our understanding of American society. It brings together a number of prominent African American psychologists who, in presenting their work, will help us articulate a dialogue on the sensitive and polemical issue of race. While each of the invited participants has made major contributions on the issues of racial identity and racism, their work has yet to be presented together as an important body of thought. This collaboration is designed to clarify what we know about race and to assess its impact on American culture as well as the psychological makeup of its citizens.

The American Dilemma

Ever since its emergence as an independent republic in the late 18th century, the United States of America has defined its mission as a unique experiment in human history founded on constitutionally guaranteed principles of equality for all. Yet that same society then consistently excluded one group among its population, namely Americans of African descent, from full participation. For centuries that group was the only one in this demographically complex multi-ethnic society whose social position was persistently defined in every aspect on the basis of skin color, an exclusively racial category. Whereas other groups also encountered initial barriers to integration as racialized categories (e.g., Jews, Irish, Italians, and later on many other groups from Asia), the dominant Anglo-Saxon population was in each case eventually willing to negotiate their inclusion. This, however, did not apply to Americans of African descent whose involuntary deportation to the New World marked them from the very beginning as truly excluded (Philogène, 2000). As such race has been the determinant factor shaping the experience of that group as well as its relationships with the rest of society.

The United States basically singled out a specific group to become the only one to be defined primarily in racial terms. Such identification was used to justify its permanent exclusion. If an essentially diverse multigroup democracy, such as the United States, commits itself to the systematic exclusion of one group in its midst, then this society should not be surprised to be fundamentally shaped by such a decision. Winant (1994) spoke in this context of *racial hegemony,* a term that applies equally well to an intergroup hierarchy of domination on the basis of skin color as it does to having made race the determinant factor in the evolution of a society.

Race can be characterized as a key cultural marker. It has permeated every facet of American culture—its laws, its language, its political ideologies. It forms the basic context for social exchange within and between groups. This strategic position of race has been recognized by such astute observers of American society as De Tocqueville (1869/1966) and Myrdal (1944). The latter study, which had a profound impact on subsequent leaders of the civil rights movement, addressed the question of Black Americans' integration into mainstream American life. Myrdal concluded that, by being institutionally marginalized solely on the basis of racial categorization, Black Americans were prevented from assimilating and joining the mainstream in their pursuit of the "American Dream."

Obviously the issue of race has evolved and found new symbolic expressions over time. The civil rights movement succeeded in removing the most explicit mechanisms of race-based discrimination and exclusion almost 40 years ago. However, centuries of first slavery and then segregation have left their indelible marks on America. Their painful legacy lives on. Race continues to shape many of the social practices and debates in the United States.

The System of Segregation

For over a century, following the Civil War, intergroup relations between Black and White Americans were defined by the notion of two separate societies in one country. Segregation was organized around the legal paradigm of "separate but equal." Whereas historiography shows segregation to have originally been advocated by moderates and liberals (Cell, 1982), the application of the idea soon degenerated into a new system of exclusion that appeared as the logical extension of slavery based on the idea of humans as property. It was this notion of subhuman–human that persisted after the abolition of slavery in 1865 and manifested itself in legislation as well as social practices of separation and exclusion.

Segregation was, of course, much more than just Black–White separation or the restriction of contact between the groups. It fostered a pervasive social–

psychological condition of American society, one that could be characterized as a state of mind as well as a constructed daily reality. A dynamic structure articulated around the issue of race gave meaning to social life and organized intergroup relations. This institutionalized form of exclusion marked the core of America's history by centralizing the issue of race as a normative and prescriptive component of social life.

Even though the National Association for the Advancement of Colored People (NAACP) under the leadership of Charles Hamilton Houston had already begun its assault on the "separate but equal" doctrine in the 1930s, it was only after World War II that one could see a systematic and widespread attack on segregation. Black soldiers contrasted their experiences to those of other GIs in the United States. Most of them were soldiers who had been sent abroad to fight for American ideals but now found themselves in a system of repression and discrimination not entirely dissimilar to those unjust societies they had helped to defeat overseas. Once they began to question the legitimacy of segregation as a normative system in direct contradiction to America's professed ideals of equality for all, mass mobilization toward change and militancy increased rapidly.

Changing the segregating patterns of intergroup dynamics proved difficult because of deeply entrenched customs and conventions. The federal government played a crucial role in this gradual transformation as it became more responsive to the needs of those segregated. It did so by denouncing the practices of exclusion. From President Roosevelt onward, the role of the federal government acquired growing importance to the point of being perceived as the strongest factor capable of affecting the pace of changing race relations.

During the Kennedy–Johnson years, at the height of the civil rights movement, the U.S. government became a mediator attempting to resolve the collective/social dissonance between American ideals of equality and justice for all and societal reality of inequality, segregation, and racial prejudice. As protector of the common citizen and embodiment of American ideals, the federal government was seen as the only force capable of propelling the divided country toward a resolution of its dissonance. Its laws could impose new societal norms of civil rights and equal status, and thus change the racial dynamics between the two groups.

Any effective alternative to segregation would have to allow for total inclusion of Black Americans into the mainstream of American life. The process began with the Supreme Court decision in May 1954 to outlaw segregation in school. This decision, known as *Brown v. Board of Education,* is acknowledged as one of the most important judicial decisions of the 20th century. It was made under the premise that, apart from being psychologically damaging to Black American children, the doctrine "separate but equal" also perpetuated ethnic prejudice and racial intolerance. The unanimous ruling of the justices was influenced by the work of social psychologists Mamie and Kenneth Clark and motivated by an optimistic climate in the aftermath of desegregation in the military. It acted on the belief that increased contact between members of two groups would translate into overall improvements in intergroup attitudes and relations.

The Civil Rights Movement

The civil rights movement of the 1960s, supported by a broad segment of American society, sought to transform social norms and values pertaining to race. To do this, and in the process break long-standing norms of exclusion, it had to address the overloaded issue of race directly. Until then, Black Americans had been excluded from full citizenship merely on the basis of their race. In its efforts to transform that two-tiered social system, the movement created new racial "subjects." It redefined the meaning of racial identity, and consequently of race itself, in American society (Omi & Winant, 1986).

The civil rights movement was fueled by a socially shared sense of injustice that motivated the cohesiveness of the Black American community. Because the entire group was discriminated against, its leaders could use this shared experience of marginalization to mobilize mass support for the objective of categorically overthrowing racial oppression. This mobilization resulted in an explicit and large-scale collective effort by the group to achieve greater inclusion and to fight racism. Black Americans had for the first time leaders who articulated goals specifically in their collective interest as a group (King, 1964).

The earlier phase of the movement, from the Montgomery bus boycott of 1955–1956 to Martin Luther King's "I Have a Dream" speech crowning the March on Washington in the summer of 1963, was propelled by an optimistic belief in the possibility of full integration. But by the end of 1963 a sense of disillusion had settled in. The new mood had built for some time below the surface in response to slow progress concerning school desegregation, continued economic discrimination, and stiff resistance in Congress to civil rights legislation. Now the threat of a violent backlash convinced activists that they needed greater cohesion within the movement to succeed. They decided to push beyond just emphasizing the need for changing racial attitudes among Whites (Carmichael & Hamilton, 1967). The movement's leaders began to focus increasingly on self-conception and self-determination among Blacks.

The civil rights movement ended abruptly. By 1970 the country's attention had shifted to the Vietnam War and the rapidly growing antiwar movement. The struggle for racial equality, which had so dominated the preceding decade, left a mixed legacy. On the positive side were major legislative achievements (e.g., Civil Rights Act of 1964, Voting Rights Act of 1965) that made it easier for many Black Americans to enter the mainstream of American society. Paving the way for political participation and opening access to professional occupations, these laws helped create a sizable Black middle class. Black Americans, albeit still in very small numbers, have been able in recent years to enter high-visibility positions at the center of those institutions controlling this complex and diverse society—law, politics, academe, the media, and arts. Their presence has already made a profound impact by beginning to adjust social relations to the multiethnic and multicultural reality of America.

Such important progress notwithstanding, the civil rights movement did not succeed in ending racial discrimination. Race remained a paramount issue, and the country continued to define itself on the basis of race. As late as the mid-1990s issues of national concern came to be defined through the prism of race and to shape public opinion accordingly. The highly charged issues of welfare and crime served as code words for the still-problematic state of race relations. Successive scandals involving Clarence Thomas, Rodney King, and O.J. Simpson profoundly reshaped the national debate on such contentious issues as sexual harassment, community relations, and domestic violence. That race-filtered context tended to polarize public opinion, with Black and White Americans looking at the same issue from very different angles.

But the 1990s were also a decade of remarkable progress. An economic boom helped reduce poverty and spur a revival of the inner cities. Welfare reform and a sustained decline of crime lessened the intensity of America's most racially charged domestic issues. While incidences of police brutality in the metropolitan centers of the North and burnings of Black churches in the South still reminded us of the persistence of racism, public reaction to these events expressed a desire to move beyond. The improving climate of intergroup relations was also fostered by the Clinton Administration's steps toward racial healing and integration. The events of 9/11 have spurred a renewed sense of national unity around a common denominator, a change which allows us to revisit the issue of race in a climate conducive to lasting progress on that particular front. The book in hand is framed within that context, projecting forward the positive role of psychology in our comprehension of race as societal construct first demonstrated by the history-making work of Kenneth and Mamie Clark half a century ago.

Structure of the Book

Black scholars in psychology have had a lot to say on the subject of race. They study the phenomenon with the objectivity of the scientific approach while at the same time being deeply and subjectively affected by it as victims. It is in the synthesis of these two perspectives that Black psychologists add their critical contribution and unique voice to our difficult struggle with equality and integration. Rare, however, are the occasions in which these scholars have had the opportunity to present their work together and at the same time connect with non-Black social scientists in search of common ground. Yet precisely such an exercise is quintessential if we are to step back and assess the "state of the art" on this topic in our discipline.

The book provides in that context an excellent occasion to honor the work of Kenneth Clark, whose contributions have fundamentally changed America. He was the first African American to receive tenure at the City College of New York and to be a member of the New York State Board of Regents. Together with his wife Mamie, Professor Clark gained national reputation as the founder and director of Harlem's Northside Center for Child Development, which for the last half century has provided an array of social services to minority children in Upper Manhattan. Best known for his writings on the effects of school segregation on students, his books include *Prejudice and Your Child* (1955), *Dark Ghetto* (1965), and *A Possible Reality* (1972). The "doll studies" by Professor Clark and his wife Mamie (Clark & Clark, 1939, 1940, 1947, 1950) demonstrating the devastating impact of segregation on the Black child, the White child, and American society as a whole laid the ground for the Supreme Court's landmark 1954 decision *Brown v. Board of Education.*

The first part of the book, introduced by Gina Philogène, is accordingly dedicated to the life and work of Kenneth Clark. In chapter 2, Frances Cherry, a historian of psychology, brings us back to the early career of Professor Clark as a social psychologist when he began to pursue a research agenda inscribed in the action-research tradition of Kurt Lewin. In chapter 3, Thomas Pettigrew, a leading scholar on the psychological manifestations of racism, assesses the broad range of Professor Clark's research agenda and its relevance to societal changes that continue to validate that body of work as path-breaking.

The second part of the book, introduced by Linwood Lewis, focuses on the creation of an identity as testimony to the integration of an initially excluded group, Americans of African descent, into a vitally important component of American culture. From the dual consciousness of DuBois (1903/1965) to the dialectical resolution of this dichotomy with the emergence of an African American identity, the process of identification has always been the basis for that group's long struggle into the American mainstream. Identifying themselves both as American and as members of a culturally distinct group, Americans of African descent have given themselves a positive outlook and resilience in the face of continued stereotyping and discrimination. Any analysis of this history reveals also a lot about American society, specifically its ability to reclaim this group and so make a virtue out of a necessity. The Clarks's studies of identity formation in Negro children cited above, which laid the theoretical foundation for the Supreme Court's reversal of school segregation in 1954, illustrate in almost chilling fashion how such group identity is formed in a broader social context. The contributors presented here continue this tradition inasmuch as their varied contributions to social psychology all focus on analyzing how identity and the process of identification are rooted in their societal context of emergence.

The concept of stereotype vulnerability, discussed by Claude Steele in chapter 4, provides us with a highly original analysis of the psychological effects associated with exposure to continuous prejudice. Stereotypes, after all, are expressions of shared beliefs about the characteristics of members of specific social groups and at the same time one of the most blatant manifestations of the ills of racism. Bridging both personality and social psychology, Enrique Neblett, Nicole Shelton, and Robert Sellers (chap. 5) examine how attitudes and behavior among Black Americans are shaped by the interaction between identity formation in individuals and their social environment. Gina Philogène (chap. 6) concludes this section by examining the emergence of a new denomination, African American, as the vehicle for a new group identity among Americans of African descent in contradistinction to Black.

The third part of the book, with an introduction by Ferdinand Jones, focuses on identity transformation through the creative input of people trying to reassert control of their lives in the face of enduring projections of negative images. This focus provides the context for a discussion of race, racism, and intergroup dynamics in the United States. It is quite rare to have an academic discussion of these issues from the target-of-discrimination perspective, with all the participants focusing on the profound dissonance in the culture at large surrounding the issue of race. That dilemma has played itself out since the very beginnings of the American experiment, continuously forcing this society to rethink and remake itself. We have gone through slavery, a civil war, segregation, and the civil rights movement to end up now with a national debate about multiculturalism as the defining vision of America in the new century. Yet at the same time issues of racism continue to explode, illustrating the deeply embedded legacy of a society polarized by race.

Kendrick Brown analyzes the physical, emotional, mental, and economic health of Black Americans in chapter 7. He shares his findings and their implications for the psychological condition of African Americans as a group while also pointing to differences between important subgroups within the population (e.g., Caribbean Americans). In chapter 8, Sandra Graham, who has looked at the social psychology of education, focuses on the applications of attribution theory to student motivation and peer-directed aggression among at-risk youths in the Black community. Jim Sidanius, a political psychologist with a special emphasis on theories of intergroup conflict in hierarchical social systems, presents his social dominance perspective to analyze oppression in chapter 9 (with coauthors Hillary Haley, Brian Lowery, and Neil Malamuth). Focusing on the pervasive influence of racism in the United States, James Jones analyzes the use of race as a variable in social psychological research and the implications of that research for the development and structure of Black personality (chap. 10).

These chapters bring a unique voice to psychological theories dealing with race-based identity and racism that reflects current trends in the discipline and lends itself therefore to dialogue with non-Black psychologists. Moreover, the issue of race affects all Americans and thus requires reciprocal engagement by all groups if we are to realize our common destiny as one society. This society is currently transforming itself into a multicultural entity within which the age-old dichotomy of a Black–White polarization gets mitigated and redefined.

The section introduced by Barbara Schecter focuses precisely on these questions. It consists essentially of non-Black social psychologists who present their own perspective on the issues to define a common ground. By highlighting how their own work moves us beyond bipolar division to a multifaceted context, these participants demonstrate the importance of dialogue within the social sciences as a vehicle for progress. Pushing further the decentralization of a Black–White dichotomy in the emergence of a multicultural America, Kay Deaux analyzes the legislative history and patterns of Black immigration in chapter 11 to illustrate the continuing interplay between race and immigration and to understand the social construction of race as well as the imagery associated with the melting pot. This review provides a fertile ground for understanding future constructions of color in the United States. The chapter by Fathali Moghaddam (chap. 12) explores the fluidity of racial identity and links it to a discussion of citizenship as it relates to the ongoing struggle for equality in opportunities. He brings forth the future challenge created by the context of third-order change in which equal treatment is supported in both formal law and the informal normative system.

The issue of race, a dominant cultural marker guiding people's thinking and actions, tells us a lot about America. Analysis of the dramatic changes in racial dynamics during the last century allows us to comprehend more clearly how our society has been transformed. Reflecting the deep embedding of this issue in people, psychology has spent a lot of time focusing on race and its impact on culture. Black scholars in psychology have had a lot to say on the subject of race. They study the phenomenon with the objectivity of the scientific approach while at the same time being deeply and subjectively affected by it as victims. It is in the synthesis of these two perspectives that Black psychologists add their critical contribution and unique voice in our difficult struggle with equality and integration. The purpose of this book is to bring together a number of prominent psychologists who, in presenting their work on this issue, will help us articulate a dialogue on the sensitive and polemical issue of race. In that context the volume provides a much-needed occasion to honor the work of Kenneth Clark, whose contributions have fundamentally changed America.

References

Bache, R. M. (1895). Reaction time with reference to race. *Psychological Review, 2,* 475–486.

Bell, D. (1992). *Faces at the bottom of the well: The permanence of racism.* New York: Basic Books.

Brown v. Board of Education, 347 U.S. 483 (1954).

Carmichael, S., & Hamilton, C. W. (1967). *Black power: The politics of liberation in America.* New York: Random House.

Cell, J. W. (1982). *The highest stage of White supremacy.* Cambridge, England: Cambridge University Press.

Clark, K. B. (1955). *Prejudice and your child.* Boston: Beacon Press.

Clark, K. B. (1965). *Dark ghetto: Dilemmas of social power.* New York: Harper Torchbooks.

Clark, K. B. (1972). *A possible reality.* New York: Emerson Hall.

Clark, K. B., & Clark, M. P. (1939). The development of consciousness of self and the emergence of racial identification in Negro pre-school children. *Journal of Social Psychology, 10,* 591–599.

Clark, K. B., & Clark, M. P. (1940). Skin color as a factor in racial identification of Negro pre-school children. *Journal of Social Psychology, 11,* 159–169.

Clark, K. B., & Clark, M. P. (1947). Racial identification and preferences in Negro children. *Personality and Social Psychology Bulletin, 5,* 420–437.

Clark, K. B., & Clark, M. P. (1950). Emotional factors in racial identification and preference in Negro children. *Journal of Negro Education, 19,* 341–350.

De Tocqueville, A. (1966). *Democracy in America.* New York: HarperCollins. (Original work published 1869)

DuBois, W. E. B. (1965). *The souls of Black folk.* Chicago: A.C. McClurg. (Original work published 1903)

Ferguson, G. O. (1916). *Psychology of the Negro.* New York: Science Press.

King, M. L., Jr. (1964). *Why we can't wait.* New York: Signet Books.

Myrdal, G. (1944). *An American dilemma.* New York: HarperCollins.

Omi, M., & Winant, H. (1986). *Racial formation in the United States: From the 1960s to the 1980s.* New York: Routledge.

Philogène, G. (2000). Blacks as "serviceable other." *Journal of Community and Applied Social Psychology, 10,* 391–401.

Terkel, S. (1992). *Race: How Blacks and Whites think and feel about the American obsession.* New York: New Press.

Winant, H. (1994). *Racial conditions: Politics, theory, comparisons.* Minneapolis: University of Minnesota Press.

Yee, A. H., Fairchild, H. H., Weizman, F., & Wyatt, G. E. (1993). Addressing psychology's problem with race. *American Psychologist, 48,* 1132–1140.

Yee, A. H., Fairchild, H. H., Wyatt, G. E., & Weizman, F. (1995). Readdressing psychology's problem with race. *American Psychologist, 50,* 46–47.

Part I

The Impact of Kenneth B. Clark: Then and Now

Introduction:

Visions of Democracy and Equality

Gina Philogène

Professor Kenneth Clark is one of America's towering figures in the social sciences. He began his rise to prominence in 1946 when, in the best Lewinian tradition of action research, he and his wife Mamie Clark founded the legendary Northside Child Development Center in Harlem. His work at the center led him to become the National Association for the Advancement of Colored People's (NAACP) psychological expert, a role which allowed him to argue convincingly that segregation was harmful to the self-image of people of African descent. His research was cited by the Supreme Court in justification of its landmark decision *Brown v. Board of Education* (1954) to desegregate American public schools.

During the 1960s Professor Clark became engaged in community activism in Harlem. As the founder and principal figure in the Harlem Youth Opportunities Unlimited—Associated Community Teams (HARYOU–ACT) program (an outgrowth of Northside) and the Metropolitan Applied Research Center, his advocacy won the admiration of President Lyndon Johnson, who quoted him as the model for the "war on poverty." This placed Clark at the center of the American discourse on race.

Professor Clark was the first person of African descent to be awarded a PhD in psychology from Columbia University, to receive a permanent professorship at the City College of New York (1942–1975), to be a member of the New York State Board of Regents (1966–1986), and to serve as president of the American Psychological Association (1970–1971). In addition, he is the recipient of numerous honorary degrees, notably winner of the NAACP's Spingard Medal (in 1961) and of the Kurt Lewin Memorial Award by the Society for Psychological Study of Social Issues.

His books include *Prejudice and Your Child* (1955), *Dark Ghetto* (1965), *A Possible Reality* (1972), *Pathos of Power* (1974), and *The Negro American* (coedited with Talcott Parsons in 1966).

That Kenneth Clark has been the first and only Black president of the American Psychological Association is testimony to progress as well as the slowness of its pace. Much work remains to be done, as Clark has himself stated repeatedly in recent years. This man has had the unique opportunity to shape a decisive turning point in American history, an honor justified by his wise vision of democracy and equality for all. But the page he helped open for us all remains to be written.

2

Kenneth B. Clark and Social Psychology's Other History

Frances Cherry

Kenneth B. Clark figures prominently in any discussion of race and identity in the 20th century, and his early career challenges us to understand the place of social identity research in the development of American social psychology. Phillips (2000) argued for understanding Kenneth Clark as "a model Afrocentric psychologist-activist" (p. 164), and while the scope of my analysis is more limited temporally, it is consistent with Phillips's attempts to draw connections among race, identity, and investigative practice.

In the course of Kenneth Clark's career, he was an action researcher in Harlem, a professor at City College of New York, an advocate for integrated education throughout America's school system, and a public intellectual much in demand beyond the local and national levels (Keppel, 1995). In these ever enlarging circles of influence, it is perhaps somewhat artificial to narrow a life as large and nationally prominent as that of Kenneth Clark to his practice of social psychology. However, much is to be regained in our understanding of the diverse origins of social psychology by locating Clark's career in the context of the tremendous growth in psychological social psychology during and after World War II (Capshew, 1995).

Clark was part of a new generation of social psychologists who had participated in research during World War II and who were ready to turn their

My research draws on the papers of Kenneth B. Clark at the Library of Congress, City College of New York, the New York Public Library's Schomburg Center for Research in Black Culture, as well as a set of seven interviews with Kenneth Clark, housed at the Columbia University Oral History Collection. I thank Stephen Berger and John Jackson Jr. for their insightful comments on an earlier version of this chapter. On several occasions, I visited the places in New York City familiar to Kenneth and Mamie Clark, to get a sense of where they grounded their working lives. I am particularly indebted to Donna Lewis, owner of Home Sweet Harlem, on W. 135th Street, who graciously allowed me to linger over great food and conversation while en route. Some of my sense of Kenneth Clark's social psychology is grounded in the social geography of Central Harlem, City College of New York, and Northside Center's various locations. I am also grateful to Minniejean Brown Trickey (see www.journeytolittlerock.com), one of the group of students (the Little Rock Nine) who integrated all-White Central High School, for her reminiscences of living with the Clark family in the late 1950s (see www.journeytolittlerock.com).

energies from international to domestic injustice. During the war years, he had contributed a chapter on the war-time morale of African Americans to *Civilian Morale,* the second yearbook sponsored by the Society for the Psychological Study of Social Issues (Clark, 1942), and he had worked on Myrdal's (1944) project on race in America. The watchwords of the immediate postwar period among many social psychologists were "social responsibility" for creating a new world order of "enduring peace" as well as the domestic pursuit of "social health," defined as groups living in harmony rather than tension, with tolerance rather than intolerance. Kenneth Clark's approach to research in the service of reaching these goals was consistent with mid-century optimism concerning the role that social psychologists could play in social health and responsibility (Chisholm, 1949; Clark, 1948).

While there has been tremendous emphasis placed on the importance of Kenneth Clark's contribution to the *Brown v. Board of Education* Supreme Court decision, there has been little discussion of the model of social psychological investigative practice within which Clark was operating. I would argue that Clark's readiness to take on *Brown* was an outgrowth of his commitment to an action-oriented social psychology that had been developing in his work throughout the 1940s.

Social Psychology After World War II

The present analysis addresses several aspects of Clark's developing social psychological practice in the period of "liberal orthodoxy" (W. A. Jackson, 1990) between 1945 and 1965. It is during this time period that psychological social psychology was transformed into a largely experimental and laboratory-based investigative practice. While social psychologists began to remove themselves from real communities and move into the laboratory where their approach to research became more narrowly defined, Kenneth Clark, among others with whom he collaborated, remained steadfastly committed to the development of an action-oriented social psychology within the context of particular ethno-cultural communities (Cherry & Borshuk, 1998).

In the post–World War II period, psychological social psychology, as it increasingly parted ways with sociological social psychology, also parted company with the study of real-life groups. As a specific style of experimentation took hold in university laboratories, the particular social identities—race, gender, and class, among others—of psychology's subjects ceased to be of interest. Danziger (2000) captured the "methodological regime" that came to dominate psychological social psychology:

> Experiments were conceptualized in terms of the demonstration of functional relationships between specific stimulus elements, now known as independent variables and specific response elements, known as dependent variables. . . . Complexity would be represented by the multiplication of variables and their essentially additive interaction. (p. 342)

The 1960s further emphasized statistical analysis, and as Danziger (2000) concluded, "The most profound effect of the new methodological regime on social psychological conceptions of the social occurred as actual social groups were gradually replaced by hypothetical groups that had a purely statistical reality" (p. 344). Statistically constituted groups of college-age students replaced socially constituted groups bearing real social identities and living in real communities.

As will be seen, the apparent neutrality of the laboratory—the way in which it masked the social identities of both experimenters and participants alike—at times appealed to Kenneth Clark but was never chosen. In fact, Clark's self-acknowledged dissonance as one of the first Black faculty at a predominantly White university in the 1940s and 1950s made clear the linkages between race and investigative practice:

> If I were not black, I think I would have been the typical objective, detached, withdrawn academician, building my prestige up on the degree of remoteness from the real world. It was always in the back of my mind, you know—Kenneth Clark, the burden, the particular burden of being black, for you, is that you really can't afford the oasis which you see so many of our colleagues enjoying. And I envied everybody. I wanted it, and couldn't do it. (Clark, 1976)

For Clark, a viable social psychology was one that attended to the differential power relations between real social groups, and one finds him involved in an array of activist projects that were under way from the 1940s through to the mid-1960s, as the civil rights movement gained momentum. Clark paid particular attention to defining the difficult role of the researcher in powerless communities in a way that is resonant with contemporary calls for community empowerment and reflexivity in research. Clark's work would come to have national prominence, and to that extent, its groundedness in the everyday Harlem community that nurtured him is lost. However, some of those details seem relevant to the investigative practice that he developed.

Clark's Early Influences

Kenneth Clark was born in the Panama Canal Zone in 1914 to Jamaican-born parents. His father, Arthur, had immigrated to Panama for employment opportunities that he had obtained with the United Fruit Company. Clark's mother, Miriam, eventually left her husband and brought 4-year-old Kenneth and his 2½-year-old sister, Beulah, to the United States, with high aspirations for their educational achievement. Economic impoverishment surrounded Clark's earliest years growing up in Harlem. His family "moved from house to house, and from neighborhood to neighborhood within the walls of the ghetto in a desperate attempt to escape its creeping blight" (Keppel, 1995, p. 152). However, there were numerous counteracting sources of personal strength and racial pride.

Clark drew strength both from his immediate family and from the community migrating from the Caribbean to New York in the early part of the 20th century.[1] His mother was a Garveyite[2] who, according to Clark, embraced the racial pride fostered by that movement. Clark was a bookish young person and, as a high school student, spent many hours in the New York Public Library, 135th Street Branch. The library was a place of refuge and, for many of Harlem's residents, a place for forging Black historical identity. Eventually Clark ascended to the third floor of the library that housed the Division of Negro History, Literature and Prints, where he met the director, bibliophile, and collector, Arthur Alfonso Schomburg. Schomburg immigrated to New York City from Puerto Rico in 1891 and dedicated much of his life to collecting the books and artifacts of international Black achievement. Schomburg's biographer Elinor Des Verney Sinnette (1989) learned from interviewing Kenneth Clark that during his visits to the library, he had been permitted

> to handle some of the rare items and to view the works of black artists. It was through the collection that Clark was first exposed to books that justified slavery and rationalized racial prejudice. . . . At a point when Clark might have become dejected and immobilized by the distortions and falsehoods perpetrated against blacks, Arthur Schomburg skillfully guided him to a discovery of the outstanding contributions of black people to the history of the world. (p. 183)

Clark credited Schomburg with playing a key role in his intellectual, cultural, and personal growth and thought of himself as one of his protégés. Clark continued to stay in touch with Schomburg while attending Howard University and visited him at the library when he returned to New York City for doctoral studies at Columbia University (Sinnette, 1989, p. 184).

Clark's Howard University years, from 1931 to 1936, provided him with a rich array of mentors as well as opportunities to demonstrate his commitment to activism.[3] In particular, Clark was guided by Francis Cecil Sumner, the first African American to receive a doctorate in psychology. It was Sumner who recommended Clark to study at Columbia University, where from 1937 to 1940, he completed his doctoral studies as Columbia's first African American

---

[1] For further details of the migration of West Indians to New York during the early part of the 20th century, the reader is referred to Mary C. Waters's (1999) book, *Black Identities: West Indian Immigrant Dreams and American Realities,* chapters 1 and 2, in particular. Waters made the argument that some West Indians already had their experience of race relations as immigrants to Panama, for example, on which to draw. This would likely have been the case for the Clark family.
[2] Marcus Garvey (1887–1940) organized and was president of the Universal Negro Improvement Association (UNIA), a worldwide social movement to promote race consciousness and independence for African peoples in the early part of the 20th century (Campbell, 2001).
[3] It is interesting to note that Kenneth Clark began his studies as a premedical student at Howard University and told an interviewer in the mid-1970s, "if I were white, I think I would have gone into neurophysiology" (Clark, 1976). While an abiding commitment to advancing social justice took him in another direction, he did, in fact, teach physiological psychology at City College and collaborated on anoxia research with two of his colleagues (Hertzman, Smith, & Clark, 1949).

graduate student in psychology. At Columbia, Gardner Murphy and Otto Klineberg were developing an approach to social psychology that stressed methodological eclecticism and sociocultural context (Pandora, 1997).

Kenneth Clark met Mamie Phipps at Howard University. She was the daughter of a prominent Arkansas physician who had encouraged his daughter's studies, which she began in 1934, at age 16. Mamie switched from mathematics to psychology, and both she and Clark spent 1937 commuting between New York City and Washington, DC. They married in 1938 (Guthrie, 1990, 1998; Keppel, 1995; Lal, 2002; Markowitz & Rosner, 1996; Phillips, 2000; Sawyer, 2000).

The Clarks's Early Identity Studies and the Founding of Northside

It was during the summer of 1938 that Mamie had an opportunity to begin studying Black preschoolers in Washington, DC (Clark & Clark, 1939a, 1939b). Kenneth and Mamie coauthored several studies of racial identity based on data collected between 1939 and 1942, some of which formed Mamie's master's thesis (Clark & Clark, 1939a, 1939b, 1940, 1947, 1950; Cross, 1991). She began her doctoral studies at Columbia University as the psychology department's second African American student in 1940 and graduated in 1943. For her doctoral research, Mamie Clark chose the challenge of working with Henry Garrett, a proponent of inherent racial differences and a later opponent to integrated schooling. Kenneth, on the other hand, studied with one of the more liberal members of the department, Otto Klineberg, whose work pointed to the greater role of culture in personality and identity formation (M. P. Clark, 1983; Collier, Minton, & Reynolds, 1991; Guthrie, 1998; Richards, 1997).

Several of the social scientists at Columbia were an integral part of the growing opposition to the biological determinism of race psychology. In a very real sense, however, both race psychology and the "culture and personality" school of the 1920s were reductionist approaches and limited in their capacity to address the complexity and diversity of African American identity. It was more the shift from "race" psychology to social psychological "studies in prejudice" (Samelson, 1978) that engaged Kenneth and Mamie Clark, as this perspective began to explore the nuances of the bigot as well as prejudice from the target's perspective. The more psychodynamic writings on inferiority complex by Alfred Adler as well as the writings on minority group identity by Kurt Lewin were of particular importance for building a social psychology from a minority group perspective (Cross, 1991; Lewin, 1948).

As has already been stated, in the world of laboratory-investigative practice taking hold in psychological social psychology, the social identities of investigators and their participants were becoming increasingly insignificant; the laboratory was a space for constructing knowledge outside race, gender, and other particular identities, which effectively neutralized discussions of group power differences. However, very few of Kenneth Clark's writings leave out a discussion of power differences between groups.[4] The reality of ghettoization permeating American society had placed limitations on both Kenneth and Mamie Clarks' own possibilities for contributing to the field of psychology. While Kenneth Clark was hired as the first African American by the Department of Psychology at City College of New York in 1942, Mamie Clark's possibilities were more severely limited by race and gender. Reflecting on the early part of her career, Mamie wrote, "following my graduation it soon became apparent to me that a black female with a Ph.D. in psychology was an unwanted anomaly in New York City in the early 1940s" (M. P. Clark, 1983, p. 271). At first, Mamie found positions well below her qualifications, but then she worked as a psychological consultant, testing and counseling homeless Black girls at the Riverdale Home for Children. It was this experience that enabled her to recognize and act on the need for mental health services for Harlem's minority children and youths (Lal, 2002). When the Clarks together were unable to convince already existing agencies to expand their services, they decided to open their own center. It can be argued that experiences with systemic racism, more so than any particular school of psychology, motivated the Clarks to build meaningful psychological services in the Harlem community, to battle for civil rights in the courts, and to confront the resistance to change in the dominant society.

In 1946, with the financial support of Mamie's family, the Northside Testing and Consultation Center (later renamed the Northside Center for Child Development) was established in its first location on 155th Street at the northern edge of Harlem. In 1948, the much expanded center moved to 110th Street at the southern edge of Harlem, and was now supported by a "working alliance between a group of white philanthropists committed to supporting black and white professionals in providing the most up-to-date services to an integrated clientele previously defined as outside the scope of any such individualized care" (Markowitz & Rosner, 1996, p. 41).

Both Kenneth and Mamie Clark had realized their vision of a multiethnic center for children of African, European, and Hispanic heritages and an equally multiethnic team of professionals. Over the next 20 years, Northside would move from a traditional psychological approach to one of community action, much in keeping with the needs of the Harlem community for a broader and more relevant array of services. Kenneth Clark argued extensively for a broad psychosocial approach to children at Northside with greater attention paid to the importance of cultural factors in both diagnosis and treatment (Chess, Clark, & Alexander, 1953). In fact, early on both Kenneth and Mamie were involved in the combined activities of evaluation and advocacy related to IQ testing with minority children, when it was found that these children were being incorrectly and illegally placed into classes for retarded children (M. P. Clark, 1983; Guthrie, 1990). Markowitz and Rosner (1996),

---

[4] Explicit discussions of power in Kenneth Clark's writings emerged in the 1960s. Keppel (2002) has looked at Clark's increasing pessimism about the possibilities for racial justice and the greater focus on power/powerlessness in his writings as one moves from *Prejudice and Your Child* (1955) to *Dark Ghetto* (1965) to *Pathos of Power* (1974).

in their history of Northside, summarized the Clarks's approach to child intervention:

> [The children] would see therapists, yes, but they would also be evaluated for reading difficulties, family dislocation, or other problems of poverty that social workers, educators, or family counselors could address.
>
> The Clarks were engaged in a struggle on two fronts. On one side, they sought to convince the social-service community that black children could benefit from and must not be denied up-to-date therapeutic diagnosis and intervention. On the other side, they sought to convince psychiatry and psychology to incorporate race and ethnicity more rigorously into their paradigms. (p. 85)

The Laboratory Versus the Community

The Clarks were adamant that distortions of both personality and behavior were fostered by enforced segregation, a structural barrier that stood in the way of full and healthy development of both Black and White Americans. Kenneth and Mamie Clark worked as a team in all of their efforts toward dismantling legalized barriers in employment, housing, and education, and to do so required the retention of an investigative practice grounded in power relations among social rather than statistical groups. In their identity studies of the late 1930s and early 1940s, Kenneth and Mamie Clark had built the foundations of a social psychology of prejudice understood from the target's perspective. The vantage point of the target prescribed a somewhat different paradigm for social psychological research wherein advocacy on behalf of the targets of injustice and objectivity in obtaining the facts of that injustice were intertwined.

Lubek and Apfelbaum (2000) argued that the laboratory was a safe place for social psychologists in American political culture of the 1950s. The activist scholar model fostered in the Depression of the 1930s was detrimental for social psychologists in the anti-Communist climate of the McCarthy era (Harris, 1998; Nicholson, 1998). Investigations of several social psychologists by the American federal government and the cold war changed the agenda of social psychologists (Apfelbaum, 1992). Talk of enduring international peace, of organized labor, of social responsibility and social health, defined at mid-century as the building of racial and religious tolerance, became dangerous insofar as it connected one to sympathies for communism. Lubek and Apfelbaum (2000) wrote:

> Thus in the 1950s, one witnessed a wholesale retreat of researchers with their graduate students . . . to the safe harbor of the apolitical scientific laboratory, with white lab coats, dyadic simulations, and mathematical models, all acting as symbolic protective talismans against the risk of being politically vulnerable in their social formulations. (p. 423)

In this context, it is all the more interesting to examine those social scientists, Kenneth Clark most prominent among them, who remained committed to the examination of social groups in real communities.

There were two action-oriented organizations with which Kenneth Clark was connected in the post–World War II period that reflected progressive liberalism and ethnic pluralism, namely, the Commission on Community Inter-relations (CCI) of the American Jewish Congress and the Society for the Psychological Study of Social Issues (SPSSI). At mid-20th century and prior to the turn toward university-based laboratory investigation, these two groupings of social psychologists in the United States offer a glimpse of greater methodological eclecticism used within the context of an activist-scholar model than what was to follow (Cherry & Borshuk, 1998).

CCI was the result of Kurt Lewin's efforts to found an applied social psychological unit to complement the Research Center on Group Dynamics at Massachusetts Institute of Technology. Both were established in 1944, and for three years until his death in 1947, Lewin shuttled between Cambridge and CCI's headquarters in New York City, nurturing the work of both organizations. During its brief history as an applied social psychology organization from 1944 to 1952, Isidor Chein, Kenneth Clark, Mary Collins, Stuart Cook, Marie Jahoda, John Harding, Claire Selltiz, and Brewster Smith, among others, were on staff or consulted for CCI on three broad areas of research: auditing discrimination through community self-surveys, testing programs that taught citizens to respond constructively to publicly expressed bigotry, and researching positive minority identity in an effort to buffer the impact of prejudice and discrimination (Cherry & Borshuk, 1998; Marrow, 1969).

By the early 1950s, many of the researchers at CCI had moved to the Research Center for Human Relations at New York University and, under the direction of Stuart Cook, were integrally involved in setting up graduate study in social psychology. Many of the social psychologists working at CCI were also involved in SPSSI in the postwar period, and under the auspices of that organization's Committee on Intergroup Relations, "the somewhat wayward child" of Gordon Allport's original proposal for a book on the measurement of prejudice was published (Jahoda, Deutsch, & Cook, 1951, pp. vi–vii). The two volumes of *Research Methods in Social Relations* present a more far-ranging eclectic and multidisciplinary approach to research that drew on interview, observational, projective, archival, group discussion, community self-survey, and experimental techniques for analyzing prejudice and discrimination. By examining Kenneth Clark's involvement with both organizations from the mid-1940s and throughout the 1950s, one can see the kind of priorities and practices he articulated for a social psychology responsive to power inequities and social groups.

Kenneth Clark and Black–Jewish Relations

In 1944, Kenneth Clark was asked to join CCI as a research associate just as CCI's first project was about to get off the ground. A fight had broken out in front of a synagogue in Coney Island on the evening of the Jewish holy day of Yom Kippur. The community had seen several incidents, and Clark was involved in surveying the community of Italian, African, and Jewish Americans with the goal of bringing to light and resolving some of the intergroup tensions

(Bellow et al., 1947–1948). Clark (1946/1992) wrote with candor on Jewish–Black relations, addressing both anti-Black sentiment among Jews and Black anti-Semitism. He wrote of the situation in the 1940s:

> To be sure, each group has a relatively insecure status in the dominant American culture; each suffers from the psychological threats of humiliation; each has been the victim of organized bigotry. But it is naïve to assume that, because Negroes and Jews are each in their own way oppressed and insecure, this will necessarily lead to a feeling of kinship and understanding. (p. 14)

In fact, for Clark Black–Jewish antagonisms were not a "special, isolated phenomenon" but served "to indicate the extent to which the pathologies of the dominant society infect all groups and individuals within that society" and to illustrate the political, economic, and psychological functions that prejudice served (Clark, 1946/1992, p. 98).

Kenneth Clark's contacts in the Jewish American community were substantial and complex, but his stay at CCI until 1946 was not without personal frustration. He had been hesitant to accept the invitation because of his primary attachment to teaching, another research commitment to the Council for Democracy, and his "personal misgivings about the professional competence and personality stability of a member of the staff" with whom Clark had been working on the Coney Island project. Clark's skills and experience were being restricted, and he wrote to CCI's research director, Charles Hendry, that

> as long as these conditions prevail I would not be honest with myself and with the C.C.I. if I did not state that I feel that I am being employed on a token, rather than genuine, basis. It would also be necessary for me to state frankly that the idea of racial or personal discrimination as a possible explanation of this patently confused and distorted situation has occurred to me.
>
> It is not easy to reconcile such an interpretation with an organization whose purpose is to combat unfavorable racial attitudes and their manifestations. I do not by any means intend to suggest that the discrimination, if it is the case, is deliberate and conscious. On the other hand, a fact of discrimination is more meaningful in terms of effect rather than in terms of intent. (Clark, 1945, p. 5)

Clark saw it as a "professional requirement" as well as a matter of good personal and workplace relationships to examine one's prejudices, and he made concrete suggestions for improving the situation at CCI, not the least of which was to review the method of determining assignments to various projects based on comparisons of experience and credentials. While it is not clear how the matter was resolved, the memo Kenneth Clark wrote to CCI's director as the organization was getting off the ground is instructive in showing Clark's forte in responding directly to discrimination, while at the same time pursuing opportunities to build alliances that would address systemic racism.

Clark's participation in the work of CCI provided the terrain for building alliances with progressive forces in the Jewish community, which would later be important in mounting broader legal action against segregated housing, employment, and education. Several of his colleagues at CCI, both Jewish and non-Jewish—Stuart Cook, Isidor Chein, and Brewster Smith—would become involved in the court cases leading up to and including *Brown v. Board of Education*. Clark's work with CCI was part of what Cornel West (1994) has called not "*a golden age* in which blacks and Jews were free of tension and friction" but a "*better age* when the common histories of oppression and degradation of both groups served as a springboard for genuine empathy and principled alliances" (p. 104). It was Clark's directness and perseverance in building principled alliances that gave him a unique and credible vantage point to articulate research and action relevant to both Black anti-Semitism and Jewish anti-Black racism.

While at CCI, between 1944 and 1946, Clark formulated several research questions regarding Black–Jewish relations that were fundamental to the later stream of identity research that CCI supported and to his own thinking on social identity. During his brief time at CCI, Clark commented on various documents related to Black–Jewish relations and laid out a set of questions for CCI staff to consider regarding the possibility and desirability of cooperative Black–Jewish relations (Clark, 1945, 1946/1992). He was interested in the perceptions each group had of the other as well as the extent of contact and the motivations for animosity that existed. Clark thought strategically about what ends justified cooperative intergroup activity and the obstacles that stood in the way of cooperative efforts. He questioned whether Blacks and Jews saw one another as having greater advantage or liability. And finally, he set out a plan to explore which activities between Black and Jewish organizations had been effective, and to develop possible joint research projects, community action programs, as well as social, legislative, and educational activities that would further the goals of both groups. Conflicts among religious and ethnic groups preoccupied much of his time, with the case of Jews and Blacks being only one instance.

A Principled Alliance

One of Kenneth Clark's most dedicated allies in the lead-up to *Brown v. Board of Education* was another social psychologist—Isidor Chein, a graduate of City College and a Columbia University PhD who graduated in 1939. The two social psychologists were both instructors at the City College of New York in the night division. Chein was a director of research at CCI from 1946 to 1952, from whence he moved to New York University's Research Center for Human Relations and he was active in SPSSI. Clark and Chein were both passionately interested in minority identity and had been influenced to an extent by Kurt Lewin's writings on the subject (Lewin, 1948).

Isidor Chein had been raised as an orthodox Jew with a strong penchant for cultural pluralism within Jewish life and an abiding belief that one did not have to choose between Jewish and American identities. Isidor Chein's writings of the post–World War II period were dedicated to understanding Jewish children's identity at a time of increasing diversification within Jewish religious practice and a lessening scope of Jewish life as a barrier to participation in mainstream American society (Chein, 1948, 1949, 1952). Chein's hopes for positive Jewish identity were premised on the notion that despite diversification, the experience of a unity of identity would prevail.

It was Chein and Clark's dialogue about minority identity that helped to shape the comprehensive document on the impact of discrimination on children for the Mid-Century White House Conference on Children and Youth.[5] Kenneth Clark had been invited to present his findings to the White House Conference in 1950, and Isidor Chein was a panelist in the session on the psychological effects of prejudice as well as a resource person in the corresponding working group. It was this working document, in turn, that would become the basis for court cases starting in 1951, and that would culminate in the highly revised document that formed part of the Appellants' Brief to the Supreme Court in 1954.

Chein and Clark shared an interest in minority identity and drew frequently on comparisons between Jewish and African American experiences of involuntary segregation in the writings of Kurt Lewin. In fact, in the first draft of the working materials prepared for the group leaders at the Mid-Century White House Conference on Children and Youth, Kenneth Clark expressed what he had come to see as the differential consequences for Jewish and African Americans, namely,

> the greater possibility of assimilation into the dominant society, the absence of differences in skin color as a concrete determinant of minority status, and possibly a generally higher economic status among Jews, must be recognized as factors which would result in a different pattern of personality consequences resulting from the minority status of the Jew. (Clark, n.d., p. 113)

Relative economic and White skin privilege were central facts for Clark in his observations of the journey of Jewish Americans. The comparison afforded Clark a view of the overarching and overdetermining impact of ghettoization along color lines—a structural barrier to diversity—that was "the basic determinant of prejudice in America" (p. 118) as well as the basis for Black children's internalizations of societal prejudice.

The Activist Scholar

In 1951, Kenneth Clark was sought out by Robert Carter, of the Legal Defense Fund of the National Association for the Advancement of Colored People

---

[5] I have found limited correspondence between Chein and Clark in either's papers, although an almost complete set of Isidor Chein's writings on group belongingness are in Kenneth Clark's papers at the Library of Congress. In an interview with Isidor Chein's widow, Norma Chein, I did learn that the Clarks and the Cheins traveled to the White House Conference in Washington together. Once there, they were required by law to stay in different hotels and eat in different restaurants. Working in New York as they both did on a variety of projects afforded numerous possibilities for conversations now lost to the archival record.

(NAACP), which was preparing to bring cases against segregated schooling largely building on the work done throughout the 1940s and in the immediate post–World War II period. At the same time as Clark was attending meetings with the NAACP lawyers, he was also working with the SPSSI's Committee on Intergroup Relations, of which he had been a member since 1945. It was the Mid-Century document that was revised several times to form the Social Science Statement that was the Appendix to Appellants' Briefs (Clark, 1989, pp. 166–184; J. P. Jackson, 1998, 2001) cited in *Brown v. Board of Education,* and from which Footnote 11 was drawn, and which was eventually made accessible for a larger audience in *Prejudice and Your Child* (Clark, 1955). Much of the work in preparing the Social Science Statement was done by a group of social psychologists, Isidor Chein among them, involved with the SPSSI, and it was this group that Clark mobilized around *Brown v. Board of Education.* As Clark (1976) described the network:

> in the fifties and early sixties, we had a working network of social psychologists who shared certain basic values . . . social values and research interests, and . . . every social psychologist whom you see appended to the social science appendix to the brief of the Brown decision cases was part of that network, in the metropolitan area.

Chein proved to be an invaluable ally in Clark's mobilization of social science expertise and expert witnesses in the courtroom (Chein, 1949; Deutscher & Chein, 1948). Continuing into the 1950s, Chein and Clark worked together on building the necessary documentation and testimony that proved significant in court challenges to segregation, primarily through the joint efforts of the NAACP, SPSSI, and both the Commission for Legal and Social Action and the Commission for Community Interrelations of the American Jewish Congress.

J. P. Jackson (1998) outlined thoroughly how Isidor Chein, Stuart Cook, and Kenneth Clark produced several drafts that gradually culminated in the 1953 document titled "The Effects of Segregation and the Consequences of Desegregation: A Social Science Statement," which provided scientific expertise in a form useful to a legal forum. As Jackson (1998) noted, "the final version would not stir the blood as the original version did, however it certainly was more in keeping with the objective tone of a scientific paper" (p. 151). The final 18-page document drew on a broad range of research that made two central points: that segregation harmed minority and majority group members alike and that desegregation would be successful if it proceeded without delay. The Statement was appended to the main appellant's brief for the Supreme Court. SPSSI did not release the statement under its auspices, but rather Kenneth Clark and Isidor Chein continued to collaborate on a campaign for signatures to append to the Statement (Benjamin & Crouse, 2002; J. P. Jackson, 1998).

It was argued for some time following that Kenneth Clark had lost the differentiation between objectivity and social activism in his work on *Brown.* J. P. Jackson (1998) made the case that for social psychologists like Clark, it was an artificial distinction. And in fact, his work in the 1950s serves as an early instance of the activist scholar model he was to champion throughout the rest of his career. Kenneth Clark's version of social action research moved more strongly into grassroots community change in which the key element in this type of research was the empowerment of community members through their own investigative practices.

In the 18-month period in the early 1960s, during which Kenneth Clark and many others studied the young people of Central Harlem, these basic principles of a community learning about itself to enhance its well-being were more clearly articulated. Regardless of the political battles that engaged Kenneth Clark in Harlem in the 1960s (and they were ferocious!), *Youth in the Ghetto: A Study of the Consequences of Powerlessness and a Blueprint for Change* (Harlem Youth Opportunities Unlimited, Inc. [HARYOU], 1964) is probably one of the most complete models for action research available to social psychologists.

For Clark and others involved in HARYOU, social interventions in a community were to be judged by the "persistent emphasis and insistence upon social action rather than dependence upon mere social services" (HARYOU, 1964, p. 388). The overriding philosophy was one of

> social action, [which] in its operational sense, means and demands the stimulation of concern among individuals who share a common predicament, who are victims of long-standing community problems and injustices, who can be induced not only to identify these problems but to seek to determine the methods by which they can be resolved, and who are able to develop and sustain the initiative for the type of collective action which, in fact, does resolve or ameliorate these problems. (p. 388)

For Clark, this was a process that engaged "indigenous community leadership," "grassroots critical involvement with neighborhood level programs" (HARYOU, 1964, p. 390), and a "continuous process of program refinement and action." Clark emphasized the importance of going beyond "hard statistical data." In the planning process, there were in fact statistical data, but there were also unstructured small group discussions, questionnaires, depth interviews, and observations of community activity, methodologies much more in keeping with the eclecticism of the first edition of *Research Methods in Social Relations* (Jahoda et al., 1951) than the growing trend toward guidelines for experimenters in the subsequent volumes of the *Handbook of Social Psychology* (Lubek & Apfelbaum, 2000; Stam, Radtke, & Lubek, 2000).

In the HARYOU document, it was noted that "the usual methods of public opinion polling and attitude testing" (p. 46) were not sufficient to "plumb the depth or complexities of attitudes, feelings, conflicts, inconsistencies, contradictions, and anxieties which are involved in relating to a community as complex as Harlem" (p. 47). It was the "contradictions in data" that "produced new insights" (p. 54) that most interested Clark and his associates. While HARYOU's work in the early 1960s became embroiled in power politics, it is fair to say that Harlem community residents along with social science experts were actively creating an alternative research methodology to the university laboratory subjects of the same period.

In *Youth in the Ghetto,* one finds an early exemplar of contemporary notions of intersubjectivity in statements about researchers and research participants, for example, that "there is a general agreement that all data collection involves establishing a relationship between the researcher and his subjects" and "information elicited from a subject is greatly shaped by the nature of that relationship" (HARYOU, 1964, p. 48). In speaking of his research in Harlem, Clark wrote (1965/1989):

> I could never be fully detached as a scholar or participant. More than forty years of my life had been lived in Harlem. I started school in the Harlem public schools. I first learned about people, about love, about cruelty, about sacrifice, about cowardice, about courage, about bombast in Harlem. For many years before I returned as an "involved observer," Harlem had been my home. (p. xxix)

Indeed, he further pointed out the difficulties in training an "involved observer," noting that

> there is at present nothing in the vast literature of social science treatises and textbooks and nothing in the practical or field training of graduate students in social science to prepare them for the realities and complexities of this type of involvement in a real, dynamic, turbulent, and at times seemingly chaotic community. (p. xxix)

Clark drew attention to some of the similarities of the involved observer with the participant observer in the sociological and anthropological tradition. The central difference between the participant and the involved observer was that the latter, as Clark very definitely found out, was likely to get caught up in the community's conflicts and struggles for power to the point of self-doubt.

Clark lived in several everyday worlds of social psychology simultaneously, for example, as an academic at City College geographically separated from research participants in Central Harlem. He very tellingly captured the unique and sometimes difficult struggle he had with both insider and outsider vantage points: "The return of a former inhabitant to the Harlem ghetto appears to be a matter of personal choice, but who can say how free the choice really is. Can the prisoner ever fully escape the prison?" (Clark, 1965/1989).

On more than one occasion, Clark retreated to City College, which offered the "protection of reflective academia, an indulgence which I thought I could not have afforded before, but always wanted interestingly enough" (Clark, 1976). But he never retreated for very long. In 1965, with a year's distance from the HARYOU project, Clark devised the Social Dynamics Research Institute. Dedicated to further action oriented investigations, Clark enlisted his City College colleague Larry Plotkin and hired Claire Selltiz, who had been a researcher first at CCI and then at the Research Center for Social Relations at New York University. Some years after the Institute, the Metropolitan Applied Research Center (MARC) was founded.

Conclusion

Kenneth Clark's action-oriented approach to social psychology came out of the everyday resistance African Americans encounter to their full participation in American society. These circumstances did not afford Clark the luxury of escaping to the laboratory, even if he sometimes thought that might be an attractive option. Even in the face of continual resistance, he remained convinced that integrationist goals were correct (Phillips, 2000).

In 1970, the call for "a social psychology of black consciousness" (White, 1980) was answered with new models for African American identity (Cross, 1991; Jones, 1997, among others) that extended beyond the possibilities that Clark had envisaged. However, as one broadens the time frame for examining issues of social identity across the 20th century, one can see that a social psychology of minority consciousness has been a constant project at the margins of psychological social psychology (Gaines & Reed, 1995). Such a project is unlikely to occupy center stage in a still largely experimental field, in which social groups remain eclipsed by statistical groups and advocacy remains separated from investigative practice. However, we are challenged by Kenneth Clark's approach to social psychology to reflect on the field's alternative origins and goals.

References

Apfelbaum, E. (1992). Some teachings from the history of social psychology. *Canadian Psychology, 33,* 529–539.

Bellow, B., Blum, M. L., Clark, K. B., Haas, M., Haydon, E. M., Hogrefe, R., et al. (1947–1948). Prejudice in "seaside"; a report of an action-research project. *Human Relations, 1,* 98–120.

Benjamin, L. T. Jr., & Crouse, E. M. (2002). The American Psychological Association's response *to Brown v. Board of Education*: The case of Kenneth B. Clark. *American Psychologist, 57,* 38–50.

Campbell, H. (2001). Pan-Africanism. In M. E. Crahan, L. R. Jacobs, W. A. Joseph, G. Nzongola-Ntalaja, & J. A. Paul (Eds.), *The Oxford companion to politics of the world* (2nd ed., pp. 631–633). Oxford, England: Oxford University Press.

Capshew, J. (1995) *Psychologists on the march: Science, practice, and professional identity in America, 1929–1969.* New York: Cambridge University Press.

Chein, I. (1948). The problem of belongingness: An action research perspective. *The Jewish Center Worker, 9,* 14–17.

Chein, I. (1949). What are the psychological effects of enforced segregation. *International Journal of Opinion and Attitude Research, 3,* 229–234.

Chein, I. (1952, June). *Securing our children against prejudice.* Paper presented at the 53rd Annual Meeting of the National Conference of Jewish Communal Service, Chicago, IL.

Cherry, F., & Borshuk, C. (1998). Social action research and the Commission on Community Interrelations. *Journal of Social Issues, 54,* 119–142.

Chess, S., Clark, K. B., & Alexander, T. (1953). The importance of cultural evaluation in psychiatric diagnosis and treatment. *Psychiatric Quarterly, 27,* 102–114.

Chisholm, B. (1949). Social responsibility. *Science, 109,* 27–30, 43.

Clark, K. B. (n.d.) *Effect of prejudice and discrimination on personality development* (First draft: Working material prepared for the use of group-leaders, Mid-Century White House Conference on Children and Youth). Washington, DC: Kenneth B. Clark Papers, Library of Congress.

Clark, K. B. (1942). Morale among Negroes. In G. Watson (Ed.), *Civilian morale: Second yearbook of the Society for the Psychological Study of Social Issues* (pp. 228–248). Boston: Houghton Mifflin.

Clark, K. B. (1945). [Memo to H.E. Hendry, Harold Levy, Juliet Bell, dated April 10, 1945]. Washington, DC: Kenneth B. Clark Papers, Library of Congress.

Clark, K. B. (1946). Candor about Negro-Jewish relations. (Reprinted in *Bridges and Boundaries: African Americans and American Jews,* pp. 91–98, by J. Salzman, A. Back, & G. S. Sorin, Eds., 1992, New York: George Braziller)

Clark, K. B. (1948). Social science and social tensions. *Mental Hygiene, 32,* 15–26.

Clark, K. B. (1955). *Prejudice and your child* (1st ed.). Boston: Beacon Press.

Clark, K. B. (1965). Introduction to an epilogue. In K. B. Clark, *Dark ghetto: Dilemmas of social power* (2nd ed., pp. xxvii–xxxix). Hanover, NH.: Wesleyan University Press.

Clark, K. B. (1974). *Pathos of power.* New York: HarperCollins.

Clark, K. B. (1976). *Interview with Ed Edwin* (Columbia University Oral History Collection, Interview 7). New York: Columbia University.

Clark, K. B. (1989). *Dark ghetto: Dilemmas of social power* (2nd ed.). Hanover, NH: Wesleyan University Press.

Clark, K. B., & Clark, M. K. (1939a). The development of consciousness of self and the emergence of racial identification in Negro pre-school children. *Journal of Social Psychology, 10,* 591–599.

Clark, K. B., & Clark, M. K. (1939b). Segregation as a factor in the racial identification of Negro preschool children: A preliminary report. *Journal of Experimental Education, 9,* 161–163.

Clark, K. B., & Clark, M. K. (1940). Skin color as a factor in racial identification of Negro preschool children. *Journal of Social Psychology, 11,* 159–160.

Clark, K. B., & Clark, M. K. (1947). Racial identification and preference in Negro children. In T. M. Newcomb & E. L. Hartley (Eds.), *Readings in social psychology* (pp. 169–178). New York: Holt.

Clark, K. B., & Clark, M. K. (1950). Emotional factors in racial identification and preference in Negro children. *Journal of Negro Education, 19,* 341–350.

Clark, M. P. (1983). Mamie Phipps Clark. In A. N. O'Connell & N. F. Russo (Eds.), *Models of achievement: Reflections of eminent women in psychology* (pp. 266–277). New York: Columbia University Press.

Collier, G., Minton, H. L., & Reynolds, G. (1991). *Currents of thought in American social psychology.* Oxford, England: Oxford University Press.

Cross, W. E. (1991). *Shades of Black: Diversity in African-American identity.* Philadelphia: Temple University Press.

Danziger, K. (2000). Making social psychology experimental. *Journal of the History of the Behavioral Sciences, 36,* 329–347.

Deutscher, M., & Chein, I. (1948). The psychological effects of enforced segregation: A survey of social science opinion. *Journal of Psychology, 26,* 259–287.

Gaines, S. O., & Reed, E. S. (1995). Prejudice: From Allport to DuBois. *American Psychologist, 50,* 96–103.

Guthrie, R. V. (1990). Mamie Phipps Clark (1917–1983). In A. N. O'Connell & N. F. Russo (Eds.), *Women in psychology: A bio-bibliographic sourcebook* (pp. 267–278). New York: Greenwood Press.

Guthrie, R. V. (1998). *Even the rat was white: A historical view of psychology* (2nd ed.). Boston: Allyn & Bacon.

Harlem Youth Opportunities Unlimited, Inc. (1964). *Youth in the ghetto: A study of the consequences of powerlessness and a blueprint for change.* New York: Author.

Harris, B. (1998). The perils of a public intellectual. *Journal of Social Issues, 54,* 79–118.

Hertzman, M., Smith, G. M., & Clark, K. B. (1949). The relation between changes in the angioscotoma and certain Rorschach signs under prolonged mild anoxia. *Journal of General Psychology, 41,* 263–271.

Jackson, J. P., Jr. (1998). Creating a consensus: Psychologists, the Supreme Court, and school desegregation, 1952–1955. *Journal of Social Issues, 54,* 143–177.

Jackson, J. P., Jr. (2001). *Social scientists for social justice: Making the case against segregation.* New York: New York University Press.

Jackson, W. A. (1990). *Gunnar Myrdal and America's conscience: Social engineering and racial liberalism, 1938–1987.* Chapel Hill: University of North Carolina Press.

Jahoda, M., Deutsch, M., & Cook, S. W. (1951). *Research methods in social relations, with especial reference to prejudice* (Vols. 1 and 2). New York: Dryden Press.

Jones, J. M. (1997). *Prejudice and racism* (2nd ed.). New York: McGraw-Hill.

Keppel, B. (1995). *The work of democracy: Ralph Bunche, Kenneth B. Clark, Lorraine Hansberry, and the cultural politics of race.* Cambridge, MA: Harvard University Press.

Keppel, B. (2002). Kenneth B. Clark in the patterns of American culture. *American Psychologist, 57,* 29–37.

Lal, S. (2002). Giving children security: Mamie Phipps Clark and the racialization of child psychology. *American Psychologist, 57,* 20–28.

Lewin, K. (1948). *Resolving social conflicts: Selected papers on group dynamics.* New York: Harper-Collins

Lubek, I., & Apfelbaum, E. (2000). A critical gaze and wistful glance at "official" handbook histories of social psychology: Did the successive accounts by Gordon Allport and successors historiographically succeed? *Journal of the History of the Behavioral Sciences, 36,* 405–428.

Markowitz, G., & Rosner, D. (1996). *Children, race, and power: Kenneth and Mamie Clark's Northside Center.* Charlottesville: University Press of Virginia.

Marrow, A. J. (1969). *The practical theorist: The life and work of Kurt Lewin.* New York: Basic Books.

Myrdal, G. (1944). *An American dilemma: The Negro problem and modern democracy.* New York: HarperCollins.

Nicholson, I. A. M. (1998). "The approved bureaucratic torpor": Goodwin Watson, critical psychology, and the dilemmas of expertise, 1930–1945. *Journal of Social Issues, 54,* 29–52.

Pandora, K. (1997). *Rebels within the ranks: Psychologists' critique of scientific authority and democratic realities in New Deal America.* Cambridge, England: Cambridge University Press.

Phillips, L. (2000). Recontextualizing Kenneth B. Clark: An Afrocentric perspective on the paradoxical legacy of a model psychologist-activist. *History of Psychology, 3,* 142–167.

Richards, G. (1997). *"Race", racism and psychology.* London: Routledge.

Samelson, F. (1978). From "race psychology" to "studies in prejudice": Some observations of the thematic reversal in social psychology. *Journal of the History of the Behavioral Sciences, 14,* 265–278.

Sawyer, T. F. (2000). Francis Cecil Sumner: His views and influence on African American higher education. *History of Psychology, 3,* 122–141.

Sinnette, E. D. (1989). *Arthur Alfonso Schomburg: Black bibliophile and collector.* New York and Detroit: New York Public Library & Wayne State University Press.

Stam, H. J., Radtke, H. L., & Lubek, I. (2000). Strains in experimental social psychology: A textural analysis of the development of experimentation in social psychology. *Journal of the History of the Behavioral Sciences, 36,* 365–382.

Waters, M. C. (1999). *Black identities: West Indian immigrant dreams and American realities.* New York: Russell Sage Foundation.

West, C. (1994). *Race matters.* New York: Random House.

White, J. L. (1980). Toward a Black psychology. In R. L. Jones (Ed.), *Black psychology* (2nd ed., pp. 5–12). New York: Harper & Row.

3

Racial Integration Today: Revisiting Kenneth B. Clark's Vision

Thomas F. Pettigrew

Kenneth Clark has lived his life in the single-minded pursuit of his vision for a better America. He has held unswervingly to this vision through discouraging as well as promising times. He has maintained his determined stand in the face of criticism from many sides. As an old friend, there are many things I admire about Clark. But it is his courage and resolve never to surrender his vision that I admire and appreciate the most.

Clark's vision consists of two basic components: the problem and the remedy. In setting out the problem, Clark has never tolerated obfuscations. He has simply held racism in all its forms to be a tragic, four-century-long national nightmare. To see the problem as anything less, he insists, means one can never fashion realistic remedies and redress.

The second part of his vision holds racial integration of Black and White Americans as equals—not mere desegregation as unequals—to be the essential remedy for the nation's major domestic tragedy. His famous "doll studies" with his wife Mamie, his influential participation in the historic 1954 ruling of the U.S. Supreme Court that found public school segregation unconstitutional, his probing television interviews with James Baldwin, Malcolm X, and Martin Luther King Jr. (Clark, 1963), and his well-known books—*Prejudice and Your Child, Dark Ghetto,* and *Pathos of Power* (Clark, 1955, 1965, 1974)—all these efforts aimed at this ultimate remedy.

Is Clark's vision viable today? Is his position, shaped in mid-20th century, still relevant in the 21st century? Has his determined stand been ahead of its time? I believe the answer to these queries is an unqualified "yes." To advance this view, this chapter revisits Clark's vision from three directions. First, it briefly reviews the status of African Americans today—in attitudes, interracial interaction, politics, education, employment, criminal justice, housing, financial resources, health, and intermarriage. Next, the chapter discusses six racial myths in current American thought that deter the attainment of Clark's vision. And, finally, the chapter closes with a brief consideration of lessons learned for future use.

The Status of African Americans Today

Clark has never claimed that the realization of his vision would be easy. Though some of his critics infer such naïveté, he has consistently emphasized throughout his career the depth of the problem of American racism. In papers prepared for the Supreme Court, Clark (1953) made a prophetic prediction about racial progress that has held true for the past five decades. After reviewing the uneven patterns of racial desegregation emerging at that time, he held that racial change of the future would be a direct function of how firmly and forcefully authorities supported the process. Leaders must be "clear and unequivocal" in their support; they must firmly enforce the policy and be willing "to deal with violations"; they cannot "engage in or tolerate [evasive] subterfuges"; and they should appeal to "the American traditions of fair play and equal justice" (Clark, 1953, p. 54).

The disappointing reality is that we have not witnessed such firm and forceful leadership in race relations over the past half-century. Presidential actions involving racial change have ranged from the conditioned endorsement of Lyndon Johnson to the open opposition of the Nixon, Reagan, and Bush eras (Orfield & Eaton, 1996). Just as Clark predicted, racial change has made two steps forward and one backward in near lockstep with these shifting political tides. In virtually every domain reviewed, one will find this mixed pattern of gains and losses.

Today, the American right-wing prefers to view the racial alterations of the 1960s, which it bitterly opposed, as having solved the problems of racial prejudice and discrimination in the United States. The right-wing concedes that problems for Black Americans remain but claims these problems are largely self-inflicted that only Blacks themselves can ameliorate (e.g., D'Souza, 1995). Observers on the left, especially young African Americans who never experienced the harsh racial past, often claim that nothing has fundamentally changed in the nation's race relations over the past half-century. Both are wrong. As this brief review will reveal, basic changes have occurred, but they have been highly uneven. Moreover, the slow progress has led to the emergence of new difficulties.

Attitudes

Howard Schuman and his colleagues provided an invaluable and comprehensive view of both Black and White racial attitudes expressed in surveys over the past six decades (Schuman, Steeh, Bobo, & Krysan, 1997). They showed that White racial attitudes have shifted markedly since the 1940s, but the present pattern is complex. For example, there is far more White willingness to interact with Blacks than a half-century ago. But this willingness rapidly dissipates for situations in which Whites are the minority. Principles of equal treatment in such major realms as jobs, schools, residential choice, and public accommodations are now widely accepted. But implementing these principles is resisted. Hence, efforts for educational integration and affirmative action programs meet increasing resistance even by the President. In January 2003, President Bush announced his opposition to the University of Michigan's modest affirmative action program. He did so on national television on Martin Luther King Jr.'s birthday with a picture of the slain leader in the background.

The most problematic White racial belief today involves causal attributions for inequality. To account for African American disadvantage, the most popular White explanation is that Blacks simply lack the motivation to achieve. The dominant perception is that racial discrimination did exist in the past but has largely been eliminated. Thus, African Americans themselves must be responsible for ending the inequalities that persist. This gross misperception underlies many of the other negative racial attitudes that Whites hold.

In sharp contrast, Black Americans regard present-day discrimination to be the primary reason for continuing racial inequalities. Eighty-one percent of African American respondents agreed with the survey question, "Do you think blacks have worse jobs, income, and housing is mainly due to discrimination?" (Schuman et al., 1997, p. 275). They experience discrimination regularly and hesitate to tell even White friends about it for fear of being viewed as "too racially sensitive"—a common "put-down" (Feagin & Sikes, 1994). This attribution of discrimination is not a phenomenon limited to the poorest segments of the Black population. Actually, surveys show repeatedly that it is well-educated African Americans who focus on discrimination, feel civil rights change has been too slow, and think White Americans "don't care about blacks" (Schuman et al., 1997, pp. 276–277). Black American interaction with White Americans shapes this phenomenon.

Interracial Interaction

Play by the rules, work hard, obtain a good education, and the American dream will apply to you—that was the promise long made to and believed by African Americans. But those Blacks with the opportunity to follow this advice and gain middle-class status now find to their chagrin that the curse of racism still haunts them. Many blatant racist forms occur in interracial interaction. Almost half of a national probability sample of adult Blacks reported in 2000 that they had experienced discrimination within the last 30 days (Smith, 2000). Common occurrences for even middle-class Blacks involve rude service in restaurants, empty cabs refusing to stop, and store employees following them as suspected thieves.

More threatening examples involve racial profiling by police or, as it is popularly called, being stopped for "driving while Black" (Ruffin, 1999). A recent national Black survey found that 69% believe that the police regularly engage in racial profiling and only 21% disagree. Significantly, upper-status respondents are just as likely as other Blacks to believe that police profiling is widespread (Bositis, 2001). And progress on this issue has been difficult. Even California's former Governor Gray Davis, although elected with strong Black support, bent to police pressure and vetoed legislation that merely required the gathering of relevant data on the race of drivers stopped.

Politics

The Voting Rights Act of 1965 was without question the most effective civil rights legislation of the 1960s. Just prior to the act, only about 100 Black Americans held elected office in the entire United States; by January 2001 more than 9,100 Blacks occupied elected office. These gains have been most notable in the South, with more than 60% of the total of Black office holders (Joint Center for Political and Economic Studies, 2002a). Without the marked increase in Black votes, the Rev. Jesse Jackson's 1988 run for the presidency would not have been possible. Nor would Harvey Johnson have become mayor of Jackson, Mississippi. It is also encouraging that African American politicians have gained high office in areas where White voters are a large majority, such as the governorship in my native state of Virginia, a member of the U.S. House of Representatives from rural Georgia, and mayors of Rochester, New York and Minneapolis, Minnesota.

These political advances, however, are only part of the story. There remains a darker side to American politics. David Duke, a Ku Klux Klan leader, has repeatedly run for high office in Louisiana. In 1988, George Bush conducted one of the most racist campaigns in modern American presidential history—featuring the threatening "Willie Horton" television advertisement. North Carolina's Senator Jesse Helms made an art form of using racism to win repeated elections. Yet upon his announced retirement, the nation's mass media generally praised him and failed to note his lifelong adherence to and political exploitation of blatantly racist beliefs and practices.

Most alarming of all was the mistreatment of African American voters in the disputed 2000 presidential election. Across the nation, a survey found that 1 of every 10 Blacks sampled reported voting problems, twice that reported by Whites (Dawson & Bobo, 2000). Indeed, this issue is at the core of Florida's hotly disputed voting returns. The U.S. Commission on Civil Rights reports that African American voters in Florida were five times more likely to have their ballots rejected than were other voters (Garber, 2001a), a disparity that drew scant attention from the mass media in their fascination with "pregnant chads." Florida's return to its racist political practices of the past may have decided the presidential election, because 93% of those Black Floridians who did manage to cast their votes supported Vice President Gore.

Education

Clark's major concerns have involved Black youths. Together with the NAACP Legal Defense and Education Fund, his integration efforts have focused on establishing interracial public schools. And the past half-century has witnessed notable Black progress in median school years completed and high school and college graduation rates. In 1940, African Americans over 24 years of age had a median of only a sixth-grade education, and only 7% had graduated from high school. Today African Americans over 24 years have a median of some college training, and two thirds have graduated from high school (U.S. Bureau of the Census, 1999). These two indices are among the few that reveal a narrowing of differences between Black and White Americans.

But the key question now becomes the quality of the education Black children are receiving. Just as Thurgood Marshall and Kenneth Clark argued a half-century ago, quality is tightly intertwined with desegregation. Yet the 1990s recorded an accelerated retreat in racial desegregation of the public schools. By 1999, Black children were more likely to be attending predominantly Black schools than at any point in recent decades. In 2000, 70% of the nation's Black children attended predominantly Black schools, and 37% attended schools with 90% or more Black students. The greatest retrogression during the 1990s occurred in the South, the region that had previously witnessed the greatest gains (Orfield, 2001; Orfield & Eaton, 1996).

Employment

An old rule of thumb gauged Black unemployment to be roughly twice that of White unemployment through both good and bad economic times. Unfortunately, the rule still holds true. In January 2001, for instance, the Black and White American unemployment rates were about 7% and 3%, respectively (Simms, 2001b).

For employed African Americans, job upgrading in many areas has been substantial. Significant percentage gains have occurred in many areas of skilled blue-collar and white-collar employment, whereas domestic service has dramatically declined since 1950. Nevertheless, compared with White Americans of equal educational attainments, African American workers today occupy lower status jobs on average and receive smaller earnings from their employment. These racial differentials are especially large for Black men but much less so for Black women because White women also face job and income discrimination (U.S. Bureau of the Census, 1999; U.S. Bureau of Labor Statistics, 1999).

Criminal Justice

Whereas other domains have witnessed positive racial trends, the nation's criminal justice system has no such trends to offer. The United States now has the highest incarceration rate in the world. With 690 people per 100,000 in jail, the nation's rate is 4 to 6 times higher than that of other countries and up to 10 times that of industrialized countries in Western Europe. And this massive internment largely reflects the imprisonment of minorities, especially young African American men (Oliver, 2001).

Over the past 30 years, the number of Americans behind bars has increased five times and now approaches 2 million people. Many factors explain this rapid escalation of imprisonment, but a dramatic rise in actual crime is not one of them. The politicization of crime, however, is a prominent factor underlying the many changes in the criminal justice system that have taken place, such as the so-called war on drugs, restrictions on judicial discretion, longer sentences for drug offenses, "three-strikes-and-you-are-out" legislation, and a doubling in constant dollars of public funding for the police and prisons (Oliver, 2001; Western, 2001).

There has long been a racial differential in incarceration rates. Yet this phenomenon has fundamentally changed in recent decades. Black rates were roughly twice those of White rates in 1975; today the difference approaches seven times. Whereas White imprisonment rates have roughly doubled over these years, Black rates have risen about seven times. Sharp racial differences in both the arrest and imprisonment rates for less serious crimes are at the core of the issue. Oliver (2001, p. 29) calculated "that if the rate of imprisonment per arrest were the same for Blacks and Whites in all offense categories, the Black imprisonment rate would be about half of what it is." It is hardly cynical to suspect that this vast, post–civil-rights-era incarceration of young Black men serves in part as a social control mechanism against the threat of racial change.

The harmful ramifications of this phenomenon are extensive. Prison time reduces the lifelong earnings and employment of those jailed, and thus it directly contributes to the creation of Black female-headed households and Black poverty. Indeed, as a source of economic deprivation and family disruption, Oliver (2001) suggested that the massive imprisonment of young Black men may well increase rather than decrease crime rates. In any event, the phenomenon conceals the true level of Black unemployment and importantly adds to the economic distress of poor Blacks (Western, 2001).

Another effect involves voting. Restrictions that keep felons and ex-felons from voting affect about 13% of the African American adult population. In the contentious Florida presidential returns in 2000, there were about 200,000 disenfranchised ex-felons (Mauer, 2001). Ex-felons are routinely allowed to vote in the vast majority of other industrial nations.

Housing

Residential segregation between Black and White Americans has declined roughly 19% over the past three decades. But Blacks remain by far the most segregated of all American minorities. The dissimilarity index of 65 in 2000 means that the complete elimination of segregation would require 65% of all Black households now living in a predominantly Black census tract to move to a predominantly White tract (Harrison, 2001). Though this index declined slightly during the 1990s, the slow rate of improvement would not eliminate Black–White housing segregation for 150 years.

The percentage of Black Americans who own their homes has doubled since 1940 (23% to about 45%) but remains far below that of White Americans (about 70%; U.S. Bureau of the Census, 1999). A dual pattern emerges. Those Black families that have benefited the most from racial changes have often moved to the suburbs for better housing and schools. At the same time, central city ghettoes have grown larger, poorer, and more desperate. Not surprisingly, one study of 29 cities found Black Americans comprised 58% of the homeless (Conrad & Lindquist, 1998).

These two trends combine to establish an intense confluence of residential segregation with poverty. Massey and Denton (1993, p. 146) demonstrated that this massive ghettoized poverty triggers "a series of ancillary changes in the social and economic composition of neighborhoods. By concentrating poverty, segregation also concentrates other [deleterious] conditions that are associated with it"—such as inferior schools (Orfield, 2001).

This situation is a direct consequence of an intense nationwide pattern of racial discrimination. Only one other urban group suffers this segregation and poverty combination: dark-skinned, but not light-skinned, Puerto Ricans (Massey & Denton, 1993). Consider, too, the findings of a large, $2 million study of housing discrimination by the U.S. Department of Housing and Urban Development (Yinger, 1995). This research conducted 3,745 field audits of advertised housing sales and rentals in 25 metropolitan areas, half with Black versus White and half with Latino versus Anglo testing teams. These audits uncovered widespread discrimination in all 25 areas against both Blacks and Latinos, but especially against African Americans in areas with large Black populations. From these results, Yinger (1995, p. 133) estimated that "discrimination has produced a deficit in net housing wealth of about $414 billion for blacks and $186 billion for Hispanics."

Financial Resources

Yinger's (1995) estimates underscore the major racial disparity in financial resources—wealth. At every income level, 1995 census data reveal that White household wealth is far greater than that of Black households (Simms, 2001a). Similarly, Black-owned businesses garner less than half of 1% of total business receipts in the American economy. Though these concerns increased in number during the 1990s, they are concentrated in the service industry and are largely individually owned and unincorporated (Garber, 2001b).

In annual income, there has been limited improvement for Black Americans. The median Black family income in 1950 was only 52% that of Whites'; by 1970 it had risen significantly to 64%, but by 1990 it had declined to only 58% of median White family income. Moreover, income gains that have occurred in Black America are limited to particular sectors. In constant dollars, median family income between 1971 and 1990 for African Americans living in the North and West actually declined. Gains occurred during these years in the South and among the most highly educated. Indeed, family income trends highlight the growing split within Black America between the have's and have-not's. In constant 1990 dollars, the percentages of Black families obtaining more than $35,000 annually and those obtaining less than $10,000 *both* increased between 1970 and the 1990s (U.S. Bureau of the Census, 1999). The growing poverty segment particularly affects Black children. In 1998, 37% of Black children lived in households below the federal poverty line compared with 10.6% of non-Hispanic White children (Joint Center for Political and Economic Studies, 2002b).

It is instructive to see how the unprecedented prosperity during the Clinton years of 1992–2000 affected Black citizens. It took about 6 of the 8 years before the boom finally reached the less educated and most residentially segregated of the Black population. Only then did urban Black unemployment rates begin to fall significantly, and a host of income-related problems, such as crime and health, begin to improve in the nation's largest ghettoes. But if history repeats itself, this improvement is likely to be brief, with Black unemployment rising and income declining more rapidly than that of Whites during the economic downturn of the early years of the century.

Health

Gross racial health indices show progress. In 1940, the average life expectancy for African American newborns was only 53 years; today it is slightly more than 70 years. This gain is larger than the White American gain from 65 to 76 years (U.S. Bureau of the Census, 1999). Black infant mortality has declined by two thirds since 1960, but so has White infant mortality with a rate that remains about half that of Blacks (Joint Center for Political and Economic Studies, 1998).

Once again, however, there are also negative trends. African Americans are disproportionately victims of AIDS (Leigh, 1996). And recent research exposes the harsh fact that Blacks routinely receive poorer medical care than Whites. For instance, Black patients are significantly less likely than Whites to undergo the preferred diagnostic use of cardiac catheterization after acute myocardial infarction (Chen, Rathore, Radford, Wang, & Krumholz, 2001; Schulman et al., 1999). And Blacks with early-stage, large-cell lung cancer are more likely than Whites to die largely because they receive less surgical treatment (Bach, Cramer, Warren, & Begg, 1999).

Intermarriage

This issue has not been a major concern of Black Americans since the U.S. Supreme Court ruled in 1967 that state laws prohibiting intermarriage were unconstitutional. Nonetheless, anti-intermarriage legislation represented the ultimate racist laws, and intermarriage rates serve as a sensitive indicator of racial change. During the past half century, the Black–White marriage rate has increased slowly, but it remains small. During these same years, other interracial marriage rates have increased substantially. By 1992, half of all Native American marriages and almost a third of all Asian American marriages involved a White partner. The comparable figure for African Americans was only 6.5% (U.S. Bureau of the Census, 1998). Thus, low intermarriage rates and the confluence of residential segregation with poverty sharply distinguish Blacks from other minorities in modern American society.

Summary

Three rough generalizations summarize what has been reviewed about the African American situation today. First, if the social condition is a negative one, such as infant mortality rates, African Americans usually have twice or more of the condition than White Americans. By contrast, if the condition is a positive one, such as median family income, African Americans usually have about half as much as White Americans.

Second, in gauging changes over the past half century, African Americans have advanced sharply on most social indices when one makes *intraracial* comparisons between 1950 and today. But if one makes *interracial* comparisons, many Black–White discrepancies have not narrowed. In other words, many Black Americans are in much better condition than they were in 1950; but so are many White Americans. Thus, serious racial disparities remain.

Third, the social class structure of Black America has greatly expanded over the past five decades. So averages for the entire group are now often misleading. Gains typically reflect the progress of the expanding Black middle class, whereas the losses typically reflect those Blacks still trapped in poverty, jail, and urban ghettoes.

In short, we have only begun the task of addressing racial disparities and attaining Clark's vision for his country. Moreover, racial myths have developed to rationalize the failure to make progress in recent years.

Six Current Racial Myths

Because White Americans generally encounter Blacks in interracial job situations if at all, they are typically aware of the prospering "haves" among African Africans but unaware of the "have-nots." This differential association process has contributed to the rise of six interrelated myths in White America concerning Black–White relations (Pettigrew, 1999).

Myth 1: Modern America has achieved racial equality. A national survey conducted in 2000 showed that a majority of White Americans believe this fiction. Thirty-four percent believe racial equality has been achieved already; another 18% believe that it will soon be achieved. Living with the inequality, African Americans understandably strongly disagree. Only 6% believe the nation has attained racial equality, whereas 59% believe they will never see it in their lifetimes (Bobo, Dawson, & Johnson, 2001).

Myth 2: Today's White opposition to policies that benefit African Americans largely reflects "principled conservatism" and not prejudice. Paul Sniderman and his colleagues (Sniderman, Piazza, Tetlock, & Kendrick, 1991; Sniderman & Tetlock, 1986a, 1986b) have argued that most White Americans do not oppose governmental policies that benefit Blacks for racist reasons. Rather, he maintained, Whites oppose these liberal policies simply on the grounds of their "principled conservatism." This thesis has provoked an entire shelf of rebuttals in the social psychological literature (e.g., Kinder, 1986; Kinder & Sanders, 1996; Meertens & Pettigrew, 1997; Sears, Sidanius, & Bobo, 2000; Sidanius, Pratto, & Bobo, 1996). All this work invalidates the principled conservatism claim. For example, Kinder and Sanders (1996), in their extensive volume, *Divided by Color,* showed that controls for such values as patriotism and moral conservatism do not influence the effects of racial prejudice on the 1988 presidential vote.

Myth 3: Racial segregation is a concern of the past. The residential segregation that remains is largely a function of economics and personal preference, not racial discrimination. Demographers and economists have repeatedly countered this misconception (Massey & Denton, 1993; Yinger, 1995). As noted previously, racial discrimination in both rental and owner housing markets remains far more important than economic and preference factors combined (Yinger, 1995).

Myth 4: Major Black problems today, such as teenage pregnancies and rampant crime, are largely self-inflicted and not a result of racial discrimination. Only Blacks themselves can solve these problems that are internal to Black communities. In this latest version of "blaming the victim" (Ryan, 1976), the core issue involves causal attribution. The myth views Blacks as the cause of social disorganization; social science analyses demonstrate that intense segregation and economic deprivation are the causes of the disorganization (e.g., Massey & Denton, 1993). Tellingly, when the prosperity of the waning years of the last century finally reached down to the Black poor, both teenage pregnancies and crime in Black areas declined sharply.

Myth 5: Although the Black poor still have problems, ambitious and talented Blacks face little discrimination today as they form a growing Black middle class that has successfully entered previously all-White institutions. This fiction also represents a dispositional attribution for racial problems. Note how it is the Black middle class that most resents continued differential treatment. And extensive research validates their claims (Crosby, Bromley, & Saxe, 1980; Feagin & Sikes, 1994). Even among business executives in large corporations, Blacks face not a "glass ceiling" but a "brick wall" in promotions (Collins, 1997).

Myth 6: For whatever reasons, the United States has not and cannot achieve racial integration. Clark's fanciful idea that government and major institutions could achieve such integration is now discredited. Most American institutions have never made full-faith efforts to integrate racially. Professional sports and the armed services, in which such efforts have begun, have achieved considerable success (Moscos & Butler, 1996). Clark was right in his 1953 contention that integration would proceed in direct correspondence with forceful leadership. Where such leadership exists, glimpses of Clark's steadfast vision come into view. Where such leadership has failed to develop, America's racism continues to fester.

Past Lessons for Future Use

Despite the failure of political leadership and the persistent racial myths, an unfolding, if halting, pattern of racial change has taken place. What lessons can we draw from the turbulent last half-century that could be useful in the future?

One lesson of recent years is that *racial prejudice and discrimination have become more subtle and indirect.* Blatant forms are still very much in operation, as David Duke and Jesse Helms will not let us forget. But the six myths used to justify inaction, together with an enormous research literature (e.g., Gaertner & Dovidio, 2000; Katz & Hass, 1988; McConahay, 1986; Pettigrew & Meertens, 1995; Sears, 1988), demonstrate that resistance to racial change is now often cloaked in ostensibly nonprejudicial forms. These subtle forms have much the same effect on their victims, but they are far more difficult to root out—or even to recognize as prejudice.

The signal characteristic of today's subtle prejudice is its persistent use of ostensibly nonracial reasons for anti-Black attitudes and actions (Gaertner & Dovidio, 2000). Racist attitudes and motivation are typically denied, even to one's self. But socially acceptable rationalizations are found to justify the action.

Another lesson is that *fundamental structural change must come first.* Sweeping change requires top-down institutional pressure and leadership. But this raises the question of how to achieve such structural change. Social psychology, importantly influenced by Clark's many contributions, has identified at least four underlying processes that operate to generate White acceptance of racial advances: the perception of inevitability, changed behavior leading to changed attitudes, optimal intergroup contact, and the disconfirmation of intergroup fears (Pettigrew, 1991). Let us consider briefly each of these processes.

1. *The perception of inevitability is a critical ingredient in the acceptance of social change generally.* The responses of the White South to the varying firmness of the U.S. Supreme Court's rulings on public school desegregation illustrate the point. With an uncompromising, nine-to-zero decision, the High Court's striking down of racially separate public schools as unconstitutional in 1954 generated a strong sense of inevitability even in the Deep South.

Widespread organized resistance did not begin until the next year, 1955, when the High Court retreated in its implementation order to a vague "all deliberate speed" formula (*"Brown II"*). But the White South is all too deliberate and rarely speedy. Only when this weak order undermined the sense of inevitability did the antidesegregation Citizens' Councils form and southern politicians become uniformly defiant. Now the opposition took heart that they could effectively defeat *Brown*. This point is not to claim that *Brown II* is solely responsible for the violent opposition that followed. But it is to say that the weak implementation order contributed to the opposition by removing the strong sense of inevitability that had prevailed.

This serious mistake by the U.S. Supreme Court delayed the implementation of school desegregation by at least a dozen years. The region's school desegregation did not take hold until the federal courts finally lost patience between 1968 and 1972 (Orfield, 1978). Current defenders of the Supreme Court's action maintain that it could do little else (e.g., Patterson, 2001). Worried by the certain opposition of the White South and without strong support in the North or from President Eisenhower, the divided Court believed they could not establish the needed guidelines and timetable. This perspective is undoubtedly how the High Court viewed matters in 1955. But this defense overlooks the extensive damage *Brown II* rendered by obliterating the crucially important sense of inevitability.[1] Even quite modest guidelines and a gradual timetable would have been preferable.

---

[1] I suspect current defenders of *Brown II* simply do not believe that the White South in 1954 so widely regarded the racial desegregation of the public schools as inevitable. And I doubt if they had the opportunity as I did to witness this phenomenon personally. I was in my native South at this time. And I collected my doctoral thesis data on White southern racial attitudes in the summer of 1955 immediately after *Brown II* was handed down (Pettigrew, 1959). The White South's collective sigh of relief was loud and clear.

2. *Behavior change typically leads to attitude change.* Conventional wisdom holds that attitude change must first take place before new behavior is adopted. But one of the best-established principles in social psychology is that behavior change is far more often the precursor of attitude change—as advanced by Festinger (1957, 1964) in his theory of cognitive dissonance and shown in the famous forced compliance experiment by Festinger and Carlsmith (1959). The very act of new interracial experiences for both Blacks and Whites leads to new attitudes, especially if the behavior is public and positively rewarded. Public acts commit us before significant others and further our need to have our behavior and attitudes appear consistent.

3. *Optimal intergroup contact improves racial attitudes.* Another well-established social psychological process involves optimal contact. The conditions for such contact include equal status of the groups in the situation, common goals, interdependence of the groups in achieving the goals, the potential for intergroup friendships, and authority sanction (Allport, 1954; Pettigrew, 1998). A recent meta-analysis of more than 500 studies shows that intergroup contact meeting many of these conditions alleviates prejudice substantially (Pettigrew & Tropp, 2000, 2003). It is interesting that affective rather than cognitive processes appear to be central in this effect. Favorable contact alters feelings and liking for the outgroup more than it improves stereotypes. This finding is important, because research shows that affect is more predictive of intergroup behavior than stereotypes (Esses & Dovidio, 2002; Esses, Haddock, & Zanna, 1993; Stangor, Sullivan, & Ford, 1991).

4. *The disconfirmation of racial fears and expectations reduces prejudice.* The many fears and expectations of Black and White Americans that have historically bedeviled American race relations are often so extreme and irrational that it is easy to disconfirm them. Put differently, the exaggerated nature of most racial fears makes it more likely that they are baseless. When change occurs and the fears are unsubstantiated, considerable improvements in racial attitudes can and do occur even without actual contact (e.g., Hamilton, Carpenter, & Bishop, 1984). But the two processes often operate together; optimal contact affords the opportunity to disconfirm unrealistic fears and expectations.

We can apply these processes to the present racial scene to explain the current impasse in American race relations. The sense of the inevitability of racial change has receded. Many blame continuing problems on African Americans themselves. Resisters to change are emboldened to oppose all progress in the name of principled conservatism. With the resegregation of such key institutions as the public schools, limited behavioral change is occurring among children to further attitude change. Nor is there a national focus on improving the conditions of intergroup contact. Critics typically attribute the problems of interracial institutions to the desegregation process itself rather than to the far-less-than-optimal conditions that exist. Finally, this period of entrenchment constrains the disconfirmation of racial fears. Such problems as voting fraud and differential policing only heighten and confirm fears. Note, too, that the failure of national political leadership thwarts all these processes for change—Clark's (1953) critical argument of a half-century ago.

This bleak perspective might make one give up on Clark's vision. But the gains that have been achieved and the lessons learned during the past half-century provide guidance for renewed efforts. And change efforts today possess greater political and economic resources than they did 50 years ago. The struggle continues, and we must follow Clark's example of hope, steadfastness, and determination in the future.

References

Allport, G. W. (1954). *The nature of prejudice.* Reading, MA: Addison-Wesley.

Bach, P. B., Cramer, L. D., Warren, J. L., & Begg, C. B. (1999). Racial differences in the treatment of early-stage lung cancer. *New England Journal of Medicine, 341,* 1198–1205.

Bobo, L. D., Dawson, M. C., & Johnson, D. (2001, May/June). Enduring two-ness. *Public Perspective, 11,* 12–16.

Bositis, D. A. (2001). Generational shift among Black elected officials. *Focus* (Joint Center for Political and Economic Studies), *29*(7), 5–6.

Chen, J., Rathore, S. S., Radford, M. J., Wang, Y., & Krumholz, H. M. (2001). Racial differences in the use of cardiac catheterization after acute myocardial infarction. *New England Journal of Medicine, 344,* 1443–1449.

Clark, K. B. (1953). Desegregation: An appraisal of the evidence. *Journal of Social Issues, 9,* 1–79.

Clark, K. B. (1955). *Prejudice and your child.* Boston: Beacon Press.

Clark, K. B. (1963). *The Negro protest: James Baldwin, Malcolm X, Martin Luther King talk with Kenneth B. Clark.* Boston: Beacon Press.

Clark, K. B. (1965). *Dark ghetto: Dilemmas of social power.* New York: Harper Torchbooks.

Clark, K. B. (1974). *Pathos of power.* New York: Harper & Row.

Collins, S. M. (1997). *Black corporate executives: The making and breaking of a Black middle class.* Philadelphia: Temple University Press.

Conrad, C., & Lindquist, M. (1998). Homeless population grows. *Focus, 26*(6), 4d.

Crosby, F., Bromley, S., & Saxe, L. (1980). Recent unobtrusive studies of Black and White discrimination and prejudice: A literature review. *Psychological Bulletin, 87,* 546–563.

Dawson, M. C., & Bobo, L. D. (2000). The racial divide. *The Polling Report, 16*(24), 1, 6–7.

D'Souza, D. (1995). *The end of racism: Principles for a multiracial society.* New York: Free Press.

Esses, V. M., & Dovidio, J. F. (2002). The role of emotions in determining willingness to engage in intergroup contact. *Personality and Social Psychology Bulletin, 28,* 1202–1214.

Esses, V. M., Haddock, G., & Zanna, M. P. (1993). Values, stereotypes, and emotions as determinants of intergroup attitudes. In D. M. Mackie & D. L. Hamilton (Eds.), *Affect, cognition, and stereotyping: Interactive processes in group perception* (pp. 137–166). San Diego, CA: Academic Press.

Feagin, J. R., & Sikes, M. P. (1994). *Living with racism: The Black middle-class experience.* Boston: Beacon Press.

Festinger, L. (1957). *A theory of cognitive dissonance.* Stanford, CA: Stanford University Press.

Festinger, L. (1964). *Conflict, decision and dissonance.* Stanford, CA: Stanford University Press.

Festinger, L., & Carlsmith, J. M. (1959). Cognitive consequences of forced compliance. *Journal of Abnormal and Social Psychology, 47,* 382–389.

Gaertner, S. L., & Dovidio, J. F. (2000). *Reducing intergroup bias: The common ingroup identity model.* Philadelphia: Psychology Press.

Garber, M. K. (2001a). Report finds racial disparities in Florida election. *Focus* (Joint Center for Political and Economic Studies), *29*(6), 4b.

Garber, M. K. (2001b). SMOBE shows large increases in number of minority-owned businesses. *Focus* (Joint Center for Political and Economic Studies), *29*(4), 4b.

Hamilton, D. L., Carpenter, S., & Bishop, G. D. (1984). Desegregation of suburban neighborhoods. In N. Miller & M. B. Brewer (Eds.), *Groups in contact: The psychology of desegregation* (pp. 97–121). New York: Academic Press.

Harrison, R. J. (2001). The status of residential segregation. *Focus* (Joint Center for Political and Economic Studies), *29*(7), 3–4, 8.

Joint Center for Political and Economic Studies. (1998). *Infant mortality rates.* Retrieved May 7, 2003 from htpp://www.jointcenter.org/DB/table/databank/children/health/infmort/infant.txt

Joint Center for Political and Economic Studies. (2002a). *Black office holders.* Retrieved May 7, 2003 from htpp://www.jointcenter.org/DB/table/graphs/beo—00.PDF

Joint Center for Political and Economic Studies. (2002b). Children living in poverty. *Focus* (Joint Center for Political and Economic Studies), *28*(6), 4a–4b.

Katz, I., & Hass, R. G. (1988). Racial ambivalence and value conflict: Correlational and priming studies of dual cognitive structures. *Journal of Personality and Social Psychology, 55,* 893–905.

Kinder, D. R. (1986). The continuing American dilemma: White resistance to racial change forty years after Myrdal. *Journal of Social Issues, 42,* 151–172.

Kinder, D. R., & Sanders, L. M. (1996). *Divided by color: Racial politics and democratic ideals.* Chicago: University of Chicago Press.

Leigh, W. (1996). The faces of AIDS. *Focus* (Joint Center for Political and Economic Studies), *24*(9), 6–7.

Massey, D. S., & Denton, N. A. (1993). *American apartheid: Segregation and the making of the underclass.* Cambridge, MA: Harvard University Press.

Mauer, M. (2001). Polls closed to many Black men. *Focus* (Joint Center for Political and Economic Studies), *29,* 7–8.

McConahay, J. B. (1986). Modern racism, ambivalence, and the modern racism scale. In S. L. Gaertner & J. Dovidio (Eds.), *Prejudice, discrimination, and racism: Theory and research* (pp. 91–126). New York: Academic Press.

Meertens, R. W., & Pettigrew, T. F. (1997). Is subtle prejudice really prejudice? *Public Opinion Quarterly, 61,* 54–71.

Moscos, C. C., & Butler, J. S. (1996). *All that we can be: Black leadership and racial integration the army way.* New York: Basic Books.

Oliver, P. E. (2001). Racial disparities in imprisonment: Some basic information. *Focus* (Institute for Research on Poverty, University of Wisconsin), *21,* 28–31.

Orfield, G. (1978). *Must we bus? Segregated schools and national policy.* Washington, DC: Brookings Institution.

Orfield, G. (2001). *Schools more separate: Consequences of a decade of resegregation.* Cambridge, MA: Harvard University Civil Rights Project.

Orfield, G., & Eaton, S. E. (1996). *Dismantling desegregation: The quiet reversal of Brown v. Board of Education.* New York: Norton.

Patterson, J. T. (2001). *Brown v. Board of Education: A civil rights milestone and its troubled legacy.* New York: Oxford University Press.

Pettigrew, T. F. (1959). Regional differences in anti-Negro prejudice. *Journal of Abnormal and Social Psychology, 59,* 28–36.

Pettigrew, T. F. (1991). Advancing racial justice: Past lessons for future use. In H. Knopke, R. Norrell, & R. Rogers (Eds.), *Opening doors: Perspectives on race relations in contemporary America* (pp. 165–178). Tuscalossa: University of Alabama Press.

Pettigrew, T. F. (1998). Inter-group contact theory. *Annual Review of Psychology, 49,* 65–85.

Pettigrew, T. F. (1999). Sociological analyses confront fashionable racial fallacies. *Sociological Forum, 14,* 177–184.

Pettigrew, T. F., & Meertens, R. W. (1995). Subtle and blatant prejudice in Western Europe. *European Journal of Social Psychology, 57,* 57–75.

Pettigrew, T. F., & Tropp, L. (2000). Does intergroup contact reduce prejudice? Recent meta-analytic findings. In S. Oskamp (Ed.), *Reducing prejudice and discrimination: Social psychological perspectives* (pp. 93–114). Mahwah, NJ: Erlbaum.

Pettigrew, T. F., & Tropp, L. (2003). *A meta-analytic test of inter-group contact theory.* Manuscript submitted for publication.

Ruffin, D. C. (1999). The perils of "driving while Black." *Focus* (Joint Center for Political and Economic Studies), *27*(3), 3–4.

Ryan, W. (1976). *Blaming the victim* (Rev. ed.). New York: Vintage Books.

Schulman, K. A., Berlin, J. A., Harless, J. A., Kerner, J. F., Sistrunk, S., Gersh, B. J., et al. (1999). The effect of race and sex on physician's recommendations for cardiac catheterization. *New England Journal of Medicine, 340,* 618–626.

Schuman, H., Steeh, C., Bobo, L., & Krysan, M. (1997). *Racial attitudes in America: Trends and interpretations.* Cambridge, MA: Harvard University Press.

Sears, D. O. (1988). Symbolic racism. In P. A. Katz & D. A. Taylor (Eds.), *Eliminating racism: Profiles in controversy* (pp. 53–84). New York: Plenum Press.

Sears, D. O., Sidanius, J., & Bobo, L. (Eds.). (2000). *Racialized politics: The debate about racism in America.* Chicago: University of Chicago Press.

Sidanius, J., Pratto, F., & Bobo, L. (1996). Racism, conservatism, affirmative action, and intellectual sophistication: A matter of principled conservatism or group dominance? *Journal of Personality and Social Psychology, 70,* 476–490.

Simms, M. C. (2001a). Assets of African-American households. *Focus* (Joint Center for Political and Economic Studies), *29*(7), 4c–4d.

Simms, M. C. (2001b). Unemployment inches up. *Focus* (Joint Center for Political and Economic Studies), *29*(3), 4c–4d.

Smith, T. W. (2000). *Taking America's pulse II.* New York: National Conference for Community and Justice.

Sniderman, P. M., Piazza, T., Tetlock, P. E., & Kendrick, A. (1991). The new racism. *American Journal of Political Science, 35,* 423–477.

Sniderman, P. M., & Tetlock, P. E. (1986a). Reflections on American racism. *Journal of Social Issues, 42,* 173–187.

Sniderman, P. M., & Tetlock, P. E. (1986b). Symbolic racism: Problems of motive attribution in political debate. *Journal of Social Issues, 42,* 129–150.

Stangor, C., Sullivan, L. A., & Ford, T. E. (1991). Affective and cognitive determinants of prejudice. *Social Cognition, 9,* 359–380.

U.S. Bureau of the Census. (1998). *Race of wife by race of husband: 1960, 1970, 1980, 1991, and 1992.* Retrieved May 7, 2003 from htpp://landview.census.gov/population/socdemo/race/interractab1.txt

U.S. Bureau of the Census. (1999). *The Black population in the United States* (March update, PPL-103). Washington, DC: U.S. Government Printing Office.

U.S. Bureau of Labor Statistics. (1999). *Usual weekly earnings of wage and salary workers: First quarter 1999.* Washington, DC: U. S. Government Printing Office.

Western, B. (2001). Incarceration, unemployment, and inequality. *Focus* (Institute for Research on Poverty, University of Wisconsin), *21,* 32–36.

Yinger, J. (1995). *Closed doors, opportunities lost: The continuing cost of housing discrimination.* New York: Russell Sage Foundation.

Part II ——————————————

Racial Identity

Introduction:

Creating an Identity: An Analysis of Kenneth B. Clark's Influence on the Psychology of Identity

Linwood J. Lewis

One of the most controversial elements of Kenneth Clark's work is his contribution to the psychology of African American identity. Dr. Clark's work with his wife Mamie Phipps Clark on self-hatred in Negro identity from their "doll studies" (Clark & Clark, 1939, 1940, 1950) formed the basis of their contribution to Footnote 11 of *Brown v. Board of Education* in 1954, although the doll studies were not themselves cited by the justices. The importance of the Clarks's contribution cannot be understated; Footnote 11 was the first time psychology had been used in American public policy to support African American liberation (see chap. 13, this volume). Initially, this work was considered in a positive light; most of the controversy surrounding the Clarks's work concerned whether or not segregation was harmful to African American children's self-concept. However, after the civil rights movement and the rise of Black Power, criticism of Kenneth Clark's work converged on his *perceived* focus on the negative aspects of African American urban life and his connections with a social science narrative of dysfunctional African American culture (Cross, 1991; Phillips, 2000).

For those of us interested in African American identities, the Clarks's work seems to hold a mixed message. The emphasis on self-hatred as an aspect of African American identity seems dated and "counterrevolutionary" when seen nearly 40 years after the civil rights movement. However, Kenneth Clark's discussion of resistance to prejudice and other oppressions, as well as his position that the effects of racism must be studied in Whites as well as African Americans, seems to presage approaches found in current psychological and sociological inquiries. The chapters in this section extend the work of Kenneth Clark in ways I believe he would have applauded.

For example, Steele (see chap. 4, this volume) provides a useful recontextualization of Clark's work in relation to damage/deficit models, to allow current readers of Clark's work to assess his impact within his own sociohistorical milieu. A central criticism of Clark is that his work extends perceptions of African Americans as a damaged people, particularly in his classic work *Dark Ghetto* (1965). Steele rightfully points out that such critiques of Clark are often decontextualized and do not take into account the historical progression of damage imagery that led to Clark's narrative. The balance of Steele's chapter summarizes his and his colleagues' work on stereotype threat, the deficit in performance of a task that occurs when a person perceives the threat of confirming a negative stereotype about one's social group. Steele also lays out the outline of a general model of social identity threat, which attempts to specify the social contextual cues in which stereotype threat tends to occur. For me, this work is exciting because it captures the sense that some aspects of African American "psychological damage" exist in the social space between people rather than being an inherent part of African American psyches.

Sellers and his colleagues have done much to enrich our understanding of the complexity of racial identity by unpacking its constituent constructs of salience, centrality, and regard (Sellers, Rowley, Chavous, Shelton, & Smith, 1997; Sellers, Smith, Shelton, Rowley, & Chavous, 1998). In their contribution to this volume, Neblett, Shelton, and Sellers (see chap. 5, this volume) point out the change in focus from negative to positive aspects of racial identity over the past 40 years, although there may be strands of a resilience approach even in *Dark Ghetto,* the most damage-focused of Clark's books. Neblett and colleagues explore the relationship among aspects of racial identity, interpretation of daily racial hassles, and the mental health of African Americans. Their findings that centrality, nationalist ideology, and public regard are significant predictors of the amount of racial hassles experienced by their participants are certainly interesting. Their longitudinal finding that mental health sequelae (anxiety, stress, and depression) are associated with the amount of racial hassles is sobering and has important implications for African American public health.

In exploring future directions for their research, Neblett, Shelton, and Sellars point out that these findings may be accounted for not only by attributional sets of individuals but also by the reactions of others to the behavior of individuals who espouse particular ideologies. Thus, the relationship between racial identity and discrimination experiences may be attributed more to social transactions between people than to cognitive schemas of the individual. Once again, this highlights the social nature of racial identity in ways consistent with Clark's approach.

In the final chapter in this section, Philogène (see chap. 6, this volume) uses social representations theory to explore the importance of the name used to describe Americans of African descent, and its implications for African American racial identity. Philogène traces historical changes in name from Negro to Black in the early 1960s and from Black to African American in the early 1990s and conducts a sociohistorical analysis of the cultural tensions between the use of the terms *Black* and *African American.* For me, Philogène's contribution is the most evocative of Kenneth Clark's oeuvre, particularly his later work in *Dark Ghetto* (1965) and *Pathos of Power* (1974), in which he explores the social implications of his work.

In describing her empirical work, Philogène relates how, for both African American and non-African American participants, the term *Black* is associated with race and evokes images of irresponsibility, loudness, rudeness, and musical ability, whereas the term *African American* is associated with religiosity, hard work, intelligence, and ambition. Interestingly, Kenneth Clark himself used the term *Negro* until fairly late in his career. He rejected the use of the term *Black,* which he saw as a litmus test by Black Nationalists for agreement with the militant thrust of the movement, a movement with which he had many disagreements (Clark, 1974, p.118). He correctly noted the pejorative connotation of *Negro* as an Uncle Tom or apologist for the racial status quo for many African Americans in the 1960s, a connotation that continues to the present day.

It has been a particular pleasure for me to introduce these chapters; I have used the work of all three contributors in my own teaching and writing (e.g., Lewis & Kertzner, 2003). In reading these chapters and participating in the 2001 conference from which these chapters come, I began to question Clark's relationship to damage imagery and his relevance to my work in ethnicity, sexuality, and HIV prevention. The lens through which I examine Clark's work is that of social constructionism, which holds that "facts" are created, mediated, and interpreted through the agency of historical and social forces.

As is well known to readers of this volume, after World War II, social science came to focus on the psychological causes and effects of racial prejudice (Scott, 1997). Analysis of individual psychological effects of discrimination on African American psyches again gained ascendance, albeit with a greater focus on quantification of psychological harm than past analyses of damage (e.g., DuBois, 1903/1990). Racial liberals began to use damage imagery within a psychological frame to alert White Americans and force change in race-related social policy; postwar American concerns about prejudice and social justice increased the effectiveness of such an approach. The Clarks's work in support of the legal challenges to racial segregation was essential to the successful challenge of racial segregation. Kenneth Clark's (1950) publication of a monograph based on the Mid-Century White House Conference on Children and Youth, his recruitment by the National Association for the Advancement of Colored People (NAACP) legal team led by Thurgood Marshall, and his consequent rise as a public intellectual and commentator on racial matters have been discussed elsewhere (see chap. 13, this volume; Kluger, 1975). I question the later connection between Clark and damage imagery, primarily made in regard to his writing in *Dark Ghetto* (Scott, 1997).

Kenneth Clark and Damage Imagery

Phillips (2000) discussed the controversy surrounding Clark's book *Dark Ghetto* and the conflict between Clark and other social scientists sympathetic to a *strengths* approach or to Black Nationalism. Clark's work was seen as supportive of a cultural deprivation approach, which places the blame for damage on cultural beliefs and practices that interfere with the ability of African Americans to achieve academic or economic success (Phillips, 2000). In part, this association with cultural deprivation occurred because of his association with Daniel Patrick Moynihan, a former student of Clark's and author of *The Negro Family: The Case for National Action,* which places responsibility for lack of upward economic mobility of African Americans on matriarchal family patterns in African American culture (Moynihan, 1965). His analysis in *The Negro Family* ignored the effects of racial discrimination, or indeed of any force outside of African American culture, on economic mobility.

Clark did spend significant narrative space in *Dark Ghetto* detailing the "institutionalized pathology" of the urban African American ghetto (Clark, 1965, p. 81). But Clark explicitly challenged ideas of "inherent racial differences" and "cultural deprivation theories" (Clark, 1965, p. xxii) as manifestations of an unchanging core African American identity engendered by the culture of the ghetto. He argued that cultural deprivation theories that present African American economic or academic inferiority are akin to racial inferiority theories; both associate the privileged status of dominant racial groups with innate intellectual characteristics (Clark, 1965, p. 131). For Clark, the ghetto and the pathology stemming from the psychology of the ghetto are not indicative of the essence of African American identity but are the culmination of present structural inequalities such as economic and housing segregation and expected human reactions to such conditions. Clark (1965) stated: "Chronic and remediable social injustices corrode and damage the *human* personality. . . . Racial segregation . . . debases all human beings—those who are victims, those who victimize, and . . . those who are merely accessories" (p. 63).

Because these structural inequalities and their effects on human psyches are experienced in the present, Clark's conception leaves open the possibility of constructive change through the transformation of these inequalities and the social forces that allowed their creation. This constructive change is not centered on the adaptation by African Americans of middle-class White American cultural values, as Moynihan suggested in *The Negro Family.* Nor is it centered on Erik Erikson's recitation of the psychological "realities" of Negro identity. Erikson, who was a contributor to Parsons and Clark's *The Negro American* (Erikson, 1965), cited African Americans as the most flagrant case of an American minority forced by the pressures of tradition and racial exclusion to "identify with its own evil identity fragments, thus jeopardizing whatever participation in an American identity it may have earned" (Erikson, 1950, p. 216). These "solutions," or rather conceptions of damage, can be seen as blaming the victim. Clark (1963, 1965) stated that the effects of the ghetto must be fully understood by both African Americans and Whites to sustain the exercise of power needed to effect change. Thus, Clark's presentation of pathology is seen as the first step in racial reconciliation and reform.

Clark clearly does not see the ghetto as a defining characteristic of African American culture; in fact his critique of both Black Nationalism and (White) racial superiority theories is that both see segregation as a virtue and the ghetto as the authentic representation of African American life (see Clark, 1974, for his detailed critique of Black Nationalism). The ghetto and the inequalities that create it are challenges that African Americans must contend with, whether living within its boundaries or outside of it. In Clark's view, the ghetto does exert an influence on African American identity. The experience of the ghetto carries much currency in pre–civil rights social science and popular culture because the majority of African Americans lived in largely African American communities. African Americans who physically or psychologically left the ghetto still negotiated the influence of the ghetto in their lives. Issues of authenticity also arise as African Americans who leave the ghetto expand their visions of the world beyond the ghetto. Part of the self-pathology Clark (1965) perceived in the ghetto is in its rejection of such individuals: "the Negro who dares to move outside of the ghetto . . . runs the risk of retaliatory hostility at worst, or of misunderstanding, at best" (p. 194). Those who violate the basic rules of the ghetto by giving precedence to issues other than race or criticizing other African Americans are considered racial deserters. It is clear that Clark rejected such litmus tests in theory and in his own life, leading to estrangement from Black Nationalists and other Black identity movements (Cross, 1991; Phillips, 2000).

Clark's conception of African American identity is predicated on the possibility of change, and it is this possibility that separates him from social scientists such as Erikson and Moynihan, who see the psychological and social damage placed on African Americans as a "permanent loss" (Erikson, 1950, p. 213; see Lewis, 2003, for a detailed analysis). There is an optimism underlying Clark's work that I admire, in a discipline that often focuses on the negative aspects of the human condition in general (Seligman & Csikszentmihalyi, 2000) and of African Americans in particular (Bacigalupe, 2001; Graham, 1992; Gynther, 1972; Staples, 1986/1995). I also admire his critique of the objective stance in positivist psychology in the face of human suffering and his call for social science to "dare to study the real problems of men and society, [to] use the real community, the marketplace, the arena of politics and power as its laboratories" (Clark, 1965, p. xxi).

At times, Clark sounds positively postmodern in his criticism of such a stance. Modernist scientific narratives present data as objective information, free from subjective distortion and bias. In contrast, Clark (1965) discussed at length the interpretive nature of his work and the use of the objective stance as "subconscious protection from personal pain and direct involvement in moral controversies" (p. 76).

> A few years ago a highly respected friend . . . interrupted a humorous but somewhat serious discussion by observing that I would not permit "the facts to interfere with the truth". . . . What are generally labeled the *facts* of the ghetto are not necessarily synonymous with the *truth* of the ghetto. . . . To obtain the truth of Harlem, one must interpret the facts. . . . Fact is empirical while truth is interpretive. (Clark, 1965, pp. xxiii–xxiv)

I wonder, as Steele does in his essay (see chap. 4, this volume), what Kenneth and Mamie Clark would do if they were entering psychology today. Kenneth and Mamie Phipps Clark's commitment to a morally relevant psychology opened the door to other socially relevant investigations of African American identity–health relationships; what would they make of African American lives in the 21st century? HIV/AIDS is arguably the Number 1 problem facing people of African descent today. The prevalence rate of HIV in some parts of

Africa exceeds 25%; for example, 38.8% of all adults (15–49 years) in Botswana are HIV positive (United Nations Children's Fund [UNICEF], 2003). If present trends continue, a 15-year-old boy in Botswana has a 90% chance of contracting HIV by the end of his life—if the prevalence rate drops by half, he still has a 70% chance. (T. C. Quinn, personal communication, November 2001). In the United States, African American men and women are disproportionately represented in the total of all reported AIDS cases, accounting for approximately 47% and 63% of all AIDS cases, respectively (White House Office of National AIDS Policy, 2000). Why are there such ethnic/racial disparities in HIV prevalence in the United States, even among people living in poverty? There are no good answers, although Kenneth Clark's connection of prejudice, structural inequalities, and social pressures inherent in segregation and their effects on personal identity and mental health may be a good place to start. I like to think that he would have admired Rafael Diaz's work with Latino gay men, which is one of the best examples of the linkage among inequalities, identity, physical, and mental health in HIV research (Diaz, 1998). Diaz outlined barriers to enactment of safer sex intentions. His examination of poverty and racism's effect on safer sex behavior point to fatalism and decreased sense of personal control as factors militating against condom usage in Latino gay men:

> Latino gay men have subjectively experienced one history of prejudice, discrimination and social alienation. Being poor, brown and gay are deeply intertwined in an overwhelming sense of being different. . . . For many men I interviewed, it was clear that being brown and poor went together. (Diaz, 1998, p. 116)

Just as in Clark's work, this fatalism is not an essential characteristic of Latinos or Latino gay men but an expected reaction to disempowering contexts experienced by these men. Expectations of powerlessness by both Latino men and a mainstream White, middle-class gay community suggest that Latino men have less agency to press safer sex practices with White partners. Diaz (1998) explored the effects of cultural scripts such as machismo and family loyalty on gay identity and safer sex practices, mirroring Clark's approach to the ghetto–identity relationship.

In research with African American men who have sex with men (MSM), African American men are less likely to consider themselves gay than men of other ethnicities (Centers for Disease Control and Prevention, 2000; McKirnan, Stokes, Doll, & Burzette, 1995; Stokes, McKirnan, & Burzette, 1993). This has implications for HIV prevention messages targeted for gay men. These messages may not resonate for African American MSMs who do not have a strong sense of themselves as *gay* men. This research has not explored the reasons for these differences but posits a combination of stigma and alienation from gay communities as possible explanations. Much of the blame for increased rates of HIV infection for heterosexual African American women has been laid at the feet of these men. There have been many reasons advanced for African American homophobia, including the Black church and social constructions of hypermasculinity, and it has been suggested that many gay African American men have internalized this homophobia, although these reasons have been contested (Crawford, Allison, Zamboni, & Soto, 2002; hooks, 1990). Explanations like these lay the "burden" of living gay on African American culture—a more nuanced examination of these men suggests a more complex negotiation of masculinity, sexuality, and perhaps more distal factors such as employment status and strong family ties as reasons for continuing to live on the down low (closeted) rather than coming out as gay men. This area of research would benefit from Clark's approach.

Given the above, it is important to reclaim Clark as a critic of modernist narratives of African American dysfunction. It is clear that Clark's arguments have relevance for *fin-de-siecle* social scientists. "Social scientists who compromise the fundamental humanity of dark-skinned children . . . are not only accessories to the perpetration of injustices; they become indistinguishable from the active agents of injustice" (Clark, 1974, p. 128). It is hoped that a widespread revival of the Clarks's approach might transform 21st-century African (American) lives, as their research did almost 50 years ago.

References

Bacigalupe, G. (2001). Is positive psychology only White psychology? *American Psychologist, 56,* 82–83.

Brown v. Board of Education, 347 U.S. 483 (1954).

Centers for Disease Control and Prevention. (2000). HIV/AIDS among racial/ethnic minority men who have sex with men—United States, 1989–1998. *MMWR, 49,* 4–11.

Clark, K. B. (1950). *The effects of prejudice and discrimination on personality development (Mid-Century White House Conference on Children and Youth).* Washington, DC: Federal Security Agency, Children's Bureau.

Clark, K. B. (1963). *Prejudice and your child.* Boston: Beacon Press.

Clark, K. B. (1965). *Dark ghetto: Dilemmas of social power.* New York: Harper & Row.

Clark, K. B. (1974). *Pathos of power.* New York: Harper & Row.

Clark, K. B., & Clark, M. P. (1939). The development of consciousness of self and the emergence of racial identification in Negro pre-school children. *Journal of Social Psychology, 10,* 591–599.

Clark, K. B., & Clark, M. P. (1940). Skin color as a factor in racial identification of Negro pre-school children. *Journal of Social Psychology, 11,* 159–169.

Clark, K. B., & Clark, M. P. (1950). Emotional factors in racial identification and preference in Negro children. *Journal of Negro Education, 19,* 341–350.

Crawford, I., Allison, K. W., Zamboni, B. D., & Soto, T. (2002). The influence of dual identity development on the psychosocial functioning of African American gay and bisexual men. *Journal of Sex Research, 39,* 179–189.

Cross, W. E., Jr. (1991). *Shades of Black: Diversity in African-American identity.* Philadelphia: Temple University Press.

Diaz, R. M. (1998). *Latino gay men and HIV: Culture, sexuality and risk behavior.* New York: Routledge.

DuBois, W. E. B. (1990). *The souls of Black folk.* New York: Vintage Press. (Original work published 1903)

Erikson, E. H. (1950). *Childhood and society.* New York: Norton.

Erikson, E. H. (1965). The concept of identity in race relations: Notes and queries. In T. Parsons & K. B. Clark (Eds.), *The Negro American* (pp. 227–253). Boston: Houghton-Mifflin.

Graham, S. (1992). "Most of the subjects were White and middle class": Trends in published research on African Americans in selected APA journals, 1970–1989. *American Psychologist, 47,* 629–639.

Gynther, M. D. (1972). White norms and Black MMPIs: A prescription for discrimination. *Psychological Bulletin, 78,* 386–402.

hooks, b. (1990). *Yearning: Race, gender, and cultural politics.* Boston: South End Press.

Kluger, R. (1975). *Simple justice: The history of Brown v. Board of Education and Black America's struggle for equality.* New York: Random House.

Lewis, L. J. (2003). *Erikson, Moynihan and Kenneth Clark: Exploring essentialist aspects of African American damage imagery.* Manuscript in preparation.

Lewis, L. J., & Kertzner, R. M. (2003). Toward improved interpretation and theory building of African American male sexualities. *Journal of Sex Research, 40,* 383–395.

McKirnan, D. J., Stokes, J. P., Doll, L., & Burzette, R. G. (1995). Bisexually active gay men: Social characteristics and sexual behavior. *Journal of Sex Research, 32,* 65–76.

Moynihan, D. P. (1965). *The Negro family: The case for national action.* Washington, DC: U.S. Department of Labor, Office of Policy Planning and Research.

Phillips, L. (2000). Recontextualizing Kenneth B. Clark: An Afrocentric perspective on the paradoxical legacy of a model psychologist-activist. *History of Psychology, 3,* 142–167.

Scott, D. M. (1997). *Contempt and pity: Social policy and the image of the damaged Black psyche, 1880–1996.* Chapel Hill: University of North Carolina Press.

Seligman, M. E., & Csikszentmihalyi, M. (2000). Positive psychology: An introduction. *American Psychologist, 55,* 5–14.

Sellers, R. M., Rowley, S. J., Chavous, T. M., Shelton, J. N., & Smith, M. (1997). Multidimensional Inventory of Black Identity: Preliminary investigation of reliability and construct validity. *Journal of Personality and Social Psychology, 73,* 805–815.

Sellers, R. M., Smith, M. A., Shelton, J. N., Rowley, S. A. J., & Chavous, T. M. (1998). Multidimensional model of racial identity: A reconceptualization of African American racial identity. *Personality and Social Psychology Review, 2,* 18–39.

Staples, R. (1995). Stereotypes of Black male sexuality: The facts behind the myths. In M. S. Kimmel & M. A Messner (Eds.), *Men's lives* (3rd ed., pp. 375–380). Boston: Allyn & Bacon. (Original work published 1986)

Stokes, J. P., McKirnan, D. J., & Burzette, R. G. (1993). Behavior, condom use, disclosure of sexuality, and stability of sexual orientation in bisexual men. *Journal of Sex Research, 30,* 203–213.

United Nations Children's Fund (UNICEF). (2003). *At a glance: Botswana.* Retrieved January 13, 2004 from http://www.unicef.org/infobycountry/botswana—statistics.html

White House Office of National AIDS Policy. (2000). *Youth and HIV/AIDS 2000: A new American agenda.* Washington, DC: White House.

4

Kenneth B. Clark's Context and Mine: Toward a Context-Based Theory of Social Identity Threat

Claude M. Steele

The first time I saw Kenneth Clark he was on television. I was in high school at the time, and my whole family was crowded into the small hallway that served as our TV room. It was summertime in 1964 and a "race riot," as they were called then, had just broken out in New York City. We were caught up in the urgency of the events. But I remember how struck we were by the image of Clark himself. He was a commentator on the broadcast. Perhaps he was a familiar public figure in New York City at the time, but he was unknown to my family of Chicagoans. He wore dark-rimmed glasses, spoke with a resonant voice, and seemed effortlessly articulate. He talked about human development and how the experience of being Black in America had profound psychological consequences. His presence inspired hope. With such intelligence at work on the problem, could better times be far away? And the way he spoke—I wanted to be that way. Yet, I do not remember feeling any epiphany. After the broadcast I probably went outside to try, yet again, my losing hand at basketball. But somehow I had been deflected; I had seen a new possibility.

Later in college I had become interested in psychology. Soon I was to encounter the deeper side of Kenneth Clark, his research and writings. Again, I felt a natural connection. His work dealt with phenomena that were personally relevant. But it also revealed the power of science, of empirical research, of working ideas out against empirical evidence. Through the portal of Clark's work, I could better see the reach of science, how it could elucidate things I cared about.

But his work—and here I am referring to his first book *Prejudice and Your Child* (1955)—also addressed society. It explained the importance of racial integration. This work was clearly psychology. Indeed, it turned out to be influential psychology, foreshadowing several subfields of inquiry into the effects of race on the self-concept and identity development, as well as reactions to stigmatization. But it was bigger than that. It gave American society a framework for dealing with a problem that, more than any other, had frustrated its ideals of fairness and openness: the problem of incorporating a long stigmatized group into its mainstream.

Kenneth Clark's journey to this epitome begins, as nearly everyone knows, with his and Mamie Clark's "doll studies" (Clark & Clark, 1947). The core finding of this research is that Black children as young as 5 or 6 years of age, when given a choice between white and brown dolls, showed a distinct preference for the white dolls when asked such questions as which one they preferred and which one they liked the most. These findings still fascinate us. Sixty years after their publication, I would argue that we still do not satisfactorily understand them.

But they were soon to attain a broader significance than their relevance to psychology. They are one among a small group of psychological studies that have come to characterize an era, or at least a defining problem of an era. I would put Milgram's (1965) experiments on obedience in this category, also the emergency intervention studies of Latané and Darley (1970) and the Zimbardo (1972) prison experiment. These studies illustrate a problem of major concern to society during a given era and offer an illuminating, if nonobvious, explanation for it. Science is never kind to particular explanations; its job is to press further. But at the very least, these studies injected into public discourse a new way of understanding something of importance. And this has to be the larger significance of Kenneth and Mamie Clark's doll studies. They helped change the way people thought about the racial segregation that was the order of that day.

Beginning as early as the late 1920s, a group of National Association for the Advancement of Colored People (NAACP) lawyers that included such men as Thurgood Marshall, Robert L. Carter, and later Jack Greenberg had been leading a legal assault on racial segregation. This system had been constructed around the 1896 "separate-but-equal" Supreme Court ruling of *Plessy v. Ferguson*. At the time the doll studies appeared, virtually every aspect of American life was racially segregated: schools, housing, public facilities from water fountains to swimming pools, working conditions, unions, the military, restaurants, hotels, and so on. These lawyers aimed to legally overcome this segregation and the Supreme Court ruling on which it was based. Toward the end of the 1940s, a strategy began to emerge.

In his 1997 book, *Contempt and Pity,* historian Daryl Scott described the development of this strategy. In his account, it was Robert L. Carter who came up with the basic idea. The Supreme Court had just ruled against racial segregation of Black and White law schools in Oklahoma on the grounds that it prevented Blacks from having access to the "intangible" advantages of the White school: "reputation of the faculty, the 'experience of the administration,' the influence of the alumni, 'standing in the community' " (from *Sweatt v. Painter,* in Scott, 1997, p. 121). Carter reasoned that if he could come up with an "intangible" negative consequence of racially segregated schools, then he might have the grounds on which to overturn *Plessy v. Ferguson*. But what could that intangible be?

It was apparently to answer this question that Carter, now in contact with Kenneth Clark, spawned what Scott (1997) called the *psychic damage* strategy: the idea that racial segregation of American public schools caused a psychic damage in Negro children. With this stroke, Carter and Clark had identified the intangible cost of school segregation that they were after. The idea that Blacks might harbor feelings of inferiority, even self-hatred, as a result of living in a segregated society that was saturated with negative images of their group was not a new idea. As Scott's research documents, it dated back at least to the beginning of the 20th century. It was present in the work of W. E. B. Dubois. But what Carter, Clark, and the other lawyers and social scientists who participated in this case had done was to make a legal wedge out of it, a wedge to upend racial segregation. Its rationale was "therapeutic"; the only way this damage could be undone was to desegregate America's schools.

Kenneth and Mamie Clark's doll studies provided the scientific basis for this wedge, the demonstration that gave tangible evidence to the idea of an intangible psychic damage. The studies came to have a place of their own in the discourse over school desegregation, a place that, in some respects, was different from their place in the scientific discourse over these issues. As Scott (1997) described, there were alternative findings and points of view about the connection between racial segregation and psychic damage in the scientific literature. Some social scientists believed that it was racial integration, not segregation, that undermined the self-esteem of Black school children. They produced evidence to support this claim (e.g., Davis, 1943; Lewin, 1941). Clark himself had waffled on how to interpret his own evidence. For example, he changed his interpretation of the finding that northern Black children in integrated schools got more upset when they chose a white doll than did southern Black children in segregated schools. Initially, he had been quite open about what this finding said about segregation. But as the psychic damage strategy unfolded, he published the view that southern black children's calm acceptance of their choice reflected an internalized sense of inferiority that was a consequence of their school segregation.

This was a hugely important historical moment. Clark had not picked himself to play the role he was given. And almost the entire social science community supported him for the sake of the larger goal: desegregation of American society. It was in this way that the doll studies, interpreted as showing the inferiority-making effects of racial segregation, were catapulted into the national consciousness and into history in a way that, as Benjamin and Crouse (chap. 13, this volume) have noted, was not to happen to any other psychological finding.

Beyond the Deficit Model

And it was probably in this way—embedded in the intellectual framework that opposed segregation—that the rather disturbing idea of Black psychic damage stemming from racial segregation and oppression went relatively unopposed for some time, well into the 1960s. But by the late 1960s, the idea, better known in psychology as the *deficit model,* came under serious attack, first in attacks against Patrick Moynihan's (1965) use of it in his description of the African American family, but then in attacks against Clark's use of it in his characterization of the African American ghetto in his second book, *Dark Ghetto*

(1965). Up to this point several things seemed to have shielded this idea from resistance:

1. It was an idea that was completely consistent with the dominant psychological theory of the day. Gordon Allport's well-known quote in his 1954 book, *The Nature of Prejudice,* suffices to make this point: "One's reputation, whether false or true, cannot be hammered, hammered, hammered, into one's head without doing something to one's character" (p. 142).

2. Prior to the era of desegregation and civil rights, the barriers against Black progress were so vividly obvious that pointing out the psychic damage these barriers might cause would not likely be seen as blaming the victim.

3. And then, of course, against the wretchedness of legalized racial segregation, noting the damage it might cause would have seemed to have a reasonable ring of truth.

But as society changed, the idea of a Black deficit born of racial oppression played itself out over a different backdrop. Water fountains, dressing rooms, swimming pools, and even college classrooms were becoming integrated. African Americans had turned their attention from civil rights to their self-image, launching a movement of self-definition that projected a positive identity grounded in their cultural and historical contributions to society. And this is where the damage and deficit models, as well as most strictly psychological explanations, began to feel awkward.

In explanation of the lingering racial inequalities that persisted in every walk of life—education, health outcomes, income, and the like—these ideas often seemed to point a finger of blame at the victims. This is not an inherent feature of these explanations—as I shall argue. But it happens because psychology easily slips into historical, decontextualized characterizations of behavior and psychological functioning. That is, it rarely specifies the ongoing circumstances to which a psychological state, trait, or process is an adaptation. And thus, it can wind up characterizing unequal group outcomes as caused by something about the psychology of the victim, missing or deemphasizing the role of context and circumstance.

Thus the arguments of that earlier era, so powerfully shaped by Clark, had led to an awesome achievement, one that had inspired many of us to become psychologists. But ironically, it had also left us with a searing challenge: how to explore the psychology of racial experience and social identity more broadly, without portraying that experience as leading, inevitably and exclusively, to deficit and incapacity.

This challenge was soon picked up by a number of African American psychologists, many of whom are contributors to the present volume. William Cross, Janet Helms, Thomas Parham, James Jackson, Jean Phinney, Robert Carter, and more recently, Robert Sellers, Nicole Shelton, and many others have created and sustained a subfield of developmental and personality psychology studying African American identity development and self-concept. This work acknowledges that discrimination and negative group images in society can affect the psyche of a group, and even that in some instances these images can be internalized by targets. But they cast this process in the larger context of identity development, an active process that while affected by "encounters" with racism can also adapt in ways that produce a fully developed, undamaged personality, one even characterized by distinctive strengths. Others such as James Jones, Wade Boykin, and Wade Nobles explored the strengths and resources of African American culture, and in particular, the role that these cultural factors play in coping with the devaluing experiences attached to racial identity.

At the root of this work, I suggest, is a basic insight, shared by, among others, the African American novelist Ralph Ellison. Some years earlier, in his essay titled "What Would America Be Like Without Blacks" (1970), Ellison conveyed his fatigue with the way Blacks were portrayed in the social sciences. He used the device of showing how nearly every aspect of American life—language, music, architecture, body movement, the centrality of the value for freedom, and so on—had been shaped by the presence of Americans of African descent. Their experience, he argued, had been an inextricable tributary to American culture, that America, in significant part, was Black.

In this portrayal was a central theme: African Americans had not been passive to their status and treatment but had always responded to it with resilience and creativity. Behind their "invisibility," in Ellison's terms, was a fully human people actively engaged in resisting and transforming their oppressive experience, and in the process, creating some of the defining forms of American society and culture. This energy, ill gotten as it was, was a defining American energy. From what capacities of African Americans, of human beings, did it come? How can people cope with a sustained experience of group-based devaluation, marginalization, and threat? Exploring the psychological nature of this resilience and transformative creativity has been a central task of the post-Clark generation of especially African American psychologists. And as this book reveals, they have taken it quite a distance.

But when it comes to seeing the limitations and costs of the deficit model of African American experience, we latter-day psychologists—Black and non-Black—had a distinct advantage over Clark: We were not under the press of having to develop an essentially therapeutic rationale for desegregating American society. That task fell to him. Would he agree with the critiques of the deficit model? Would he press for a deeper understanding of the psychic and cultural resources with which African Americans cope with prejudice and marginalization? Would he recognize the cultural achievements of African Americans and their role in coping with oppression? I cannot help but believe that the answer to all of these questions is a resounding yes. He is a man of prodigious intellect on whose shoulders fell a task that had to be done before those following him could do other tasks.

One contribution that someone's work can make is to lay out the intellectual landscape—the central issues, questions, and challenges—that subsequent work in an area must address. For anyone interested in the psychological effects of being prejudiced against, Kenneth Clark's work laid out that landscape. And at its center remains a challenge: how to understand the psychology of this experience without falling into a language and paradigmatic way of thinking that loses sight of the ongoing context with which the person is contending.

Theories of Threat

In answer to this challenge, the work of my colleagues and I has evolved toward a particular strategy: Before describing the psychology of this experience, we have tried first to describe the ongoing context to which that psychology is an adaptation. That is, we have tried to integrate some characterization of the person's ongoing life context into our characterization of the person's psychology and behavior.

This approach has its origins in my long-standing interest in how people cope with self-image threat—threats that can arise from the judgments of others but that can also arise from one's own behavior in the form of failure or self-contradiction. Initially this work focused on general self-image threats that could happen to anyone: for example, the threat experienced when called a negative name (Steele, 1975) or that experienced from self-contradictory behavior of the sort induced in cognitive dissonance experiments (e.g., Steele & Liu, 1983). Our focus was less on the nature of the threat than on the psychological resources people could summon to deal with it. In a general theory of self-affirmation (e.g., Steele, 1988), I argued that the capacity to recover from one self-image threat by affirming a valued aspect of the self, even when that aspect was unrelated to the provoking threat, gave people a great deal of resiliency and flexibility in coping with self-image threat.

But over the years, spurred by an effort to understand academic underperformance among certain groups in society (e.g., minority group students and women in math), the work of my colleagues and I began to focus more on the nature of the threat itself, in particular, on how certain forms of self-image threat seemed to be attached to certain social identities in certain situations. Here we began to etch out a conceptualization of how the context of one's life could be shaped by one's social identity: Based on that identity, one could be exposed to preconceptions and stereotypes about one's group and self that would have to be contended with on an ongoing basis.

Our work on stereotype threat (e.g., Steele, Spencer, & Aronson, 2002) is a prime example. We define this threat as follows: Whenever one is in a situation in which a negative stereotype about one of one's social identities is relevant, one can feel in jeopardy of fulfilling the stereotype, or of being judged and treated in terms of it. When the stereotype in question is negative and encompassing of the self—as, for example, when it denigrates intelligence—and when it is relevant to important situations in life—such as academic performance—then this form of threat can be a rather serious condition of life. Here, then, is a characterization of the burden of prejudice and stereotypes that begins with a characterization of how they shape one's life context. Rather than skipping over a specification of the context to get to the psychic deficit it would presumably cause, this approach begins by trying to elaborate an understanding of the context itself—a more precise specification of the threatening predicament that stereotypes cause for particular identities in particular situations.

When the goal of such an analysis is to understand the negative outcomes experienced by certain groups—as in the case of explaining the academic underperformance of certain groups—this approach can yield a more compassionate explanation. But more important, it yields a more complete understanding of the relevant psychology, psychology that is now understood in context.

Using this approach, we have uncovered several facts about the academic underperformance of groups whose abilities are negatively stereotyped:

1. *Stereotype threat contributes to underperformance.* The underperformance of such groups—underperformance that is often attributed to group-based deficits in ability, expectations, and confidence—can stem in significant part from stereotype threat, the threat of confirming or being seen to confirm negative stereotypes about their group's abilities in critical performance situations. Our early research showed that this pressure could undermine the standardized test performance of motivated women students taking a difficult math test (Spencer, Steele, & Quinn, 1999) and motivated African American students taking a difficult verbal test (Steele & Aronson, 1995). It is frustration on the test that initiates the threat. It makes the negative stereotype about their group's abilities—something that is always "in the air" of the students' life context—relevant to them personally as they take the test. Then, if they are identified enough with the content of the test to care about their performance, the prospect of confirming or being seen to confirm this stereotype can be upsetting enough to undermine their performance.

Importantly though, when this pressure is removed, the performance of these groups goes up to match that of equally skilled test-takers who are not members of ability-stereotyped groups. To remove this pressure, one has to somehow make the group stereotype irrelevant to the person's performance. Most commonly, this has been done in this research by telling participants that the particular test they are about to take is either nondiagnostic of ability—making any stereotype about ability irrelevant to performance on the test—or that the test does not show group differences in performance—meaning that any frustration on the test could not suggest a group-based limitation of ability alleged in the stereotype because the test does not measure such differences.

This improved performance among ability-stereotyped test-takers when stereotype threat is removed makes the point that their lower performance under normal test-taking conditions—when the stereotype is left relevant to their performance—is, in some significant part, due to stereotype threat. That is, this form of threat is a feature of the context in which they take tests in real life, and most likely, when the critical conditions are in place, it impairs that performance. The students' abilities, then, as evidenced by test performance, cannot be adequately understood without reference to the identity-based context in which they take these tests.

2. *Stereotype threat is not restricted to particular groups.* Research over the years also makes it clear that stereotype threat's impairment of performance is not restricted to particular groups. It can happen to any group performing in an area wherein their abilities are negatively stereotyped, and it can happen for behaviors other than test-taking. Stone, Lynch, Sjomeling, and Darley (1999), for example, reported a series of experiments that make both points. They found that the performance of White, college-level athletes on a miniature golfing task was impaired relative to that of Black athletes when the task was represented as a measure of "natural athletic ability," a representation that

makes the stereotype about White athletes not having as much natural ability as Black athletes relevant to their task performance. But the tables were turned in another condition in which the task was represented as a measure of "sport strategic intelligence." There, the task representation made the stereotype about Blacks' intelligence relevant to their performance on the golf task, and accordingly, they performed worse than White athletes in this condition. As these findings illustrate, stereotype threat can affect the performance of essentially any group on a variety of behaviors. It is seen to arise not from a predisposition of the group but from the relevance of a negative group stereotype to a specific performance, that is, from a context of stereotype threat linked to a specific social identity in a specific situation.

3. *Higher skills and motivation leave one susceptible to stereotype threat.* Also, contrary to the idea that low self-regard is necessary for stereotype threat to impair performance, research shows that the impairing effect of stereotype threat is greatest for people with the strongest skills and motivation to succeed in the domain, and occurs hardly at all for people who do not care about the domain. This latter group performs poorly regardless of whether they are under stereotype threat. But the skilled and motivated vanguard of a negatively stereotyped group—for example, strong women math students identified with doing well in math—reliably show the effect. It is they for whom the prospects of being reduced to a negative group stereotype in the domain is upsetting, and thus, disruptive to performance. Blascovich, Spencer, Quinn, and Steele (2001) have shown that performing under this pressure significantly elevated the blood pressure of African American participants, a fact that suggests their underperformance results less from giving up than from their trying too hard.

Stereotype threat is indeed a contextual threat. Tied to stereotypes about one's group in the larger society, it is part of the context with which one must contend in situations in which those stereotypes apply. But it is felt most acutely by members of the stereotyped group who are the most identified with the domain in which the threat exists. In fact, one protection against stereotype threat that we have proposed is disidentification with the domain in which it occurs (see Steele, 1997), a point that leads nicely to our last point about the stereotype threat research.

4. *Disengagement from the performance domain is a defense against stereotype threat.* Domain disidentification is a process that helps to explain how a person can be exposed to negative stereotypes about his or her group and not have those stereotypes "hammered in" to the point of its lowering his or her self-esteem—a typical meaning of psychic damage. That is, although the burden of stereotype threat may be an inevitability that is certain to occur in situations in which relevant negative stereotypes about a person's group could be applied, psychic damage as a consequence may not be. Stereotype threat research reveals people to be rather strong resisters of these stereotypes. They consistently put forth great effort to perform despite the possibility of being negatively stereotyped, almost in resistance to it. Thus, if psychic damage occurs from being in a negatively stereotyped group, it does not seem to occur because people passively accept the negative stereotype. No matter how broadly held the stereotype is in the larger society, its targets first seem to resist it. And

this is especially true in domains that are broadly valued in society such as schooling and academic achievement.

The research of Crocker and Major and their colleagues (e.g., Crocker & Major, 1989) shows that in this resistance, people have a rather fulsome set of attributional weapons. They can even use the negative stereotype or stigma itself to help protect their self-esteem. For example, they can blame failures and setbacks on prejudice toward them that may derive from the stereotype; they can evaluate themselves in relation to only other people who endure the stereotype, and so on.

And then, domain disidentification (and disengagement) is an almost surgically precise weapon in the fight against the effect of stereotypes and stigma on self-esteem. One disengages one's self-evaluation from precisely the domain in which the stereotype applies. The price, of course, is less intrinsic motivation in the domain. And when the domain in question is academic achievement in the form of test and grade performance, this price can be considerable. Accordingly, the adaptation of disidentification is likely to be slow to come and painful. But when the threat is strong and persistent, disengagement may turn into full-blown disidentification in a domain, and the seeking of other domains on which to base one's self-evaluation.

These are ways, then, that people can protect their self-esteem from the threat of negative stereotypes and stigma. But what about internalization of the negative stereotype? Do people eventually yield to the hammering that Allport (1954) described and come to accept the negative stereotype as true of their group, and even of themselves? The above strategies do not rule out the possibility that a person could still come to believe the stereotype. This has been a long-standing suspicion about the psychology of negatively stereotyped groups; one that was, in no small part, fueled by the Clark doll studies themselves.

To this question, stereotype threat research offers a two-part answer. First, as just noted, people who are the targets of negative stereotypes seem to first resist them. Second, the theory behind this work has a clear implication about when such internalization, if it happens, could happen: when a person has never been identified with the domain in question or has disidentified with the domain. As long as a person is enough identified with a domain for it to be a basis of his or her self-evaluation, he or she should resist internalizing the domain-relevant negative stereotype.

The larger point here is that internalization of a negative group stereotype in the form of chronic self-doubts and low performance expectations, especially about something as societally important as school achievement, is best understood as a domain-specific reaction to a perceived threat in the domain, and as something that is resisted until the person loses the stamina to remain identified with the domain. It does not happen automatically or through passivity.

A Model of Social Identity Threat

This research shows the power of one's life context to influence a behavior as important as standardized test performance and school achievement more generally. And in so doing, it makes the larger point that psychological functioning and behavior cannot be well understood outside the context to which they are adaptations. This research also shows that contextual factors, such as the possibility of being stereotyped in certain settings, are literally attached to social identities. They go around with the person holding the identity, waiting to emerge as a contingency of behavior and psychological functioning in situations in which they are relevant.

From these conclusions, it is not too large a step to reason that beyond the particular phenomena of stereotype threat there could be a more general phenomenon of social identity threat. That is, a person could experience a sense of being at risk of devaluation or marginalization in a setting based on a social identity even when the source of the threat is not the relevance of a negative stereotype. For example, individuals could recognize that on the basis of one of their social identities they are a small outgroup minority in a setting— for instance, a Methodist on a softball team that is 90% Catholic. Even when no negative stereotype about their group is relevant to them in the setting, they could worry that they might be marginalized in the setting, kept outside the "ingroup." This sense of threat, then, can derive from more cues in a setting than those signaling the relevance of a negative group stereotype. In fact, stereotype threat could be a specific form of more general social identity threat. And like stereotype threat, social identity threat should affect a broad range of psychological functioning and behavior (e.g., intergroup relations) as well as particular performances.

This reasoning takes another step away from the idea of psychological functioning as something that is largely "inside the head" and strongly stable across situations. It suggests instead that it is a pattern of transaction with aspects of a person's environment. Thus to understand the broader effects of social identity on psychological functioning, one must understand the ways in which social identity shapes one's transactions with that environment.

To this end, and to extend our work on the perspective of potential targets of prejudice, my colleagues and I have begun to outline a more general model of social identity threat, one that includes the experience of stereotype threat but that tries to capture the broader experience of social identity threat. As important, this model attempts to identify a broader set of contextual cues that can cause such threat. And as we shall see, an understanding of how these cues mediate social identity threat may help in figuring out how to remedy it. The reasoning of this model is summarized in four parts:

1. All people have multiple social identities: sex, age, race, ethnicity, profession, religion, language, region, sexual orientation, and so on. As people engage a setting, the possibility exists that they could be devalued on the basis of one or more of these identities.

2. Cues that indicate the possibility of an identity-based devaluation in the setting initiate an appraisal process. This process functions as an ongoing hypothesis-testing about possible threat in the setting. Many more cues than just those relevant to prejudice in the setting are relevant to this appraisal. Cues and interpretations that confirm the hypothesized threat sustain vigilance; those that reduce the threat relax vigilance. This logic is summarized in a quote from Amin Maalouf's book, *In the Name of Identity: Violence and*

the Need to Belong (1996): "People often see themselves in terms of whichever one of their allegiances (identities) is most under attack—whether he [she] accepts or conceals it, proclaims it discreetly or flaunts it, it is with that allegiance that the person concerned identifies" (p. 26).

3. The prospect of being devalued and limited on the basis of a social identity, especially in a setting to which one wants to belong, is highly threatening. Thus the motive to be vigilant is simultaneously opposed by a motive not to see what one is most sensitized to see.

4. The resulting ruminative conflict and sense of threat (as in Dubois's [1903/1990] "double consciousness") can become a chronic feature of the person's experience in the setting. Accordingly, it can undermine performance and relationships in the setting, and over time, foster disengagement and disidentification with the setting.

A chief implication of this model is that social identity threat can be aroused by more cues than just those signaling the relevance of a negative group stereotype. It can be aroused by any cue relevant to the evaluative jeopardy of people with a given social identity. More in the interest of illustration than of describing a definitive set of such cues, we offer the following examples.

1. The number and proportion of people in the setting who share a social identity: The following quote from Arthur Ashe (1993), the African American tennis player, illustrates this point: "Like many other blacks, when I find myself in a new public situation, I will count, I always count. I count the number of black and brown faces" (p. 132).

2. Cues that signal the degree to which a setting is identity-hegemonic, that is, centered on a given social identity, and thus the degree to which other social identities may feel marginalized in the setting: Sometimes even when high numbers of minority identities are present in a setting, the setting is still deeply imbued with the cultural values of a dominant group—for example, the math class with a fair number of women in it that is still centered on a male "geek" culture. Such "centeredness" of a setting can cue the perception that the setting devalues different identities.

3. Cues that a given social identity plays a significant role in organizing the setting: This would include, for example, cues that the identity affects how people are distributed to prestigious locals and roles in the setting; that interests and preferences in the setting are organized around the identity; that the identity strongly organizes social life and relationships including romantic relationships; that it organizes where people live, the kind of activities they engage in, and so on.

4. Cues that indicate how much the setting values a diversity of groups and perspectives.

5. Cues as to the strength of the norms favoring intergroup sensitivity in speech and conduct.

We have yet to directly test the ability of cues such as these to cause social identity threat. But several studies in the existing stereotype threat literature do test the principle implication of this theory, that stereotype threat, as a form of social identity threat, can be aroused by seemingly small, incidental cues in a setting.

Inzlicht and Ben-Zeev (2000), for example, tested whether the degree of stereotype threat among women taking a difficult math test could be affected by the incidental cue of the proportion of other women in a small group of test-takers. Their findings were clear. In groups of three test-takers, women's performance on the test went down, in a linear fashion, with each man added to the group, so that women with no men in the group performed better than women with one man in the group who performed better than women with two men in the group. These data offer compelling evidence that an incidental situational cue is capable of affecting a meaningful performance, presumably through its arousal of identity threat.

Also a series of experiments by Davies, Spencer, and colleagues (Davies & Spencer, 2001; Davies, Spencer, Quinn, & Gerhardstein, 2001) found that the incidental embedding of negative stereotypic images of women in several TV commercials shown in a laboratory study lowered the subsequent math test performance of women viewers, made them less willing to work on math test items compared with verbal items, and made them report less interest in qualitative majors and professions. Again, seemingly incidental situational cues seemed to have strong identity-alienating effects.

A study by Cole and Barber (2000) examining the fate of minority college students yielded a pattern of results that, while subject to multiple explanations, fits the present line of argument. The study found that achievement outcomes (grades, graduation rates, dropout rates, etc.) of African American college students in the sample of some 35 top American colleges and universities varied across college types. They were worse at smaller liberal arts colleges than at Ivy-league universities, large public universities, or historically Black colleges and universities.

A multitude of causes are surely involved. But our reasoning suggests one possibility: The concentration of social identity threatening cues that African American students may face on smaller campuses could influence their outcomes there. Compared with the other kinds of schools, smaller liberal arts campuses may be more often geographically isolated from minority communities, have smaller minority populations, have few minorities in positions of influence, have a less diverse campus culture, and generally be more frustrating to the cultural and social interests of minority students. This configuration of cues may establish a social identity threat for African American students. In addition to making their racial identity salient to them in the setting, it may impede their achievement and persistence in the setting. We lack the evidence from this study to even provide a tentative test of this interpretation. But in light of our larger program of research, we suggest that it is an important question for future research.

It is important to stress that the experience of social identity threat is probably based less on the perception of a particular cue than on a holistic perception of the environment. Thus, while a single cue may contribute to the perception of threat, whether or not it results in the experience of threat should depend on what else is going on in the situation and on what else the person knows or believes about the setting. Likewise, the same cue, which triggers social identity threat in one setting, may not do so in another setting in which other situational features give the cue a less provocative meaning.

And herein may lie a ray of hope as to how some of the school achievement problems that launched our research—and that were, of course, a persistent concern of Kenneth and Mamie Clark's—might be remediated: Despite the many cues in a setting that can evoke a sense of threat, a remedial strategy may nonetheless be effective by refuting the threatening meaning of those cues, either directly or through recontextualizing the cues so that they have a less threatening meaning. My colleagues and I have termed this goal of a setting as that of *identity safety* (Markus, Steele, & Steele, 2000; Plaut, 2002; Purdie, Steele, Davies, & Crosby, 2001). To the extent that it is achieved in an academic setting, it should weaken the sequelae of identity vigilance, mistrust, disidentification, and underperformance.

It is beyond the scope of this chapter to detail the evidence in behalf of this idea (see Steele et al., 2002, for a complete review). But to illustrate the idea, I present a study with implications for an important schooling process, giving critical academic feedback across the racial divide.

In Cohen, Steele, and Ross (1999), my colleagues and I reasoned that the social identity threat African American students could feel in instructional settings, based on cues like those described earlier, could undermine their trust in the feedback they get from White instructors. The question we researched was, "Can such feedback be given in a way that bridges this mistrust?" To test this, we devised a simple experimental paradigm. Black and White students at Stanford University were asked to write an essay about their favorite teacher, ostensibly for possible publication in a teaching journal. Their picture was taken (with a Polaroid) and attached to their essay. They were told that should their essay be published, we would need their photograph for publication but, in fact, the photograph was included to let them know that their race was known by the person who graded their essays. Two days later, they returned for feedback on their essays, given by a White experimenter. We measured how biased participants saw the feedback to be—as the principal measure of trust—and how motivated they were to improve their essay. It was the variation across conditions in the way the feedback was given that varied the students' identity safety in this interaction. All participants received critical feedback.

It is important to note that giving participants the feedback straightforwardly, with or without a cushioning statement ("There were many good things about your essay"), did not achieve identity safety. Black participants saw this feedback as more biased than White participants did, and seeing it that way, they were less motivated to improve their essays. This is a telling finding. These were talented students given graded-blind feedback. And yet Black students were untrusting. Our theory offers an explanation: The Black students' social identity and the stereotypes attached to it ambiguated the feedback. Was it based on their essay or on images of their group? White students would not have this question. They could take the feedback at face value. For Black students, however, there was an ambiguity that was attached to their identity and the stereotypes about it. Here, then, a social identity and the "threats in the air" attached to it isolated a group of people from valuable feedback, from cultural capital.

But one form of feedback did achieve identity safety: telling students that the teaching journal used very high standards for publication, and that having evaluated their essays, the evaluator believed that the student could meet those standards. Under this feedback, Black students saw the feedback as unbiased, and seeing it that way were highly motivated to improve their essays. More students in this condition took the essay home to improve it than did students in any other condition.

Why did this strategy work? My reasoning is this: It conveyed to Black participants that they were not being seen through the lens of negative stereotypes about their group. Using high standards and being told that they could meet those standards signaled that they were not being seen stereotypically. The content of the feedback itself was a cue that led them to discount other possibly threatening cues in the setting, and thus provided them with a sense of identity safety. This finding has a hopeful implication: In a situation that would otherwise cause a trust-breaking social identity threat among Black students, as evidenced by the results in the other feedback conditions, this feedback strategy was enough to overcome the mistrust. The entire context did not have to change for trust to be achieved; one stereotype-refuting relational act was enough.

Steele et al. (2002) reviewed research examining 10 or so strategies for achieving identity safety, focusing especially on school and workplace settings. Several findings are illustrative. Materials that represented a company as recognizing and valuing group diversity increased minorities' trust in the company. The signal that group differences were valued presumably allowed minority respondents to disregard cues in the setting that would have otherwise caused social identity threat, such as there being a small number of minorities in the company (Purdie et al., 2001). Enabling university students to have cross-race conversations—by giving evidence to the fact that all groups have a range of experiences in the setting—helped minority students see their own experiences less in racial terms, and thus, to trust more, and perform better, in that university environment (Steele et al., 2002). The performance of poorly performing elementary school students was significantly improved by "expert tutors" who, in the process of teaching, were able to deflect these students' concerns about how their reputations caused them to be seen (e.g., Lepper, Woolverton, Mumme, & Gurtner, 1993).

A promise of this work is that problems that have been understood as rooted in tenacious patterns of psychological functioning—in psychic damage—often prove to be surprisingly fixable by first recognizing the contextual contingencies that produce the problem and then changing those contingencies.

As I approached the end of my college years, having decided to go into social psychology, I applied to the social psychology graduate program at the City University of New York (CUNY) with a particular dream in mind: to work with Kenneth Clark. I waited anxiously in the spring of 1967 for word of their decision. Nothing came. Finally, on April 15, the day students had to choose among the schools they have been admitted to, I called the Graduate Center at the university for some word. They had no record of my application. Later I learned that it had been misrouted to another City College campus, completely lost to the decision process. As fate would have it, I was not to be Kenneth Clark's graduate student. But I had gotten into a great social psychology program at Ohio State University that was really building steam. So, though disappointed about my miss at CUNY, I was extravagantly happy about what lay ahead. I did not meet Clark until some 20-plus years later, and then only in passing when he came to give a talk at the University of Michigan where I was then teaching. We talked briefly. He said wise things. But he could hardly have known what he meant to me and to my generation of especially African American psychologists.

I felt that my life as a social psychologist had, from its beginnings, been built on a foundation laid down by him, both in his door-opening role in the history of the field and in the substance of his work. It was through that work that I had first seen the value and excitement of psychology as a science. My generation of African American psychologists enjoyed a greater intellectual freedom than his role in society allowed him. He had cleared away certain responsibilities. We could work on a variety of problems. His context, and the challenges in it, were different from ours. But my connection to this field, if I track down its deepest root, goes back to the achievements and challenges laid down in the person and the work of Kenneth Clark.

References

Allport, G. (1954). *The nature of prejudice.* New York: Addison Wesley.

Ashe, A. (1993). *Days of grace.* New York: Knopf.

Benjamin, L. T., & Crouse, E. M. (2002). The American Psychological Association's response to *Brown v. Board of Education*: The case of Kenneth Clark. *American Psychologist, 57*(1), 38–50.

Blascovich, J., Spencer, S. J., Quinn, D. M., & Steele, C. M. (2001). Stereotype threat and the cardiovascular reactivity of African-Americans. *Psychological Science, 12,* 225–229.

Clark, K. B. (1955). *Prejudice and your child.* Boston: Beacon Press.

Clark, K. B. (1965). *Dark ghetto: Dilemmas of social power.* New York: Harper Torchbooks.

Clark, K. B., & Clark, M. P. (1947). Racial identification and preference in Negro children. In T. M. Newcomb & E. L. Hartley (Eds.), *Readings in social psychology* (pp. 169–178). New York: Holt.

Cohen, G. L., Steele, C. M., & Ross, L .D. (1999). The mentors' dilemma: Providing critical feedback across the racial time. *Personality and Social Psychology Bulletin, 25,* 1302–1318.

Cole, S., & Barber, E. (2000). *Increasing faculty diversity: The occupational choices of high achieving minority students* (A report prepared for the Council of Ivy Group Presidents). New York: Author.

Crocker, J., & Major, B. (1989). Social stigma and self-esteem: The self-protective properties of stigma. *Psychological Review, 96,* 608–630.

Davies, P. G., & Spencer, S. J. (2001). *Stereotype threat and taking charge: The effect of demeaning commercials on women's leadership aspirations.* Unpublished manuscript, Stanford University.

Davies, P. G., Spencer, S. J., Quinn, D. M., & Gerhardstein, R. (2001). *Consuming images: How television commercials that elicit stereotype threat can restrain women academically and professionally.* Unpublished manuscript, Stanford University.

Davis, A. (1943). Racial status and personality development. *Scientific Monthly, 57,* 359.

DuBois, W. E. B. (1990). *The souls of Black folk.* New York: Norton. (Original work published 1903)

Ellison, R. (1970, April 6). What America would be like without Blacks. *Time,* 32–33.

Inzlicht, M., & Ben-Zeev, T. (2000). A threatening intellectual environment: Why females are susceptible to experiencing problem-solving deficits in the presence of males. *Psychological Science, 11,* 365–371.

Latané, B., & Darley, J. M. (1970). *The unresponsive bystander: Why doesn't he help?* New York: Appleton-Century Crofts.

Lepper, M. R., Woolverton, M., Mumme, D. L., & Gurtner, J. L. (1993). Motivational techniques of expert human tutors: Lessons for the design of computer-based tutors. In S. P. Lajoie &

S. J. Derry (Eds.), *Computers as cognitive tools: Technology in education* (pp. 75–105). Hillsdale, NJ: Erlbaum.

Lewin, K. (1941). Self-hatred among Jews. *Contemporary Jewish Record: Review of Events and Digest of Opinion, 4,* 219.

Maalouf, A. (1996). *In the name of identity: Violence and the need to belong* (Barbara Bray, Trans.). New York: Arcade.

Markus, H. R., Steele, C. M., & Steele, D. M. (2000). Colorblindness as a barrier to inclusion: Assimilation and nonimmigrant minorities. *Daedalus, 129,* 233–258.

Milgram, S. (1965). Some conditions of obedience and disobedience to authority. *Human Relations, 18,* 57–76.

Moynihan, D. P. (1965). *The Negro family: The case for national action.* Washington, DC: U.S. Department of Labor, Office of Policy Planning and Research.

Plaut, V. C. (2002). Cultural models of diversity in America: The psychology of difference and inclusion. In R. A. Shweder, M. Minow, & H. R. Markus (Eds.), *Engaging cultural differences: The multicultural challenges in liberal democracies* (pp. 365–195). New York: Russell Sage Foundation.

Plessy v. Ferguson, 163 U.S. 537 (1896).

Purdie, V. J., Steele, C. M., Davies, P. G., & Crosby, J. R. (2001, August). *The business of diversity: Minority trust within organizational cultures.* Paper presented at the 109th Annual Convention of the American Psychological Association, San Francisco, CA.

Scott, D. (1997). *Contempt and pity: Social policy and image of the damaged Black psyche 1880–1996.* Chapel Hill: University of North Carolina Press.

Spencer, S. J., Steele, C. M., & Quinn, D. M. (1999). Stereotype threat and women's math performance. *Journal of Experimental Social Psychology, 35,* 4–28.

Steele, C. M. (1975). Name-calling and compliance. *Journal of Personality and Social Psychology, 31,* 361–369.

Steele, C. M. (1988). The psychology of self-affirmation: Sustaining the integrity of the self. *Advances in Experimental Social Psychology, 21,* 261–301.

Steele, C. M. (1997). A threat in the air: How stereotypes shape intellectual identity and performance. *American Psychologist, 52,* 613–629.

Steele, C. M., & Aronson, J. (1995). Stereotype threat and the intellectual test performance of African Americans. *Journal of Personality and Social Psychology, 69,* 797–811.

Steele, C. M., & Liu, T. J. (1983). Dissonance processes as self-affirmation. *Journal of Personality and Social Psychology, 45,* 5–19.

Steele, C. M., Spencer, S. J., & Aronson, J. (2002). Contending with group image: The psychology of stereotype and social identity threat. *Advances in Experimental Social Psychology, 34,* 379–440.

Stone, J., Lynch, C. I., Sjomeling, M., & Darley, J. M. (1999). Stereotype threat effects on Black and White athletic performance. *Journal of Personality and Social Psychology, 77,* 1213–1227.

Zimbardo, P. G. (1972). *The Stanford prison experiment* (Slide/tape presentation). Available from Philip Zimbardo, Inc., P. O. Box 4395, Stanford, CA 94305.

5

The Role of Racial Identity in Managing Daily Racial Hassles

Enrique W. Neblett Jr., J. Nicole Shelton, and Robert M. Sellers

Racial identity, discrimination, and psychological well-being have been linked conceptually for African Americans as early as the 1930s when some of the first investigations of African American self-concept were being conducted in African American children (see Clark & Clark, 1939, 1947). Most of the early work on African Americans was geared toward demonstrating that African Americans' experiences of discrimination in the United States resulted in a damaged self-concept (e.g., Kardiner & Ovesy, 1951). This work formed what is commonly known as the Negro self-hatred perspective. The rationale for this perspective was based on the concept of reflected appraisals in which it was hypothesized that individuals' self-concepts were derived in large part from the way in which others viewed them. Given that the rest of American society devalued African Americans, logic dictated that African Americans should internalize that devaluation in the form of low self-esteem. On the basis of the research by Kenneth and Mamie Clark, in which African American children demonstrated a preference for playing with white dolls, researchers argued that African Americans hated themselves and had low self-esteem (Clark & Clark, 1947). In the 1960s and 1970s, researchers challenged this interpretation of the "doll studies" and argued that preference for a doll was not equivalent to low self-esteem (e.g., Banks, 1976; Brand, Ruiz, & Padilla, 1974; Rosenberg & Simmons, 1971).

Fortunately, more recent work has emphasized that African Americans have a positive self-concept (e.g., Crocker & Major, 1989; Crocker, Major, & Steele, 1998). The rationale for these newer findings is based on the notion that African Americans' self-concepts are not derived from how mainstream White Americans view Blacks, but instead from how other African Americans view them (see Crocker & Quinn, 2001; Crocker & Wolfe, 2001). These other

This research was supported by a grant from the National Institute of Mental Health (NIMH 5 P01 MH58565-03). We thank the Racial Identity Longitudinal Lab Group, University of Michigan (Ann Arbor), for their help with data collection.

African Americans are not likely to stigmatize them because of their race. Moreover, other research suggests that a healthy racial identity is directly associated with positive well-being (Baldwin, 1984; Cross, Parham, & Helms, 1998; White & Parham, 1990). In general, the zeitgeist has turned from arguing that African American identity is psychologically unhealthy to arguing that it is associated with a healthy self-concept.

Not only has the zeitgeist changed in terms of how African Americans are studied, but researchers are also beginning to examine the complex ways in which racial identity, discrimination, and mental health interact in the lives of African Americans. There is a rather extensive body of literature showing that for African Americans, both racial identity and racial discrimination are directly related to psychological well-being (Arroyo & Zigler, 1995; Baldwin, 1984; R. Clark, Anderson, Clark, & Williams, 1999; Landrine & Klonoff, 1996; Munford, 1994; Parham & Helms, 1981; Phinney & Alpuria, 1990; Pyant & Yanico, 1991; Rowley, Sellers, Chavous, & Smith, 1998; Sanders-Thompson, 1996). Furthermore, in recent years, researchers have postulated that racial identity may protect individuals from the negative impact of discrimination on psychological well-being. However, there has been little empirical work addressing the role of racial identity as a protective factor. The theoretical argument about the protective benefit of racial identity suggests that experience with discrimination is not as straightforward as researchers had once postulated.

The importance of addressing the complexity of the relationships among racial identity, discrimination, and mental health cannot be overemphasized. First, racial discrimination is a very real aspect of the African American experience as evidenced by research that suggests that more than 60% of African American adults typically encounter racial discrimination over the life course (Kessler, Mickelson, & Williams, 1999; Landrine & Klonoff, 1996; Sanders-Thompson, 1996; Williams, Yu, Jackson, & Anderson, 1997). Even more disturbing is the link between racial discrimination and mental health outcomes for African Americans. Specifically, several researchers have shown that racial and ethnic minorities' personal experiences with incidences of discrimination are significantly associated with adverse mental health and psychological well-being (e.g., Kessler et al., 1999; Noh, Beiser, Kaspar, Hou, & Rummens, 1999). Given the pervasiveness of racial discrimination in the lives of African Americans in the United States and the potential deleterious effect of discrimination experiences on one's psychological health, a closer investigation of the protective effects conveyed by racial identity is certainly warranted.

The aim of the present chapter is to address the complex relationships among racial identity, discrimination, and psychological well-being. First, the daily hassles approach, adopted from the stress and coping literature, is introduced as a conceptual framework for understanding the relationships among the variables. Special attention is given to how racial identity may moderate the relationship between racial discrimination and psychological well-being. Second, we present an empirical study that explores the relationships of interest. Finally, we discuss the implications of the present study and offer directions for future research.

The Stress and Coping Paradigm as a Conceptual Framework

Several researchers have begun to conceptualize experiences with prejudice and discrimination within a stress and coping framework (see R. Clark et al., 1999; Contrada et al., 2000; Landrine & Klonoff, 1996; Miller & Kaiser, 2001; Miller & Major, 2000; Sellers, Morgan, & Brown, 2000). The stress and coping framework is useful because it incorporates racial discrimination into a larger conceptual framework that takes into consideration the transaction between person and situation characteristics to explain differences in the way in which individuals experience, cope with, and are affected by racial discrimination (Lazarus & Folkman, 1984).

Three distinct approaches to stress are prevalent in psychological research: (a) the major life events approach, (b) the daily hassles approach, and (c) the transactional approach. In the major life events approach, discriminatory experiences are major events that can change a person's entire life course (e.g., being fired because of race). In the daily hassles approach, discriminatory experiences are considered to be minor and subtle behaviors that occur much more frequently than major life events. Finally, in the transactional approach, discriminatory experiences are examined within a framework of how individuals cognitively appraise a single racist event, how they cope with that event, and the psychological consequences of the event. In the present chapter, we use the daily hassles approach as a conceptual guide for our research.

Construals in the Daily Hassles Approach

In the stress and coping literature, *daily hassles* are defined as "the irritating, frustrating, distressing demands that to some degree characterize every day transactions with the environment" (Smith, 1993, p. 18). Some researchers argue that daily hassles are more predictive of mental and physical health than major stressful life events because their cumulative effects tend to wear people down (Kanner, Coyne, Schaeffer, & Lazarus, 1981). In terms of racial discrimination, a daily hassles approach focuses on subtle experiences of racism that are likely to occur frequently in individuals' lives. Examples include being treated rudely or disrespectfully at work or school; being ignored, overlooked, or not given service; and being accused of something or treated suspiciously. Daily hassles tend to be ambiguous and must first be construed as racist to be considered a racist daily hassle. Racial identity may play an important role in this construal process.

Role of Racial Identity in the Construal of Discrimination

Although racial discrimination seems to be a common experience for African Americans, according to the stress and coping framework, individual differences should play a role in the extent to which a negative incident is perceived as racial discrimination. Crocker and Major (1989) suggested that minority group identification may be an individual difference factor that plays a role in

the construal of discrimination. Specifically, they argued that group identification might facilitate the likelihood of attributing negative treatment and
outcomes to racial prejudice. Recently, researchers have provided empirical
evidence consistent with this position. For instance, Shelton and Sellers (2000)
found that African Americans for whom race was a central component of their
identity were more likely to attribute ambiguous discriminatory events to race
than African Americans for whom race was a less central component of identity.
Additional work suggests that highly ethnically identified individuals perceive
themselves as more personally vulnerable to discrimination (Major, Levin,
Schmader, & Sidanius, 1999; Operario & Fiske, 2001). For instance, Operario
and Fiske (2001) found that high ethnically identified minorities (Asian, Black,
and Latino) reported more personal experiences with ethnic discrimination
than did less ethnically identified minorities. Taken together, these findings
suggest that racial identity plays a role in the construal process with respect
to discrimination.

Whereas previous research has focused solely on how the level of racial
identification plays a role, it is also possible that other aspects of racial identity
should affect the construal process. Sellers and colleagues (Rowley et al., 1998;
Sellers, Rowley, Chavous, Shelton, & Smith, 1997; Sellers, Smith, Shelton,
Rowley, & Chavous, 1998) argue that racial identity is the significance and
qualitative meaning that individuals attribute to their racial group membership. Sellers and colleagues suggest that there are at least four ideologies that
capture African Americans' views on what it means to be a member of their
racial group. These ideologies are (a) a nationalist ideology, which stresses the
uniqueness of being of African descent; (b) an oppressed minority ideology,
which stresses the similarities between African Americans and other oppressed
groups; (c) an assimilationist ideology, which stresses the similarities between
African Americans and the rest of society; and (d) a humanist ideology, which
stresses the commonalities of all humans. In addition, Sellers and colleagues
suggest that African Americans vary in their affective and evaluative judgments of their race. Some African Americans perceive other African Americans
favorably (positive private regard), whereas some African Americans perceive
other African Americans less favorably (negative private regard). Similarly,
some African Americans believe that non-African American others hold positive
attitudes toward African Americans (positive public regard), whereas other
African Americans believe that other groups hold more negative attitudes
toward African Americans (negative public regard). We suspect that all dimensions of individuals' racial identity, not just racial centrality (e.g., how much
one identifies with the group), affect their construals of daily hassles.

With respect to the relationships between the qualitative dimensions of
racial identity and construals of daily hassles, several hypotheses can be made.
First, individuals who endorse nationalist and oppressed minority ideologies
may be more likely to construe daily hassles in terms of racial discrimination.
Individuals who endorse these ideologies are more inclined to see racism as a
part of the African American experience. Consequently, they are more likely
to attribute race as the cause of negative personal treatment. Whereas African
Americans who endorse nationalist and oppressed minority ideologies may be
more likely to construe daily hassles in terms of discrimination, those who

endorse a humanist ideology may be less likely to do so. Individuals who endorse a humanist ideology are less likely to view themselves and others in terms of race, and, in turn, are less likely to use race in the construal of negative events. With respect to affective and evaluative judgments of race, it may be that people who believe that other groups have relatively negative opinions of African Americans (low public regard) are more likely to interpret daily hassles involving others in terms of racial discrimination. These individuals may view negative treatment from others in terms of racial prejudice because they think others view their racial group negatively. Taken together, we argue that the significance and meaning of race, not just level of group identification, will likely influence the extent to which African Americans indicate that they have experienced daily racial hassles.

Consequences of Discrimination: Identity as a Protective Factor

A negative link between stress and mental health outcomes is well documented (see Moore & Burrows, 1996, for a review). The stress and coping framework posits that the relationship between stress and mental health is moderated by person factors (Cox & Ferguson, 1991; Lightsey, 1997; Pengilly & Dowd, 2000; Taylor & Aspinwall, 1996). For instance, Lightsey (1997) found that experiencing more stressful life events was related to more depressive symptoms in a sample of undergraduate students over a five-week period. However, individuals' generalized self-efficacy beliefs seemed to moderate the impact of stressful events. Specifically, individuals with higher levels of generalized self-efficacy showed less of an effect of stressful life events on levels of depression than individuals with lower levels of generalized self-efficacy. Consistent with this finding, it is possible that the relationship between daily racial hassles and psychological well-being is moderated by racial identity. That is, although daily racial hassles can be stressful, they may not affect all racial minorities in a negative manner to the same degree. Below we describe the negative consequences of experiencing daily racial hassles and discuss how racial identity may buffer these negative consequences.

In general, experiences with racial discrimination have been associated with a variety of negative physical and mental health outcomes (Allison, 1998; R. Clark et al., 1999; Feldman-Barrett & Swim, 1998; Landrine & Klonoff, 1996; Sellers et al., 2000; Utsey, 1998). For instance, experiencing racial discrimination is associated with higher psychiatric symptoms such as intrusion and avoidance, symptoms of depression, anxiety, obsession-compulsion, and somatization among African Americans (Landrine & Klonoff, 1996; Sanders-Thompson, 1996). Additionally, the more African Americans and Hispanics experience discrimination, the more they experience anger and depression, lower levels of life satisfaction, and lower levels of happiness (Jackson et al., 1996; Salgado de Snyder, 1987). Moreover, multiple experiences of racial discrimination over time has a cumulative, negative impact on African Americans' subjective well-being (Brown et al., in press). Taken together, these studies indicate that exposure to racial discrimination can have serious mental health consequences.

Racial identity researchers have argued that a strong identification with one's group can serve as a psychological buffer against prejudice and discrimination (see Cross, 1991; Phinney, 1990, 1996). Unfortunately, as noted previously, there are few empirical investigations of this relationship. In fact, our literature review revealed only two studies (Branscombe, Schmitt, & Harvey, 1999; Williams, Brown, Sellers, & Forman, 1999). Williams et al. (1998) found that African Americans who experienced racial discrimination and felt close to most Blacks reported higher psychological well-being than those who experienced discrimination but did not feel close to Blacks. Unfortunately, their operationalization of closeness was unclear. It is unclear as to whether it is a measure of beliefs about the importance of racial group identification, private regard attitudes, or perceived similarity. Branscombe et al. (1999) also demonstrated that racial group identification buffered the psychological impact of racial discrimination. On the basis of social identity theory, they argued that attributions to racial discrimination lead to a stronger identification with one's group, which, in turn, leads to positive psychological well-being. Consistent with their predictions, they found that willingness to make attributions to racial prejudice had a direct negative effect on mental health and an indirect, positive effect on well-being that was mediated by minority group identification. Unfortunately, they focused on the proclivity to make attributions to racial prejudice, which may be different from actual experiences with discrimination. These two studies provide initial evidence that racial identity may protect African Americans from the deleterious effects of discrimination. We provide further evidence along this line later in the chapter. Our work extends the previous two studies by using a multidimensional measure of group identification. Additionally, we focus on individuals' actual experiences in daily life, not perceptions of hypothetical situations.

Empirical Evidence

In this section, we present longitudinal data from a sample of African Americans to test the hypothesis that racial identity plays a role in the construal process with respect to experiencing daily racial hassles and can also protect individuals from the adverse mental health outcomes of such hassles. Specifically, we address three research questions. First, is racial identity related to African Americans' construals of daily hassles? Second, do daily racial hassles predict subsequent mental health? Finally, does racial centrality buffer the impact of experiencing daily racial hassles on individuals' subsequent mental health?

Study Overview

In the present study, 188 self-identified African American freshman college students completed several measures of racial identity, discrimination, and psychological well-being. Participants completed the measures early during their first semester and again at the end of their second semester of college.

The students were recruited from lists of incoming African American freshmen at two predominantly White universities located in the Midwest and Southeast and one predominantly Black university also located in the Southeast. The sample was predominantly female (75%) and had a median self-reported family income of between $55,000 and $64,999.

Measures

MULTIDIMENSIONAL INVENTORY OF BLACK IDENTITY. The Multidimensional Inventory of Black Identity (MIBI) is a 56-item measure of the three stable dimensions of racial identity (Centrality, Ideology, and Regard) proposed by the Multidimensional Model of Racial Identity for African Americans (Sellers et al., 1998). Participants indicate the extent to which they agree or disagree with the items on a 7-point Likert scale. The MIBI comprises a total of seven subscales.

The Centrality scale consists of 8 items measuring the extent to which being African American is central to the respondents' definition of themselves (e.g., "My destiny is tied to the destiny of other Black people"). A higher score on the Centrality scale is indicative of race being a more important aspect of the individuals' definitions of self ($\alpha = .77$). The Regard scale is composed of two subscales, Private and Public Regard. The Private Regard subscale consists of 6 items measuring the extent to which respondents possess positive feelings toward African Americans in general (e.g., "I am happy that I am Black"). A higher score corresponds to more positive feelings toward African Americans ($\alpha = .68$). The Public Regard subscale consists of 6 items measuring the extent to which respondents feel that other groups have positive feelings toward African Americans (e.g., "Overall, Blacks are considered good by others"). A higher score on the Public Regard subscale indicates a belief that other groups have more positive feelings toward African Americans ($\alpha = .75$). The Ideology scale is composed of four subscales. The Assimilation subscale consists of 9 items measuring the extent to which respondents emphasize the similarities between African Americans and mainstream America ($\alpha = .53$). The Humanist subscale consists of 9 items measuring the extent to which respondents emphasize the similarities among individuals of all races ($\alpha = .66$). The Minority subscale consists of 9 items measuring the extent to which respondents emphasize the similarities between African Americans and other minority groups ($\alpha = .66$). The Nationalist subscale consists of 9 items measuring the extent to which respondents emphasize the uniqueness of being African American ($\alpha = .69$). The present study uses participants' responses to the MIBI during the first wave of the study.

DAILY LIFE EXPERIENCE. The Daily Life Experience (DLE) is a self-report measure that assesses the frequency and impact of experiencing 18 "microaggressions" attributed to race in the past year (Harrell, 1994). The microaggressions include such items as being observed or followed while in public places and being ignored, overlooked, or not given service. Two subscales were created by averaging across participants' responses to (a) the frequency with which the event happened (α = .89) and (b) how much the event bothered them (α = .90). Participants answered the frequency questions using a 6-point scale with the following labels: 0 = *never happened,* 1 = *one time,* 2 = *a few times,* 3 = *about once a month,* 4 = *a few times a month,* and 5 = *once a week or more.* Participants answered how bothered they were by the event using a 5-point Likert type scale with the following labels: 1 = *did not bother me at all,* 2 = *bothered me a little,* 3 = *bothered me somewhat,* 4 = *bothered me a lot,* and 5 = *bothered me extremely.*

A composite scale for racial discrimination was created by multiplying the participants' scores on both the frequency and the bother scale for each microaggression and summing across the 18 items (α = .90). A higher score on the composite scale represents greater experience of daily racial hassles. In the present study, we used participants' responses to the DLE during the first wave of the study.

CENTER FOR EPIDEMIOLOGICAL STUDIES–DEPRESSION SCALE. The Center for Epidemiological Studies—Depression Scale (CES—D) consists of 20 items that assess the presence and frequency of clinical symptoms associated with depression. Participants rated the frequency with which the symptoms occurred over the past week on a scale ranging from 1 (*less than 1 day*) to 4 (*5–7 day*). Higher scores on the composite scale indicate more depressed mood (α = .88). In the present study, CES—D scores from the second wave of the study were analyzed.

PERCEIVED STRESS SCALE. The Perceived Stress Scale (PSS) includes 14 items that assess the degree to which individuals appraise situations in their lives as stressful (Cohen, Kamarck, & Mermelstein, 1983). Participants respond how often they have had specific feelings or thoughts over the past month using a scale ranging from 0 (*never*) to 4 (*very often*). Higher scores on the composite scale indicate higher levels of stress (α = .86). PSS scores from the second wave of the study were used in the analyses.

SPEILBERGER TRAIT ANXIETY INVENTORY. The Speilberger Trait Anxiety Inventory (STAI) is a 20-item measure of the tendency of participants to generally experience symptoms of anxiety. Participants indicated how often they felt like 20 statements related to trait anxiety using a scale ranging from 1 (*almost never*) to 4 (*almost always*). Higher scores indicated higher levels of trait anxiety (α = .92). The present study used participants' responses to the STAI during the second wave of the study.

Key Findings

The relationship between racial identity and daily racial hassles was analyzed using an ordinary least squares (OLS) regression model. In this model, gender and race of school (both used as control variables) and the seven MIBI subscales were included as independent variables, and the daily racial hassles composite score was used as the dependent variable. The overall model was significant and explained roughly 15% of the variance, $F(9,174) = 4.68$, $p < .01$. Racial centrality ($\beta = .26$, $p<.01$), public regard ($\beta = -.80$, $p<.05$), and nationalist ideology ($\beta = .20$, $p<.05$) were significant predictors of amount of daily racial hassles. Individuals for whom race was more central, who felt that other groups held negative attitudes toward Blacks, and who endorsed a nationalist ideology tended to experience more daily racial hassles during the past year.

Three OLS regression models were examined to test whether racial identity and daily racial hassles measured at Wave 1 were predictive of subsequent mental health at Wave 2. The seven MIBI subscales, the daily racial hassles composite variable, and the two control variables (gender and race of school) were entered as predictor variables in three separate models to predict anxiety, stress, and depression. The predictors explained 10% of the variance in anxiety, $F(10,173) = 1.89$, ns; 8% of the variance in perceived stress, $F(10, 173) = 1.42$, ns; and 8% of the variance in depression, $F(10, 172) = 1.42$, ns. In each of the models, only daily racial hassles were predictive of the mental health outcomes. In each model, more experiences with daily racial hassles were associated with poorer subsequent mental health. The racial identity variables were unrelated to any of the mental health outcomes.

To test whether racial centrality moderated the relationship between daily racial hassles and subsequent mental health, we ran three hierarchical OLS regression models. In the first block of each of the models, gender, race of school, racial centrality, and daily racial hassles were entered. Consistent with Aiken and West (1991), the racial centrality and daily racial hassles were centered. An interaction term comprised of the product of participants' centered scores on the racial centrality scale and their centered scores on the daily racial hassles composite was entered in a second block for each of the models. In each of the models, only daily racial hassles had a direct relationship with the mental health variables. As was found in the previous analyses, participants who reported experiencing more racial hassles in Wave 1 experienced more psychological distress in Wave 2. The interaction term added a significant ($p < .05$) increase in the amount of variance explained for anxiety and depression.

To illustrate the nature of the significant interaction between racial centrality and daily racial hassles on subsequent mental health, we divided the participants into low, medium, and high groups on the basis of their distribution on their centrality scores. We then ran three OLS regression models with gender, race of school, and racial hassles predicting subsequent levels of anxiety, stress, and depression for each of the centrality groups. For each of the three mental health outcome variables, experiences with daily racial hassles resulted in significantly ($p < .05$) poorer mental health for individuals with low and medium levels of racial centrality. In contrast, experiences with daily racial hassles seemed to have no impact on the subsequent mental health of individuals with the highest levels of centrality. These results suggest individuals' levels of racial centrality has a buffering effect on the impact of daily racial hassles on subsequent mental health outcomes.

Implications and Future Directions

The results support the idea that racial identity is related to African Americans' construals of daily racial hassles. This finding is consistent with a number of studies indicating that racial centrality influences the way in which individuals interpret racially ambiguous events (Operario & Fiske, 2001; Shelton & Sellers, 2000). These previous studies primarily focused solely on how group identification influences individuals' construals. The present work extends this previous work and shows that the qualitative meaning of racial identity also plays a role in the construal process. Our research replicated previous research concerning group identification. In addition, our findings show that people who endorse a nationalist ideology and people who believe others had a negative view of African Americans are more likely to experience racial hassles. It appears that these individuals are more likely to use race in their interpretation of daily hassles.

With respect to the relationship between racial hassles and mental health outcomes, we found that individuals' experiences with racial hassles were negatively related to their subsequent levels of anxiety, stress, and depression. However, the data also revealed that racial centrality shaped the extent to which daily racial hassles were associated with these negative mental health outcomes. Among individuals for whom race was not a central component of their identity, the more they experienced daily racial hassles, the more stress, depressive symptoms, and anxiety they experienced. However, among individuals for whom race was a highly central component of their identity, there was no significant relationship between experiences with daily racial hassles and the three mental health outcomes. In other words, highly identified African Americans were buffered from the adverse impact of daily racial hassles on mental health. These findings provide empirical support to the accumulating theoretical work that suggests that the significance of race/ethnicity protects ethnic minorities from the deleterious impact of racism (see Crocker et al., 1998).

Given the pattern of relationships found in our research, there are several interesting questions to explore. Perhaps the most important task now is to begin to identify the underlying mechanisms that account for these observed relationships. Stated another way, researchers have identified the how and what but should now begin to address why these patterns exist.

With respect to the relationship between racial identity and discrimination, one interesting question is whether individuals who hold certain ideologies regarding race evoke more racially discriminatory behavior from others. Shelton and Sellers (2000) have suggested the possibility that the relationship between racial identity and racial discrimination may be accounted for not only by attributional sets or biases to ambiguous stimuli but also by the reactions of others to the behavior of individuals who espouse particular ideologies. In this sense, the relationship between racial identity and discrimination experiences is attributed more to the transaction between two or more people and is based less on the cognitive schema of the individual experiencing discrimination.

With empirical evidence that racial centrality appears to play a buffering role in the effects of racial discrimination, future research should also attempt to identify why this is the case. Could it be that individuals with higher levels of centrality spend more time thinking about race and discrimination, and as a result develop a more varied and sophisticated repertoire of coping skills for dealing with discrimination than individuals who have not (Sellers et al., 2000)? Further research that takes into account the role of racial coping in racial identity, racial discrimination, and mental health may increase our understanding of racial centrality's protective effects and also assist in the implementation of interventions designed to assist individuals who are susceptible to the damaging effects of racial discrimination.

Future research also needs to be conducted to address the potential bidirectionality of the relationship between racial identity and discrimination experiences. One major criticism of the research in this area is that the causal direction between these variables is difficult to untangle. It is possible that racial identification encourages individuals to perceive their personal experiences a certain way. However, according to social identity theory, it is also possible that experiences with racial discrimination lead one to identify more strongly with one's racial group (Tajfel & Turner, 1986). In a directionality test of this issue, Branscombe et al. (1999) found that minority group identification did not predict individuals' willingness to make attributions to prejudice. Instead, the opposite relationship was true: Willingness to make attributions to prejudice predicted minority group identification. We believe that there is a cyclical relationship between these variables such that minority group identification and willingness to make attributions to prejudice influence each other in a reciprocal manner (see Operario & Fiske, 2001). It is clear that longitudinal data collected over a large period of time may be able to yield useful information about how discrimination and mental health influence one another.

Finally, the use of multiple research methodologies will be important in any future research designed to elucidate the complex relationships among racial identity, discrimination, and mental health. The use of daily diary methods (see Swim, Hyers, Cohen, & Ferguson, 2001, who studied women's experiences with gender discrimination), for example, may reduce the need for researchers to rely solely on retrospective reports. Event-sampling and laboratory studies may also be useful in studying actual experiences with discrimination. And, as suggested above, more longitudinal research is necessary to understand the role of racial identity experiences in racial discrimination and mental health over time. The reliance on a single methodological approach will only impede the rate at which we are able to obtain knowledge regarding the complex relationships among racial identity, racial discrimination, and mental health.

Conclusion

In the present chapter, we used a stress and coping framework to address the complex ways that racial identity, discrimination, and mental health interact in the lives of African Americans. As illustrated by the empirical data, racial identity influences individuals' construals of daily hassles. Additionally, racial identity protects African Americans from the negative mental health outcomes associated with experiencing daily racial hassles. In essence, racial identity seems to serve as both a risk factor for experiencing daily racial hassles and a protective factor against the deleterious impact of those hassles on subsequent mental health. Although this may seem to complicate our understanding of the role of race in African Americans' lives, we believe this view provides a more accurate picture of how African Americans manage issues of race in the United States.

References

Aiken, L. S., & West, S. G. (1991). *Multiple regression: Testing and interpreting interactions.* Newbury Park, CA: Sage.

Allison, K. W. (1998). Stress and oppressed social category membership. In J. Swim & C. Stangor (Eds.), *Prejudice: The target's perspective* (pp. 149–170). New York: Academic Press.

Arroyo, C. G., & Zigler, E. (1995). Racial identity, academic achievement, and the psychological well-being of economically disadvantaged adolescents. *Journal of Personality and Social Psychology, 69,* 903–914.

Baldwin, J. (1984). African self-consciousness and the mental health of African Americans. *Journal of Black Studies, 15,* 177–194.

Banks, W. C. (1976). White preference in Blacks: A paradigm in search of a phenomenon. *Psychological Bulletin, 83,* 1179–1186.

Brand, E. S., Ruiz, R. A., & Padilla, E. M. (1974). Ethnic identification and preference: A review. *Psychological Bulletin, 81,* 850–890.

Branscombe, N., Schmitt, M., & Harvey, R. (1999). Perceiving pervasive discrimination among African Americans: Implications for group identification and well-being. *Journal of Personality and Social Psychology, 77,* 135–149.

Brown, T. N., Williams, D., Jackson, J. S., Sellers, S., Brown, K., Torres, M., & Neighbors, H. (in press). Being Black and feeling blue: The mental health consequences of racial discrimination. *Race and Society.*

Clark, K. B., & Clark, M. P. (1939). The development of consciousness of self and the emergence of racial identification in Negro preschool children. *Journal of Social Psychology, 10,* 591–599.

Clark, K. B., & Clark, M. P. (1947). Racial identification and preference in Negro children. In T. M. Newcomb & E. L. Hartley (Eds.), *Readings in social psychology* (pp. 169–187). New York: Holt.

Clark, R., Anderson, N., Clark, V., & Williams, D. (1999). Racism as a stressor for African Americans: A biopsychosocial model. *American Psychologist, 54,* 805–816.

Cohen, S., Kamarck, T., & Mermelstein, R. (1983). A global measure of perceived stress. *Journal of Health and Social Behavior, 24,* 385–396.

Contrada, R. J., Ashmore, R. D., Gary, M. L., Coups, E., Egeth, J. D., Sewell, A., et al. (2000). Ethnicity-related sources of stress and their effects on well-being. *Current Directions in Psychological Science, 9*(4), 136–139.

Cox, T., & Ferguson, E. (1991). Individual differences, stress and coping. In C. L. Cooper & R. Payne (Eds.), *Personality and stress: Individual differences in the stress process* (pp. 7–30). New York: Wiley.

Crocker, J., & Major, B. (1989). Social stigma and self-esteem: The self-protective properties of stigma. *Psychological Review, 96,* 608–630.

Crocker, J., Major, B., & Steele, C. (1998). Social stigma. In D. Gilbert, S. T. Fiske, & G. Lindzey (Eds.), *Handbook of social psychology* (4th ed., pp. 504–553). Boston: McGraw Hill.

Crocker, J., & Quinn, D. (2001). Psychological consequences of devalued identities. In R. Brown & S. Gaertner (Eds.), *Blackwell handbook of social psychology: Vol. 4. Intergroup processes* (pp. 238–257). Malden, MA: Blackwell.

Crocker, J., & Wolfe, C. (2001). Contingencies of self-esteem. *Psychological Review, 108,* 593–623.

Cross, W. (1991). *Shades of Black: Diversity in African-American identity.* Philadelphia: Temple University Press.

Cross, W. E., Parham, T. A., & Helms, J. E. (1998). Nigrescence revisited: Theory and research. In R. L. Jones (Ed.), *African American identity development: Theory, research, and intervention* (pp. 3–71). Hampton, VA: Cobb & Henry.

Feldman-Barrett, L., & Swim, J. (1998). Appraisals of prejudice and discrimination. In J. Swim & C. Stangor (Eds.), *Prejudice: The target's perspective* (pp. 11–36). San Diego, CA: Academic Press.

Harrell, S. P. (1994). *The Racism and Life Experience Scales.* Unpublished manuscript.

Jackson, J. S., Brown, T. N., Williams, D. R., Torres, M., Sellers, R., & Brown, T. (1996). Racism and the physical and mental health status of African Americans: A thirteen year national panel study. *Ethnicity and Disease, 6,* 132–147.

Kanner, A. D., Coyne, J. C., Schaeffer, C., & Lazarus, R. S. (1981). Comparison of two models of stress measurement: Daily hassles and uplifts versus major life events. *Journal of Behavioral Medicine, 4,* 1–39.

Kardiner, A., & Ovesy, L. (1951). *The mark of oppression.* New York: Norton.

Kessler, R. C., Mickelson, K. D., & Williams, D. R. (1999). The prevalence, distribution, and mental health correlates of perceived discrimination in the United States. *Journal of Health and Social Behavior; 40,* 208–230.

Landrine, H., & Klonoff, E. A. (1996). The Schedule of Racist Events: A measure of racial discrimination and a study of its negative physical and mental health consequences. *Journal of Black Psychology, 22,* 144–168.

Lazarus, R. S., & Folkman, S. (1984). *Stress, appraisal, and coping.* New York: Springer Pub. Co.

Lightsey, O. R. (1997). Stress buffers and dysphoria: A prospective study. *Journal of Cognitive Psychotherapy, 11,* 263–277.

Major, B., Levin, S., Schmader, T., & Sidanius, J. (1999). *Implications of justice ideology, group identification, and ethnic group for perceptions of discrimination.* Unpublished manuscript.

Miller, C. T., & Kaiser, C. R. (2001). A theoretical perspective on coping with stigma [Special issue: Stigma: An insider's perspective]. *Journal of Social Issues, 57*(1), 73–92.

Miller, C., & Major, B. (2000). Coping with stigma and prejudice. In. T. Heatherton, R. Kleck, M. Hebl, & J. Hull (Eds.), *The social psychology of stigma* (pp. 243–272). New York: Guilford Press.

Moore, K. A., & Burrows, G. D. (1996). Stress and mental health. In C. L. Cooper (Ed.), *Handbook of stress, medicine, and health* (pp. 87–100). Boca Raton, FL: CRC Press.

Munford, M. B. (1994). Relationship of gender, self-esteem, social class, and racial identity to depression in Blacks. *Journal of Black Psychology, 20,* 157–174.

Noh, S., Beiser, M., Kaspar, V., Hou, F., & Rummens, J. (1999). Perceived racial discrimination, depression, and coping: A study of Southeast Asian refugees in Canada. *Journal of Health and Social Behavior, 40,* 193–207.

Operario, D., & Fiske, S. (2001). Ethnic identity moderates perceptions of prejudice: Judgments of personal versus group discrimination and subtle versus blatant bias. *Personality and Social Psychology Bulletin, 27,* 550–561.

Parham, T. A., & Helms, J. E. (1981). Relation of racial identity attitudes to self-actualization and affective states of Black students. *Journal of Counseling Psychology, 32,* 431–440.

Pengilly, J. W., & Dowd, E. T. (2000). Hardiness and social support as moderators of stress. *Journal of Clinical Psychology, 56,* 813–820.

Phinney, J. (1990). Ethnic identity in adolescence and adulthood: A review and integration. *Psychological Bulletin, 108,* 499–514.

Phinney, J. (1996). When we talk about American ethnic groups, what do we mean? *American Psychologist, 51,* 918–927.

Phinney, J., & Alpuria, L. L. (1990). Ethnic identity in college students from four ethnic groups. *Journal of Adolescence, 13,* 171–183.

Pyant, C. T., & Yanico, B. J. (1991). Relationship of racial identity and gender role attitudes to Black women's psychological well-being. *Journal of Counseling Psychology, 38,* 315–322.

Rosenberg, M., & Simmons, R. G. (1971). *Black and White self-esteem: The urban school child* (Arnold and Caroline Rose Monograph Series). Washington, DC: American Sociological Association.

Rowley, S., Sellers, R. M., Chavous, T. M., & Smith, M. A. (1998). The relationship between racial identity and self-esteem in African American college and high school students. *Journal of Social and Personality Psychology, 74,* 715–724.

Salgado de Snyder, V. N. (1987). Factors associated with acculturative stress and depressive symptomatology among married Mexican immigrant women. *Psychology of Women Quarterly, 11,* 475–488.

Sanders-Thompson, V. (1996). Perceived experiences of racism as stressful life events. *Community Mental Health Journal, 32,* 223–233.

Sellers, R., Morgan, L., & Brown, T. (2000). A multidimensional approach to racial identity: Implications for African American children. In A. Neal-Barnett, J. Contreras, & K. Kerns (Eds.), *Forging links: African American children clinical developmental perspectives* (pp. 23–56). Westport, CT: Praeger.

Sellers, R. M., Rowley, S. J., Chavous, T. M., Shelton, J. N., & Smith, M. (1997). Multidimensional Inventory of Black Identity: Preliminary investigation of reliability and construct validity. *Journal of Personality and Social Psychology, 73,* 805–815.

Sellers, R. M., Smith, M., Shelton, J. N., Rowley, S. J., & Chavous, T. M. (1998). Multidimensional Model of Racial Identity: A reconceptualization of African American racial identity. *Personality and Social Psychology Review, 2,* 18–39.

Shelton, J. N., & Sellers, R. (2000). Situational stability and variability in African American racial identity. *Journal of Black Psychology, 26,* 27–50.

Smith, J. C. (1993). *Understanding stress and coping.* New York: Macmillan.

Swim, J. K., Hyers, L. L., Cohen, L. L., & Ferguson, M. J. (2001). Everyday sexism: Evidence for its incidence, nature, and psychological impact from three daily diary studies [Special issue: Stigma: An insider's perspective]. *Journal of Social Issues, 57*(1), 31–53.

Tajfel, H., & Turner, J. (1986). The social identity theory of intergroup behavior. In S. Worchel & W. Austin (Eds.), *Psychology of intergroup relations* (pp. 33–48). Chicago: Nelson-Hall.

Taylor, S. E., & Aspinwall, L.G. (1996). Mediating and moderating processes in psychosocial stress: Appraisal, coping, resistance, and vulnerability. In H. B. Kaplan (Ed.), *Psychosocial stress: Perspectives on structure, theory, life-course, and methods* (pp. 71–110). San Diego: Academic Press.

Utsey, S. O. (1998). Assessing the stressful effects of racism: A review of instrumentation. *Journal of Black Psychology, 24,* 269–288.

White, J. L., & Parham, T. A. (1990). *The psychology of Blacks: An African-American perspective.* Englewood Cliffs, NJ: Prentice Hall.

Williams, D. R., Brown, T., Sellers, S., & Forman, T. (1998). *Racism and mental health: Risk factors and resources.* Unpublished manuscript.

Williams, D. R., Yu, Y., Jackson, D. S., & Anderson, N. B. (1997). *Racial differences in physical and mental health: Socioeconomic status, stress, and discrimination.* Unpublished manuscript.

6

Choosing a Name as Filter of Group Identity

Gina Philogène

When the influence of the "doll studies" in shaping the Supreme Court decision to desegregate public schools gave Kenneth Clark his deserved moment in American history half a century ago, he was full of hope that America might one day be able to dismantle the social construct of race. His argument that institutionalized racism damaged not only Black Americans but also their non-Black compatriots pointed to the ideals of a color-blind society. That vision of true democracy and equality, which a society had to struggle for, drove his body of work over the decades.

Later in his life, however, Clark became increasingly doubtful and pessimistic about America's ability to overcome its legacy of race. The persistence of race had, in his mind, undermined even well-intended policy initiatives, such as desegregation of schools and affirmative-action policies. Having become deeply skeptical about the scope of progress for Black Americans, Clark showed little patience with symbolic changes, such as having a Black mayor in New York City. That skepticism extended obviously to the name chosen for the group. In a fascinating interview in the *New York Times* (Clark, 1995), Clark responded to the last question posed by the interviewer "You've seen the evolution from Negro to black to African American? What is the best thing for blacks to call themselves?" with a typically consistent "White."

While that answer embodies Clark's original vision of a color-blind society, it also implies that names do not matter as long as race permeates intergroup relations. How can a new name end the misery of the "kids in the ghetto"? In Clark's view, only when Blacks call themselves White will race, and all its weight on our divided society, cease to dominate. That same sentiment had also been expressed in 1928 by W. E. B. DuBois in his much-discussed response to Roland Barton, who had written a letter expressing his support of efforts within the Black American community aimed at eradicating the term Negro:

> Suppose now we could change name. Suppose we arose tomorrow morning and lo! instead of being "Negroes," all the world called us "Cheiropolidi"— Do you really think this would make a vast and momentous difference to you and to me? Would the Negro problem be suddenly and eternally settled?

> Would you be any less ashamed of being descended from a black man, or
> would your schoolmates feel any less superior to you? The feeling of inferior-
> ity is in you, not in any name. The name merely evokes what is already
> there . . . a Negro by any other name will be just as black and just as white;
> just as ashamed of himself and just as shamed by others, as today. It is not
> the name—it's the Thing that counts. (DuBois, 1928, in Bennett, 1970,
> pp. 379–380)

Group denominations per se, as both DuBois and Clark implied, are probably of no major objective consequence to the extent that they do not themselves
change the things they represent. Yet one can make an equally valid argument
that they do gain significance when used in the elaboration of one's social
reality, especially when that reality gets collectively reshaped by means of a
new name serving as vector for new meaning given to the renamed object. It
is in this broader context of changing the social reality surrounding an object
that new group names for Black Americans can make a difference.

Take, for instance, the term *African American,* which appeared in the
early 1990s as a new designation for the group hitherto referred to as Blacks.
This name has become part of everyday social life in contemporary America.
More than just a new label to identify a group, the term in question constitutes
indeed a major cultural phenomenon that formalizes behavior and orients
communication. African American originates from Black, with the purpose of
remaking the object associated with that term—those Americans of African
descent. It gets shaped therefore in contradistinction to Black, as an alternative
representation of the same object.

African American is a new name that must be understood as a new social
representation. Once we frame a new name for a group in such a broader
context, it becomes possible to see how the term acquires sufficient meaning
for people to reshape their identity, direct attitudes about that identity, and
eventually provide a figurative core for interactions between the different social
actors. So when the group is talked to or talked about, the name used defines
and represents the group for those involved in the interaction. And this collective activity turns the name into a shared reality.

One appropriate context for studying new group denominations as vectors
of identity is through the framework of social representation theory. In this
chapter we demonstrate how the use of this theoretical approach enables us
to capture the reconceptualization of a group previously referred to in primarily
racial terms as *Blacks* into a different, culturally defined group identity as
African Americans.

Names as Social Representations

Social representations facilitate our interpretation of reality by guiding our
relation to the world around us and providing a framework of shared references
that define how to think about the world. Because they concern the creation
of shared knowledge by a community, they originate in daily life, in the course

of interindividual communication. In this sense they are a societal construction, socially elaborated and collectively shared (Philogène, 2000; Philogène & Deaux, 2001). Any interaction, whether between two individuals or two groups of individuals, presupposes shared representations. It is only on the basis of these shared representations, which shape our beliefs, ideas, attitudes, and opinions, that we give meaning to things and come to understand each other. Because we elaborate them together and evoke them frequently, we let social representations become deeply embedded in our cultural fabric.

Social representations are created through interaction and crystallize around language. People elaborate such representations not least by developing a terminology for things that they share. By naming a new and unfamiliar object, people crystallize its representation in a word or words as shared thought constructs. Being endowed with a widely shared and collectively understood name allows a social object to be categorized and classified. Whenever the name is evoked, one knows what it is referring to and what the object thus named is supposed to mean. These presuppositions are based on certain assumptions that are articulated and expressed in one's social interactions.

Even though naming plays a crucial role in the anchoring of new objects, social psychologists have paid relatively little attention to the strategic significance of names. In contrast, this topic has been explored by a number of influential linguists, anthropologists, and philosophers. Their combined insights on that subject provide us with a rich framework for the inclusion of names and naming processes in social representation theory.

When we name someone or something, we make a reference whereby we establish a causal or conventional relation between the object and the symbol; that is the name. When we choose a name for an object, we place the thing so named in a system of conceptual relations and conditions, as well as factual beliefs. Indeed, in the act of naming we denote the class of all particular things to which the name applies. Names, and here we might include group designations as proper names, serve as identifying markers to the extent that they make reference to a meaningful system of commonly shared and understood characteristics. Its name associates the object being named with a preestablished category. The name chosen defines a class of objects thus named and assigns to them a defining structure of functions and properties.

People's commonly shared factual beliefs, what Chomsky (1975) termed *common-sense expectations,* automatically assume that these functions and properties exist whenever the name is used. The stipulation that a thing be given a specific name thus carries with it certain commonly shared presumptions about concepts and categories. These in turn determine how the name is understood in the minds of individuals and shape how its meaning is communicated between them.

Yet the meaning of a name, by which it connects to the object it represents, is not there a priori. Meaning has to be first established by the act of naming the thing and then contextualized in a system of language. This context has to be maintained by consistent use of the name. Such elaboration of its meaning is a fundamentally social activity. The meaning of a name thus lies entirely in how it is used in interactions. People share a language to describe what occurs outside their minds and to communicate what is on their minds. This facility enables them to agree about the meaning of a word and to maintain this agreement in their applications of it.

Hence it is safe to argue that the meanings attached to names are not the product of individual mental activity but instead the result of collective creation. Cognitive philosophers, such as Saul Kripke (1980) or Hilary Putnam (1975, 1983), have emphasized the importance of the origin and history of names in determining how they function and what they come to mean. Kripke saw the naming process commence with an "initial baptism" in which the object gets named and the reference of the name chosen is fixed by description. Putnam focused on what he termed the "historic chain of transmission," by which the name gets passed, as Kripke put it, "from link to link" to preserve the reference fixed originally in the naming process and refine it to the extent that it is commonly understood. In that process of elaboration the name becomes a social representation.

The Emergence and Diffusion of African American

As Dauzat (1956) pointed out, proper names must be analyzed in their historical evolution, within their specific cultural setting, and as a product of struggles over their meaning. This is especially true in a multicultural and multiethnic society such as the United States, where names given to groups have always played an important role in the public discourse. When an established group denomination gets replaced by a new one, we can surmise that broader changes are under way. Names, after all, are a filter for group identity as well as intergroup relations.

If we want to explore the deeper meaning underlying the switch in names from Black to African American for group identity and intergroup relations, we need to appreciate clearly the extent to which race has been a defining issue in U.S. history. From slavery and the Civil War to segregation and the civil rights struggles of the 1950s and 1960s, race pervaded American society and dominated its course of evolution. The presence of race has changed over time as the result of efforts to reconcile a dissonance between the democratic ideals of this society and its race-based discriminatory practices. It so happens that changes concerning race have usually come about during periods of social unrest. And they have often culminated in a switch of the denomination applied to Americans of African ancestry ("Slave," "Colored," "Negro," "Black," and "African American").

The term *Black,* for example, emerged out of the civil rights struggles in the late 1960s to replace *Negro.* This alternative social representation was seen as an equivalent counterweight to *White.* At the beginning, the term was especially favored by militants for precisely that reason (Carmichael & Hamilton, 1967; Wilkinson, 1990). This juxtaposition between Black and White reinforced a mutual vision of homogeneity within each group and immutable differences between them (Tajfel, 1982).

Even though the term Black became popularized with the end of segregation, it never managed to change the social representation of the group as a race apart from the rest of America. The rigidity implied by the dichotomization of this society into Black and White Americans has always been the framework defining the interactions between these two groups. Allowing for little contact between them, their peaceful coexistence was attributed to their segregated proximity. Yet Blacks in this country have also lived to become Americans, albeit with a dual consciousness that attempted to reconcile their presence in America as an excluded group (DuBois, 1903/1965).

Following the two presidential campaigns by Jesse Jackson, the first Black American to run for the highest office of the land, Ramona Edelin proposed in December 1989 at a reunion of civil rights leaders in New Orleans to use the term *African American* as the new official designation for Americans of African descent in lieu of Black. This suggestion by the then-president of the National Urban Coalition was enthusiastically endorsed by the participants of the meeting and followed up with a nationwide campaign to propagate the new term. Kripke's "initial baptism" of the term African American thus occurred as a concrete event, meant to rename and thereby explicitly re-present a group historically subjected to negative imagery in the course of centuries of racial prejudice.

Use of the new group denomination grew rapidly. Its spread was surely helped by its widespread adoption among public-opinion makers—in television shows, in the newspapers, and in the public discourse of politicians. Today the term is used almost exclusively in the media when referring to Americans of African descent as a group, indication that Edelin's initiative has indeed succeeded. Perhaps an even more important vehicle for the remarkably swift diffusion of the new group denomination was the adoption of the term by a demographically distinct subgroup as the self-chosen marker of a new group identity. A study by the Joint Center for Political and Economic Studies (1990) found that those referring to themselves as African Americans are predominantly young, male, educated, and from the urban centers of the Northeast and Midwest. Those sociodemographic characteristics have become the field of reference for the denomination, thereby providing a first filtering of its interpretation in the minds of individuals.

Several surveys, discussed in Philogène (1999), have confirmed that the term *African American* came to be used within 2 years of its introduction by fully one third of all Black Americans when referring to themselves. Those surveys also illustrate the pronounced popularity of this term among young, upwardly mobile professionals seeking their justified place in mainstream America. These empirical studies demonstrate the impressive impact of African American as a social representation in the making. Its rapidly and steadily growing use by Black Americans just after its introduction has allowed the new denomination to be anchored on their own terms, based on the interpretations they give it when switching from Black.

The real fruitfulness of demographic data about those using or preferring African American as opposed to Black remains in their interpretations, as a way of classifying the unfamiliar object. This involves an ordering process that links the new term to people's preexisting social categories. To the extent that a necessary degree of coherence within an individual's mental organization is thereby maintained, the new denomination gets anchored and becomes familiar. When African American emerged as a term of self-reference for certain Black Americans and less so for others, it became inevitably associated with different social categories that people could already relate to, such as socioeconomic background, educational level, age, or gender. The surveys mentioned above confirmed the predominance of the term African American among younger, urban Black Americans with a college education. To the extent that this subgroup has adopted the new denomination as a vehicle for group positivation, it seeks to redefine its group identity and alter intergroup relations. It is around this specific subgroup calling itself African Americans that the new social representation gets anchored.

The meaning of the new group denomination is then to a significant degree based on the projection of images resulting from the demographic profile of the subgroup calling itself African American. Contemporary America's extensive interest in demographic data lends itself to this type of information being used as adequate basis for the classification of people. The notion of what constitutes an African American gets constructed in our mind by means of seemingly objective demographic profiles, and their incorporation into preexisting categorizations makes the new term more familiar. Such familiarization is propelled by communication, a process that leads to the formation of different attitudes and opinions about African Americans in contradistinction to those held about Blacks. The media plays a crucial role in this familiarization, not least by endorsing the new term as the socially accepted denomination for the entire group. Putnam's historic transmission of African American thus has been propelled forward by two powerful vectors of propagation: a demographically distinct subgroup referring to itself as such and the media using the term as a new denomination for Americans of African descent.

Choosing a Name, Remaking an Identity

Why does it matter whether Americans of African descent are referred to or refer to themselves as African Americans rather than Blacks? How we answer this question depends on differences in consensually shared meanings that set these two group denominations apart. In other words, to what extent does African American constitute a new social representation of the group hitherto referred to as Blacks?

The sequence of different names used to identify Black Americans—from "Colored" to "Negro," then to "Black," and now "African American"—reflects incessant attempts to change perceptions and attitudes concerning the group. When the civil rights movement began to switch from Negro to Black after 1963, it did so with the intent to create a sense of pride in Blackness. We could see that attempt at group positivation crystallize around the movement's omnipresent slogans "Black Power" and "Black is Beautiful." The effort succeeded at first because of the unity of the group in its struggle against racial intolerance in America. But as the term gained acceptance in mainstream America, it lost its initial political context. With that, its negative connotations as a racial term resurfaced. The term Black applies irrevocably to one's color of skin (even though those referred to exist only in different shades of brown) and is therefore by definition associated with race. No wonder that it could never re-present the group in the eyes of the majority as anything but still a race apart.

The long-held view of people of African descent being separate and distinct from the rest of American society, as implied by the term Black, is deeply entrenched. Four centuries of group exclusion on the basis of racial difference have made sure of that. The classification of people by their race, still a subject of raging debate whenever census data are collected, is one of America's most persistent social practices. Following the abolition of slavery, racial inferiority was given a new and scientific justification. The biological paradigms that emerged in the late 19th century, most notably social Darwinism and eugenics, explained differences in physical, mental, and psychological abilities on the basis of race (Banton, 1977; Gossett, 1965; Kelves, 1985; Rose, 1968). These theories were transformed into common sense to provide society with clear definitions of race that were used to categorize and identify individuals in terms of racial groups. Once turned into a social practice, race-based differentiations last longer than they would have, had they remained a scientific theory.

The term African American tries to break this ubiquitous determinism associated with race by shifting the focus onto culture. This particular group denomination is consistent with the designation of everyone else, juxtaposing a cultural specificity to "America." The same semantic structure has also been adopted by other groups such as Italian Americans, Irish Americans, and so forth. Placed within a class of similarly structured group names for the different population facets of contemporary America, the term African American connotes equality and cultural integrity. By focusing away from race onto culture, the new term has the potential of achieving precisely what the term Black could not do in the mid-1960s, namely to change the underlying social representation of the group.

Empirical studies (see Philogène, 1999) have confirmed that both Black and non-Black participants project significantly more positive images onto African American than they do with regard to Black. When one looks at personality traits typically associated with the two terms, one finds similarly striking differences (Philogène, 2001). The traits evoked by African American are those corresponding to the ideals of mainstream America—religious, hard-working, intelligent, ambitious, family-oriented—whereas Black typically stimulates the kind of negative images anchored in racial prejudice—irresponsible, musical, happy-go-lucky, rude, loud, and so on. It helps, of course, that the subgroup referring to itself as African Americans is largely composed of young, well-educated professionals who have gained growing visibility as fully engaged and actively participating members of a thriving society.

Another major reason why the term African American seems to be the first change in name capable of re-presenting the object is its collective elaboration. Unlike the last switch from Negro to Black in the 1960s, this time the elaboration of meaning is not confined to the ingroup alone. Instead the positivation of the group has become a broad-based cultural phenomenon. Normalized by the political correctness movement on American university campuses and beyond, the term African American has in its rapidly spreading use managed to transcend group boundaries. By reflecting the pluralistic visions of America as a multicultural democracy celebrating its diversity, the name engages Black as well as non-Black Americans alike. This collective redefinition of America, embedded in the new social representation of Black Americans, is what sustains the projective qualities of African American as symptomatic of what Americans of all stripes want their society to be. Embedded in the term are widely shared anticipations of a different future in which the painful legacy of racism will have finally been laid to rest and in the realization of Martin Luther King's dream of a color-blind society. Precisely these forward-looking qualities have also been actively diffused by public opinion makers, often with renewed vigor after the events of 9/11 spurred a renewed sense of national purpose and unity not seen since World War II.

Its broad-based diffusion has created a consensus of meaning around the use of the term African American. As the term circulates more widely in public discourse and becomes increasingly familiar, it gains its capacity of re-presenting Black Americans. They are re-presented through projections of a different future for all. It is precisely through those anticipations, whose collective elaboration endows them with normative force, that a group can be redefined and repositioned with the help of a new name. While still in the making, this emerging social representation gradually transforms perceptions about the group and its relations with the rest of society.

The Social Representations of African American

Still, our break with the past is neither swift nor easy. We do not one day go to sleep thinking Black and wake up the next morning thinking African American. While the new term gains usage, it still coexists with the old term Black. Even if one half of all Americans already tend to use African American, this means that the other half is still wedded to the use of Black. More often than not, Americans use both terms intermittently. The terms thus continue to coexist as competing group denominations.

According to Jodelet (1984), a representation always originates from a previous one, having altered in the process mental and social configurations. Jodelet emphasized that the dynamic nature of a social representation, which is to be capable of continuous change, is rooted in its genesis, that is in its linkage to preexisting representations. Consequently, the full understanding of a given representation necessarily requires us to start with those from which it was born (Moscovici, 1984). Remembering its "initial baptism" in 1989–1990 as an officially selected alternative group designation, we know that African American is rooted in the earlier representation of Black. As a matter of fact, the social representation of African American takes its source directly from that of Black, with the latter representation providing a context for the reinterpretation of Black Americans into African Americans. The linkage between the old and new representations has been that of opposites, with the rapid propagation of African American during the early stages of its life cycle marked by its direct juxtaposition to Black. But the preexisting system of mental categories consists, among other things, of deeply rooted feelings about Blacks as well as various beliefs and ideologies on race. These mental categories have been shaped over a long period of time and are therefore quite solidified. They may not adjust easily to changing values and conventions that create a new social reality.

The tension between Black and African American as diametrically opposed representations of one and the same object depends in its evolution on Americans' preexisting social representations concerning race. This issue links the two denominations as the key mental category filtering each. Despite its downplaying of race-based differences, African American cannot eliminate the impact of race in its integration as a social representation. Even though the new term moves us away from race, its attempt at disassociation cannot fully neutralize the issue. The reference to Africa serves to some extent as a reminder. People's attitudes about race and racial categorization will in the foreseeable future still strongly influence what they think of African Americans.

The social representation of an existing object can only get transformed if that object appears anew. Such a mental shift occurs only, if and when the contextual setting of the object has undergone some sort of qualitative change that permits a redefinition of the object in question. In the case of African American, this means that individuals thus designated are no longer viewed as a racial category apart. For the new term to become a genuine and autonomous social representation, rather than exist just as a counterweight to Black from which it cannot be separated, it will have to have replaced race with an alternative characterization of the group as an integral part of American society. The adoption of African American may eventually become a new social representation by allowing a sort of opening, termed by Moscovici (1984) a "fissure," through which the object can be redefined—not a race apart, but a culturally distinct group sharing values and attributes with the rest of America. Such an opening can only come about by reshaping the internal structure of the preexisting representations of the same object, the central core (Abric, 1984). Providing a stable and integrative structure, the central core cannot change unless the social representation changes. This is why the positivation of Black in the 1960s could not succeed. It did not alter the social representation of Black, centered on race. Let us now examine how African American might transform the social representation by removing race from the center of the structural core in a fissure that lets culture take its place.

To understand the maturing of African American into a new and genuinely different social representation, one has to examine the context of social exchange regulating its use. It is there, in ordinary language, mediatic communication, or symbolic exchanges, that this representation takes on its full meaning by connecting individual mental processes to the social world. One crucial force driving the elaboration of the new term into a social representation are those referring to themselves as African Americans. This demographically distinct subgroup breaks down the homogenization of the group (as a race apart) implied in the term Black and reclaims the heterogeneity of a culturally determined group identity within a multicultural society.

Yet half of Black Americans still see themselves as Blacks. If so many Black Americans still perceive themselves as Blacks, they implicitly reject African American as a claimed identity for themselves. This rejection is, however, a qualified one. Many Blacks still prefer non-Black Americans to refer to them as a group in terms of African American. In this symbolic sense, as the official group designation, the new denomination serves one key purpose, namely to position all Black Americans as integrated citizens of America. The denomination grants the group an ancestral cultural system that coexists harmoniously with its American cultural definition, just like any other group of assimilated immigrants. The emergence of African American represents a beacon of hope for Blacks, no matter how excluded they still feel from the rest of America. The term signals a break with past patterns inasmuch as it shifts the attention away from the physical traits of a racially defined group to the cultural identity and experiences shared by people of African descent in America (Davis, 1991). Its widespread use by the media and in public discourse symbolizes their inclusion in a pluralistic society composed of many different peoples, each with their own institutions and cultural identity. To the extent that Blacks identify with this symbolic use of African American, they inherently project a different future for themselves in which race will have become much less important in America.

For non-Blacks, the crystallization of the new social representation might result in conflicts between a preexisting system of mental categories and fundamental changes that have taken place in American society. They may not adjust easily to changing values and conventions that create a new social reality. Hence it may be difficult for many non-Black Americans to view Blacks as African Americans. Still, the rapport non-Black Americans have with the new denomination is shaped by communication propagating the images of African American that imposes itself on individuals as an inescapable normative context. The term has today become the most acceptable way to address or discuss members of the group in public exchanges. The social content of its use tends to be one of integration and equality. Accepting and conforming to these conversational norms shapes a view of African American that is embedded in the positive image implied by its creation, as integral part of the mainstream. When the term African American is used in conversation, its normative context orients the communication toward projections that are built around a common belief in the "American dream." Motivated by an optimistic view of integration, the images created in the process are polarized in a positive direction.

Because African American sets the context for equality and inclusion of a previously discriminated group, it has a prescriptive force of orienting discussion toward a representation of that group as part of the American culture. This collective anticipation, which Black and non-Black Americans elaborate together, endows the new denomination with positive qualities. It comes to stand for everything that Black is not, and reflects what all Black Americans aspire to be in this society. African American exists as a depository for all projections concerning an inclusive resolution of America's racial dilemma that has divided the United States for centuries.

References

Abric, J. C. (1984). A theoretical and experimental approach to the study of social representations in a situation of interaction. In R. M. Farr & S. Moscovici (Eds.), *Social representations* (pp. 169–183). Cambridge, England: Cambridge University Press.

Banton, M. (1977). *The idea of race.* London: Tavistock.

Bennett, L., Jr. (1970). What's in a name? In P. I. Rose (Ed.), *Americans from Africa: Old memories, new moods* (pp. 373–383). New York: Atherton Press. (Reprinted from W. E. B. DuBois, The name "Negro." *The Crisis,* March 1928.)

Carmichael, S., & Hamilton, C. V. (1967). *Black power: The politics of liberation in America.* New York: Random House.

Chomsky, N. (1975). *Reflections on language.* New York: Pantheon Books.

Clark, K. (1995, May 7). An integrationist to this day, believing all else has failed. *New York Times,* p. E7.

Dauzat, A. (1956). *Les noms de personnes: Origine et evolution* [Personal names: origin and evolution] (4th ed.). Paris: Librairie Delgrave.

Davis, F. J. (1991). *Who is Black? One nation's definition.* University Park: Pennsylvania State University Press.

DuBois, W. E. B. (1965). *The souls of Black folk.* New York: Mentor Books. (Original work published 1903)

Gossett, T. F. (1965). *Race: The history of an idea in America.* New York: Schocken Books.

Jodelet, D. (1984). The representation of the body and its transformations. In R. M. Farr & S. Moscovici (Eds.), *Social representations* (pp. 211–238). Cambridge, England: Cambridge University Press.

Joint Center for Political and Economic Studies. (1990). *JCPES survey: Black vs. African American.* Washington, DC: Author.

Kelves, D. J. (1985). *In the name of eugenics: Genetics and the uses of human heredity.* New York: Knopf.

Kripke, S. (1980). *Naming and necessity* (2nd ed.). Oxford, England: Oxford University Press.

Moscovici, S. (1984). The phenomenon of social representations. In R. M. Farr & S. Moscovici (Eds.), *Social representations* (pp. 3–69). Cambridge, England: Cambridge University Press.

Philogène, G. (1999). *From Black to African American: A new representation.* Westport, CT: Praeger/Greenwood.

Philogène, G. (2000). Social representations. In A. Kazdin (Ed.), *Encyclopaedia of psychology.* Washington, DC: American Psychological Association and New York: Oxford University Press.

Philogène, G. (2001). Stereotype fissure: Katz and Braly revisited. *Social Science Information, 40,* 411–432.

Philogène, G., & Deaux, K. (2001). Introduction. In K. Deaux & G. Philogène (Eds.), *Representations of the social: Bridging theoretical perspectives* (pp. 3–7). New York: Basil Blackwell.

Putnam, H. (1975). The meaning of "meaning." In K. Gunderson (Ed.), *Language, mind and knowledge: Minnesota studies in the philosophy of science* (Vol. 7, pp. 131–193). Minneapolis: University of Minnesota Press.

Putnam, H. (1983). *Realism and reason: Philosophical papers* (Vol. 3). Cambridge, England: Cambridge University Press.

Rose, P. (1968). *The subject is race.* New York: Oxford University Press.

Tajfel, H. (1982). Social psychology of intergroup relations. *Annual Review of Psychology, 33,* 1–39.

Wilkinson, D. (1990). Americans of African identity. *Society, 27,* 14–18.

Part III ————————————————

Racism and Its Cultural Manifestations

Introduction:
Resilience and Self-Esteem
in African Americans

Ferdinand Jones

Members of devalued populations can have difficulty attaining and maintaining self-esteem because of the psychological detriments of racism. Assessing the presence, absence, or extent of this effect in African American individuals has been an ongoing challenge to psychologists. Unraveling what self-esteem actually means and then how to measure it are intertwined parts of that challenge. This work is important because it has implications for understanding how living as a member of a denigrated group affects African Americans' relationships and their everyday competence.

Kenneth and Mamie Clark were pioneers in researching the subject of African Americans' self-esteem in the 1930s and 1940s when the fields of personality and social psychology were in their infancy (Clark & Clark, 1939). A significant number of participants in their studies seemed to demonstrate that they were caught in self-deprecating cycles of negative comparisons with Whites. But later developments both in psychology and in American race relations in general influenced a more sophisticated and also a more optimistic understanding of the way African Americans were likely to evaluate themselves. The Clarks, incidentally, helped foster both developments. One major illumination was greater appreciation for the multifaceted intricacies of self-concept formation including, for instance, the realization that it had public and personal manifestations (Cross, 1991). Assessment methods grew more sophisticated. And the relative social condition of Black Americans in every respect evolved to be less defeating.

Recent research and theory about African Americans' psychological adaptation to racism, including the topic of self-esteem, is well represented by this section's authors. Their work dovetails with a subject I am exploring that is directly related: the resilience phenomenon in at-risk and victimized individuals. I contribute a few comments here on how I see the relationship between the two subjects.

Several psychologists, three of them authors in this volume, have developed persuasive and converging theoretical descriptions of the processes of self-esteem achievement and maintenance in African Americans. William E. Cross Jr. (1991) indicated that racial identity development is a maturational process: The competent Black individual must and often can grow to effectively negotiate the psychological hazards of the stigmatizing larger society to construct a foundation of personal satisfaction and effectiveness. Jennifer Crocker and Jason S. Lawrence (1999) found that the African American college students they studied made healthy adaptations to their significantly different cultural experience by systematically disregarding the contingency of their self-worth that depended on White's approval. Claude M. Steele's (1997) research on Black youngsters' reactions to being the targets of negative stereotyping indicated that they tended to disidentify with activities that they perceived were potentially damaging to their self-respect. James M. Jones's (1998) TRIOS concept describes a confluence of psychological mechanisms built into Black culture that allows African Americans as a group and as individuals to affirm themselves and to control their destinies. Adelbert S. Jenkins (1995) observed that Black culture socializes individuals to assert their own interpretations of reality and to therefore protect themselves from internalizing the devaluing attitudes of the dominant White society. And Gina Philogène's (1999) work on the progressive social phenomenon that the identity African American represents points to hopeful self-conceptions among Black Americans and, in turn, in the perceptions White Americans have of them.

The intersection between self-esteem and resilience in African Americans seems to me to lie in the broad conception of what we might call *psychological self-sufficiency*. I see both as processes that involve the individual's capacity to withstand the internalization of stigmatization or hardship and abuse and to become competent as agent of her or his own concerns. Targets of racism as well as survivors of trauma, abuse, and neglect can often demonstrate adaptive and creative thinking and behaviors.

The resilience construct is elusive. Is it a trait, a set of traits, an attitude, a set of skills? Can one learn to be resilient, or is one born with the capacity? Is a person who exhibits resourceful adaptation under catastrophic circumstances but not under other conditions resilient or not? And how does resourceful adaptation differ from maladaptive reactions? These are some of the many questions surrounding the construct of resilience. Some theorists believe there are too many of these seemingly irresolvable questions, and they suggest that the resilience construct does not really mean anything. But witnessing individuals' protective reactions and behaviors during times of extreme crisis convinces close observers that there must be something substantial to the concept of resilience. Natural disasters and manmade ones, like the Holocaust, the Atlantic slave trade, domestic violence, and the domestic terrorist attacks of September 11, 2001, produced reactions in affected people that ranged from recovery from the worst effects (the majority of the victims), to the impetus to extraordinary resourcefulness, to psychological disintegration (the smallest percentage). And we have seen that people's reactions change as time goes on. What does resilience mean in these circumstances? Who is or is not resilient? Can we know the answers to such questions without knowing the long-term effects on people?

The task for resilience scholars is formidable, just as it is for psychologists seeking the solution to many other psychological puzzles. Some scholars have looked retrospectively at individuals who have undergone trauma to try and find out what distinguishes the best adapted ones from the others. Other investigators have studied "at-risk" children longitudinally to see which ones fare better and why (see Luthar, Cicchetti, & Becker, 2000, for a review and critique of resilience studies). We are learning that resilience is a *multidimensional dynamic process*. This process indicates that all dimensions of the affected individual as well as the injurious circumstances themselves need to be included in comprehending an individual's adaptation to potentially damaging psychological assaults. Resilience is not something individuals either have or do not have but rather the qualities of individuals' interactions with disturbing circumstances. In sum, the elements of that interaction involve personality characteristics; social, emotional, cultural, and physical health conditions; and developmental factors plus the nature and timing of the adverse conditions.

In trying to develop a theory of resilience, and therefore of self-esteem in African Americans, some combinations of personal, cultural, and situational variables are particularly interesting to me. For instance, I have asked whether we can say that there are characteristics of African American culture that coalesce to facilitate resilience. I am thinking about the following traditional features of Black communities: ongoing social supports, a spiritual attitude, sturdy character, the capacity to find meaning in adverse situations, general resourcefulness, and flexibility in responding to fluctuating environmental circumstances. James M. Jones in his TRIOS model argues that these characteristics have been psychological lifesavers for Black Americans. They are, perhaps not incidentally, also prominent descriptors of resilient at-risk participants that have emerged as significant in longitudinal studies (Werner & Smith, 1992). They enabled the developing individuals to deal successfully with potentially damaging conditions such as chronic poverty, physical illness, and violent homes. The same set of interacting variables seems to also aid recovering victims of such traumas as rape, political imprisonment, and torture and also to be helpful to survivors of natural disasters such as earthquakes, floods, and hurricanes (Herman, 1992).

I have sought to articulate the hypothesis of resilient African Americans by pointing to certain expressive manifestations of Black culture, specifically jazz and jazz music-making. It seems logical that African Americans' artistic products would be infused with outlooks that are essential to their well-being. My explorations were spurred by Jenkins's (1995) speculation that jazz improvisation is the musical representation of a mental attitude in Black culture that accounts in large part for Black Americans' disregarding the negative stereotypes of them held by the dominant society. They have not believed that because they were Black they were intellectually weak, morally inconsistent, and mentally unstable. Their resistance is propagated by an attitude of healthy skepticism that is pervasive in African American culture. People are instructed in one way or another to challenge White Americans' false beliefs about everything, especially them. Like Jenkins, I see a parallel between this protective attitude and jazz improvisation (F. Jones, 2001). The jazz artist assumes that the given is to be interpreted and made into his or her own new meaning. This is the mind-set that directs the Black individual to be flexible in responding to disruptive stimuli. And I see this same attitude in the variables that characterized resilient individuals in several research studies and in clinical case reports. Another element of resilient processes can also be identified in the resilience studies and in observations of African American culture: constructing personal meaning in situations that are either chaotic or defined by threatening others. The resemblance of these phenomena to the protective self-esteem mechanisms—disidentification, disengagement, self-naming, and selective contingencies of worth—described by Steele, Jones, Crocker and Lawrence, and Philogène is striking.

I am aware that there are several difficulties with demonstrating this jazz improvisation–resilience analog compellingly. One hazard is generalizing any psychological phenomena onto a population that is not homogeneous. Another is attributing qualities like resilience to a group that have been mainly described in individuals. An additional problem with the hypothesis is instrumental. Just how does a cultural ethic get systematically taught to people, and how does it get passed down from one generation to the next? Another problem is accounting for how cultural values get transmitted into artistic phenomena. I am exploring answers to some of these questions and ways to find answers to others. But I have not been concerned with constructing or finding a methodology to test the validity of these ideas, and maybe I should be. The construct of resilience itself, its definition, and its efficacy, as I have noted, is controversial. All of the questions that surround it compound the ones I have listed. I am sure there are many more.

Each time I think about the enormity of the obstacles African Americans have overcome (and we can find similar courses of events in other oppressed groups) and what they have contributed to American and to world culture, I am bolstered in the conviction of African American resilience. The work of this section's authors illuminates crucial insights into African Americans' self-esteem that I think can also be included in the resilience paradigm. These scholars' careful examination of the extensive interaction of race, culture, and identity gives us a great deal more to think about too.

References

Clark, K. B., & Clark, M. P. (1939). The development of consciousness of self and the emergence of racial identification of Negro schoolchildren. *Journal of Social Psychology, 10,* 591–599.

Crocker, J., & Lawrence, J. S. (1999). Social stigma and self-esteem: The role of contingencies of worth. In D. A. Prentice & D. T. Miller (Eds.), *Cultural divides: Understanding and overcoming group conflict* (pp. 364–392). New York: Russell Sage Foundation.

Cross, W. E. (1991). *Shades of Black: Diversity in African American identity.* Philadelphia: Temple University Press.

Herman, J. L. (1992). *Trauma and recovery: The aftermath of violence from domestic abuse to political terror.* New York: Basic Books.

Jenkins, A. H. (1995). *Psychology and African Americans: A humanistic approach.* Boston: Allyn & Bacon.

Jones, F. (2001). Jazz and the resilience of African Americans. In F. Jones & A. C. Jones (Eds.), *The triumph of the soul: Cultural and psychological aspects of African American music* (pp. 127–151). Westport, CT: Praeger.

Jones, J. M. (1998). Psychological knowledge and the new American dilemma of race. *Journal of Social Issues, 54,* 641–662.

Luthar, S. S., Cicchetti, D., & Becker, B. (2000). The construct of reliance: A critical evaluation and guidelines for future work. *Child Development, 71,* 543–562.

Philogène, G. (1999). *From Black to African American: A new social representation.* Westport, CT: Praeger.

Steele, C. M. (1997). A threat in the air: How stereotypes shape intellectual identity and performance. *American Psychologist, 52,* 613–629.

Werner, E. E., & Smith, R. S. (1992). *Overcoming the odds: High risk children from birth to adulthood.* Ithaca, NY: Cornell University Press.

7

The Power of Perception: Skin Tone Bias and Psychological Well-Being for Black Americans

Kendrick T. Brown

Kenneth and Mamie Clark's doll studies of the 1930s and 1940s are among the most influential research programs involving Black people in the United States. In the doll studies, Black children were presented with a white and brown doll and were asked by an experimenter to select the doll best representing a particular characteristic. The Clarks found that Black children preferred to play with the white doll, considered the white doll to be nice and also have a nice color, and regarded the brown doll as bad (Clark & Clark, 1947). These findings, coupled with previous work (Clark & Clark, 1940), provided supporting evidence for legal arguments that racial segregation instilled harmful anti-Black sentiments in Black children and consequently proved pivotal in the U.S. Supreme Court's 1954 decision to end school segregation.

An often unrecognized aspect of the Clarks's research is their interest in how skin tone, or the shade of one's skin color, can affect Black people. From their earliest work, the Clarks made efforts to visually assess the skin tone of their child participants as "light," "medium," and "dark" (Clark & Clark, 1940, 1947). They also mentioned briefly in an early article the importance of having a Black researcher with medium complexion who would not unduly influence the children's responses during their experiment (Clark & Clark, 1940). One of their studies found skin tone differences in selections of the doll that children most wanted to "play with," considered to be a "nice doll," regarded as a doll that "looks bad," and perceived as having a "nice color" (Clark & Clark, 1947). When compared with both the medium- and dark-complexioned groups, children with light complexion showed greater favoritism toward the white doll than the brown doll. In discussing this finding, the Clarks speculated that because skin tone is a physical characteristic, skin tone identification might precede racial identification, a process based more on learned social definitions and cues (Clark & Clark, 1940). Though they did not elaborate on this idea,

I would like to thank Suman Ambwani and Keith B. Maddox for their helpful comments during the preparation of this chapter.

the Clarks maintained an interest in skin tone (Clark & Clark, 1980), an interest that is understandable considering the many ways in which skin tone influences the well-being of Black people in the United States.

Skin Tone as a Status

Skin tone can be a status marker determining how Black Americans will be perceived by others. Both White and Black perceivers use skin tone as an organizing principle for their observations and attributions. Maddox and Gray (2002, Study 1) found that more within-category errors (e.g., incorrectly attributing a statement made by a light-complexioned person to another light-complexioned person) than between-category errors (e.g., mistakenly attributing a statement made by a dark-complexioned person to a light-complexioned individual) happened when participants tried matching specific statements observed during a group discussion. In effect, perceivers recognize when a light- or dark-complexioned Black person has made a statement or engaged in a behavior even if perceivers are unable to specifically identify the correct individual. Also, a greater proportion of stereotypic traits commonly linked to Black people were applied to dark-complexioned people, and a larger proportion of counterstereotypic traits were assigned to light-complexioned people (Maddox & Gray, 2002, Study 2). Skin tone then both organizes the perceiver's perceptions and provides a cue for the characteristics that may be associated with a Black person.

In addition to perceptions and stereotypes, skin tone can influence Black Americans' socioeconomic status. Compared with darker skin tones, lighter skin tone is associated with more years of education as well as greater personal and family income (Allen, Telles, & Hunter, 2000; Keith & Herring, 1991) and greater spouse education and occupational prestige (Hughes & Hertel, 1990). These differences in resources exist for both men (Hill, 2000) and women (Hunter, 1998). Furthermore, the magnitude of the differences between light- and dark-complexioned Black people for education and occupational prestige has been found to be equivalent to the disparities between Blacks and Whites (Hughes & Hertel, 1990).

Skin tone status also has been linked to physical health outcomes. In particular, the relationship between skin tone and hypertension has received attention from researchers. Darker skin tone is associated with higher levels of blood pressure than light skin tone (Dressler, 1991; Harburg et al., 1973; Krieger & Sidney, 1996), though an individual's lifestyle can moderate this relationship between skin tone and hypertension. Specifically, Black people with darker skin tone displaying a higher lifestyle (e.g., more material goods and greater access to information) have five times the risk of hypertension than individuals with lighter skin tone evincing a lower lifestyle (Dressler, 1991). This increased risk of hypertension is thought to arise from the stress of pursuing conflicting statuses in the face of cues calling for consistency (i.e., dark skin paired with lower lifestyle).

Lastly, skin tone status has been related to mental health for Black Americans. Compared with either medium- or lighter-complexioned individuals, dark-toned people have been found to exhibit lower self-esteem (Robinson & Ward, 1995). Many studies on skin tone and mental health have focused on gender differences. Examining only Black women, Bond and Cash (1992) found that greater discrepancies between ideal skin tone and self-perceived skin tone were associated with less satisfaction with one's face. Also, desiring to change skin tone related to more negative self-evaluations of overall appearance and one's face (Bond & Cash, 1992). For men, darker skin related to greater mean ratings of sexual attractiveness than lighter skin (Wade, 1996). In one of few studies using a national sample, Thompson and Keith (2001) found gender differences in the relationship of skin tone to self-efficacy and self-esteem. Lighter skin tone was associated with higher self-efficacy for men but not women. Conversely, lighter skin tone related to higher self-esteem for women but not men.

Perception of Skin Tone Bias and Psychological Well-Being

With the exception of some research on hypertension (e.g., Dressler, 1991), perception of racially discriminatory acts (e.g., Klonoff & Landrine, 2000; Krieger, Sidney, & Coakley, 1998), and mental health outcomes, little attention has been given to the internal dynamics that a Black American may experience when confronting issues related to skin tone. In the majority of studies conducted, skin tone has been strictly conceived as a status. While this conceptualization is useful, especially when considering the attitudes and behaviors that others might direct toward Black Americans on the basis of their skin tone, it tends to direct attention away from how individuals may perceive and interpret skin tone bias from others. The Clarks were considering this point when they assessed the skin tone of the children in their study. In discussing why there might be differences based on the skin tone of the participants, the Clarks focused on how Black people's internal perceptions related to skin tone might influence their psychological well-being (Clark & Clark, 1940). The present chapter expands on this focus by examining the relationship between Black Americans' perception of skin tone bias and their psychological well-being.

The impact of perceiving that one is treated differently as a result of shade of skin color has been addressed by many works of fiction, including *The Blacker the Berry* by Wallace Thurman (1929) and *The Bluest Eye* by Toni Morrison (1972), autobiographies such as *The Autobiography of Malcolm X* (X, 1965) and *Notes of a White Black Woman* (Scales-Trent, 1995), and films by Spike Lee (1988) and Kathe Sandler (1992). These works often highlight the difficulties and pain that dark-complexioned individuals experience when trying to navigate situations favoring light-complexioned people. Some of them also describe the obstacles that light-skinned Black people must overcome or expectations that they are pressured to meet.

The negative experiences evident in these anecdotal accounts are also present in the client remarks and observations made by counseling and clinical psychologists during therapy sessions with Black Americans. Individuals disclosing their experiences of skin tone bias mention being scapegoated by some family members because they are either darker or lighter than others in the family (Boyd-Franklin, 1991; Harvey, 1995). Light-complexioned individuals recognized receiving unfair advantages and frequently expressed a sense of guilt as a consequence (Boyd-Franklin, 1991; Neal & Wilson, 1989). This awareness also bred a degree of suspicion in some light-complexioned Black people who discussed the difficulty of knowing when they receive benefits because of who they are or simply because of their light skin tone (Okazawa-Rey, Robinson, & Ward, 1987). Conversely, dark-complexioned Black people often mentioned feeling resentment and some fear about being too dark (Neal & Wilson, 1989). In some cases, the skin tone bias that they perceived drove dark-complexioned individuals to compensate by excelling in other areas of their lives, such as education (Okazawa-Rey et al., 1987).

The anecdotal accounts conveyed by literature and film as well as the observations gathered during therapy sessions offer insight into how perceiving skin tone bias may affect a Black American's psychological well-being. These sources, however, do not use large samples from nontherapy populations. This limitation hinders generalization about the perceptions that many Black people might develop as they encounter skin tone bias. The study described in this chapter addresses this limitation by using the 1995 Detroit Area Study. The Detroit Area Study includes a representative sample of more than 500 self-identified Black people from the population of individuals living in the Detroit metropolitan area.

Perception of Skin Tone Bias as a Stressor

In addition to the anecdotal and therapy accounts that indicate perceiving skin tone bias should be associated with diminished psychological well-being for Black Americans, research on the influence of perceiving oneself to be the target of discrimination suggests that stress is part of the process. Heightened physiological and psychological responses to the stress accompanying perceptions of discrimination can over time influence an individual's physical and psychological well-being (R. Clark, Anderson, Clark, & Williams, 1999). This health impact can occur even if others deem an individual's perception to not objectively reflect what happened in the situation. In accord with major views of the stress appraisal process (Lazarus & Folkman, 1984; Pearlin, 1999), it is the target's appraisal of a situation as discriminatory and therefore stressful that is important (R. Clark et al., 1999; Miller & Kaiser, 2001).

Once individuals have appraised the situation as one involving discrimination, particularly when it is based on racial characteristics such as skin color, they may be affected in a number of ways. Landrine and Klonoff (1996) found that more potentially racist events appraised as stressful correlated with greater anxiety and an increased number of somatic symptoms of stress for their Black American participants. Other research has found that more attributions of past and future experiences to racial prejudice decreased Black Americans' personal well-being (Branscombe, Schmitt, & Harvey, 1999). Also, perceiving that one has been treated badly in the last month because of race is associated with more reported health problems and health disability for Black Americans (Jackson et al., 1996).

Hypotheses

Drawing from research suggesting that perceiving skin tone bias can entail negative observations about one's interactions with others, as well as studies indicating that the perception of racial discrimination is associated with negative psychological well-being, a general hypothesis was formed to guide the work in this chapter. It was expected that perceiving that one has been treated better or worse because of skin tone will be associated with negative psychological well-being for Black Americans.

The majority of the work on skin tone bias has focused on the attitudes and behaviors that Black Americans exhibit toward one another. Though historical research (e.g., Davis, 1991; Williamson, 1980) and empirical work on the relationship between skin tone and socioeconomic status attest to the role that White Americans can have in perpetuating skin tone bias, many Black Americans may not as readily attribute their perception of bias to skin tone as much as racism when they interact with White Americans. Therefore, Black Americans may have a more difficult time identifying skin tone bias from White Americans compared with that from other Black Americans. Also, Black Americans may have more responses at their disposal to cope with bias from White Americans, who can be conceived as members of an indifferent or antagonistic out-group (Crocker & Major, 1989; Crocker, Voelkl, Testa, & Major, 1991), than bias from other Black Americans from whom in-group support might be expected. Consequently, a second hypothesis is that the perception of skin tone bias from other Black Americans will be more strongly associated with psychological well-being than perception of skin tone bias from White Americans.

Method

Participants

The present study used data from 586 self-identified Black American respondents living in the Detroit metropolitan area from April through October 1995. Women accounted for 68.4% of the sample. Respondents had a mean of 12.76 years of education, an average imputed family income of $29,004.06, a mean occupational prestige rating of 3.63 on a 6-point scale (1 = *manual labor/personal or domestic services* to 6 = *professional/technical*), and averaged 45.08 years of age.

Materials

The survey instrument used for this study was the 1995 Detroit Area Study (DAS) questionnaire. The DAS is a yearly survey that has been conducted by the University of Michigan Survey Research Center for more than 25 years. The 1995 survey focused on the relationship between various perceptions and experiences of racial discrimination and physical and mental health outcomes.

PERCEPTION OF SKIN TONE BIAS. Two questions measuring the perception of skin tone bias were presented. The first asked respondents, "Because of the *shade* of your skin color do you think White people treat you a lot better, somewhat better, no different, somewhat worse, or a lot worse than other Blacks?" Less than 3% of respondents selected "a lot better," whereas 13.3% chose "somewhat better." On the other end of the scale, 1% stated that they had been treated "a lot worse," and 9.9% gave a response of "somewhat worse." The most frequent response given was that individuals felt they were treated "no different" (72.6%). Given the low percentage of respondents choosing the most extreme scale options, "a lot better" and "somewhat better" were combined as were "a lot worse" and "somewhat worse." Collapsing these response options together resulted in a three-category variable consisting of better, no different, and worse treatment from Whites based on skin tone. Two dummy variables were then created to compare the different types of perceived treatment. The first focused on perceived better treatment (1 = *better*, 0 = *else*), and the other concentrated on perceived worse treatment (1 = *worse*, 0 = *else*). Consequently, both dummy variables used "no different" as the excluded category of comparison.

The second perception of skin tone bias question asked respondents, "Because of the *shade* of your skin color do you think Black people treat you a lot better, somewhat better, no different, somewhat worse, or a lot worse than other Blacks?" As was the case for the perception question focused on White people, relatively few respondents chose the extreme categories of "a lot better" (1%) or "a lot worse" (1%). More individuals selected "somewhat better" (8.3%) and "somewhat worse" (10.7%), but the most frequently chosen option was "no different" (78.8%). Because of the low percentage of respondents selecting the extreme categories, a similar recoding was done for this question as for the previous one. Ultimately, this recoding resulted in two dummy variables focused on perceived better treatment from Blacks (1 = *better*, 0 = *else*) and perceived worse treatment from Blacks (1 = *worse*, 0 = *else*), with "no different" as the excluded category of comparison.

PSYCHOLOGICAL WELL-BEING. Two outcome variables represented negative and positive aspects of psychological well-being. The negative aspect of well-being, psychological distress, was measured by a six-item scale asking respondents to reflect on the last 30 days and rate how often they felt (a) so sad nothing could cheer them up, (b) nervous, (c) restless or fidgety, (d) hopeless, (e) worthless, and (f) that everything was an effort. Respondents used a 5-point scale from 1 = *never* to 5 = *very often* for each of these items. The psychological distress scale had a Cronbach's alpha of .82.

Life satisfaction represented the positive aspect of psychological well-being. Respondents were presented with the following question, "Please think about your life as a whole. How satisfied are you with it—are you completely satisfied, very satisfied, somewhat satisfied, not very satisfied, or not at all satisfied?" The scale was reverse-scored such that higher responses indicated greater life satisfaction.

CONTROL VARIABLES. Several demographic variables served as control variables in this study. The first was *age,* measured in the respondents' number of years. Second was *marital status,* which was recoded to compare individuals who had never been married with those having other marital statuses (e.g., married, separated, widowed, etc.). *Gender* comparing women with men also was taken into consideration. The fourth control variable was *education,* as measured by the number of years of schooling that respondents had completed at the time of the interview. Fifth was *imputed family income,* which consisted of the respondent's self-reported family income for 1994. If individuals did not choose to disclose their income, an imputation method based on respondents with similar sociodemographic characteristics was used to arrive at an estimate of the nondiscloser's family income. This imputation was used for only 8.7% of the sample. The sixth control variable was *occupational prestige rank* as assessed by the general category into which the respondent's job could be placed. Those categories from least to most prestigious consisted of (a) manual labor/personal or domestic services, (b) operative services, (c) crafts, (d) clerical, (e) management/sales, and (f) professional/technical.

In addition to these demographic variables, respondents' self-rated skin tone ratings were included. Typically, the status approach to investigating skin tone bias assesses only the skin tone of participants. Thus, this self-rated measure was included to investigate the extent to which perceptions associated with skin tone bias are distinguishable from simply taking account of skin tone status. The self-rating question asked, "Compared with most Black people, what skin color do you believe you have?" Of the response categories given, most individuals chose "medium brown" (50.2%), followed by "dark brown" (24.7%) and "light brown" (16.8%), with both extremes of "very light brown" (4.6%) and "very dark brown" (3.6%) chosen least.

The final control variable consisted of a measure of the perception of racial discrimination. This variable was included to ensure that the perception of skin tone bias did not overlap greatly with an awareness of racism. The perception of racial discrimination was assessed by the following question, "Thinking over your whole life, do you think that you have ever been treated unfairly or badly because of your race or ethnicity?" A yes/no dummy variable with "no" as the excluded category was created.

Procedure

For the 1995 DAS, a representative sample of residents in the Detroit metropolitan area was obtained through a multistage, area, clustered, probability sampling of the population 18 years of age and older residing in Wayne, Oakland, and Macomb counties in Michigan, including the city of Detroit. At the first stage, a random sample of segments, consisting of clusters of city blocks within the tri-county area, was drawn. Next, within the selected segments, a housing unit was randomly chosen. Lastly, a Kish table was used to randomly select a respondent who was identified as living within the household.

After determining which individual in the household would be a respondent, trained interviewers conducted face-to-face interviews. Interviewing occurred in the respondent's home, or another location in which the respondent felt comfortable, and generally lasted for 1 hour. If participants were not present at the time that the interviewer visited their home, interviewers continued to attempt to contact them. After completing the interview, interviewers asked respondents if they had any questions or concerns regarding the questionnaire.

Analysis

Linear regression was used to analyze the relationship between perception of skin tone bias and psychological well-being. The six sociodemographic, self-rated skin tone, and perception of racial discrimination variables were entered first into the model, followed by the two skin tone bias perception variables focused on White people and the two perception variables concerning treatment by Black people.

Results

The correlations, means, and standard deviations for the predictor and outcome variables are presented first. Starting with perceptions of different treatment from White people because of skin tone, 15.94% of the sample respond that they have been treated better, whereas 10.92% believe that they have been treated worse. Bivariate analyses show that perception of better treatment by Whites is not independent of perception of better treatment by Black people ($\varphi = .27, p < .01$), nor is perception of better treatment by Whites independent of perception of worse treatment by Black people ($\varphi = .12, p < .01$). Examining the bivariate relationships for perceiving worse treatment by White people shows independence from perceiving better treatment by Black people ($\varphi = .02, ns$) and lack of independence with perceiving worse treatment by Black people ($\varphi = .21, p < .01$). Results of perceptions associated with Black people reveals that 9.3% of the sample disclose that they have been treated better because of skin tone and 11.72% think that they have been treated worse.

For the two psychological well-being indicators, the sample showed relatively high life satisfaction ($M = 3.48, SD = 0.87$) and somewhat low psychological distress ($M = 2.02, SD = 0.84$). The bivariate correlation between life satisfaction and psychological distress showed a moderate degree of association ($r = .29, p < .01$).

Psychological Distress

An ordinary least-squares linear regression analysis of psychological distress consisting of both controls and the perception variables was conducted. Three of the eight control variables had significant relationships with psychological distress (not shown). Greater age ($b = -.01, SE\ b = .01, p < .05$) and greater imputed family income ($b = -6.30 \times 10^{-6}, SE\ b = -.18, p < .01$) were associated with lower levels of psychological distress, whereas perceiving that one has

Table 7.1. Summary of Linear Regression Analysis for Variables Predicting Psychological Distress

Variable	b	SE b	β
Perception of better treatment from Whites (1 = *better*, 0 = *else*)	−.06	.11	−.03
Perception of worse treatment from Whites (1 = *worse*, 0 = *else*)	.05	.14	.02
Perception of better treatment from Blacks (1 = *better*, 0 = *else*)	.37*	.13	.13
Perception of worse treatment from Blacks (1 = *worse*, 0 = *else*)	.10	.13	.04
Adjusted R^2		.084*	

Note. The excluded category for each dummy variable is "treated no differently."
* $p < .01$.

been treated badly in the last month because of race was related to greater psychological distress ($b = .17$, *SE* $b = .08$, $p < .05$).

Table 7.1 shows the regression analysis involving the four dummy variables assessing the perception of skin tone bias. Only perceiving better treatment by other Black people has a significant relationship with psychological distress. Compared with not perceiving different treatment, Black American respondents believing that they have been treated better by other Black people report greater levels of psychological distress. The other three skin tone bias perceptions did not approach statistical significance.

Life Satisfaction

As with the regression analysis for psychological distress, the three control variables of age, imputed family income, and perception of racial discrimination related significantly to life satisfaction (not shown). Greater age ($b = .01$, *SE* $b = .01$, $p < .01$) and greater imputed family income ($b = 5.63 \times 10^{-6}$, *SE* $b = .15$, $p < .01$) were associated with higher life satisfaction, whereas perceiving racial discrimination in the last 30 days was associated with lower life satisfaction ($b = −.21$, *SE* $b = .09$, $p < .05$).

The regression relationships involving the four perception of skin tone bias variables are depicted in Table 7.2. None of the four perception of skin tone bias dummy variables are significantly associated with life satisfaction.

Discussion

Examining Black Americans' perceptions of how others might treat them differently because of their skin tone can provide important information about well-being. The analyses in this chapter account for perceptions of skin tone bias and reveal that individuals' interpretations of skin tone bias are associated

Table 7.2. Summary of Linear Regression Analysis for Variables Predicting Life Satisfaction

Variable	b	SE b	β
Perception of better treatment from Whites (1 = *better*, 0 = *else*)	−.11	.12	−.05
Perception of worse treatment from Whites (1 = *worse*, 0 = *else*)	.11	.14	.04
Perception of better treatment from Blacks (1 = *better*, 0 = *else*)	−.06	.14	−.02
Perception of worse treatment from Blacks (1 = *worse*, 0 = *else*)	−.01	.13	−.01
Adjusted R^2		.078*	

Note. The excluded category for each dummy variable is "treated no differently."
* $p < .01$.

with psychological well-being, depending on the racial group to which skin tone bias is attached and evaluation of that bias as positive or negative.

Psychological Distress

Although perception of skin tone bias did not exhibit significant relationships with life satisfaction, it was related to psychological distress. Specifically, Black Americans who perceived that they have been treated better by other Black people had heightened levels of psychological distress compared with individuals who did not perceive different treatment based on their skin tone. This relationship may exist because positive discrimination can be more difficult to handle than negative discrimination, especially when it comes from an unexpected source such as members of one's own racial in-group. Although there can be an in-group bias that affects many interactions between Black Americans, skin tone bias provides a clearly different rationale for that favoritism. In effect, individuals are treated more positively not because they share an important social bond with other racial in-group members but because of skin tone, a feature that often divides Black Americans. When a Black person acknowledges that he or she has been treated better because of a contentious characteristic like skin tone, the person may experience a large amount of distress for receiving unfair rewards that fail to acknowledge who the person is as an individual or member of his or her racial group.

Perceiving better treatment from other Black Americans can have this association with psychological distress more so than the three other types of skin tone bias perceptions. Because of experiences with racism, Black Americans may have a repertoire of coping responses at their disposal for dealing with perceptions of bias from White Americans. These coping responses can insulate their psychological well-being from perceptions of racially based bias associated with White Americans (R. Clark et al., 1999; Crocker & Major, 1989; Crocker et al., 1991; Miller & Kaiser, 2001). This protective process may apply to perceptions of both better and worse treatment due to skin tone bias and keep distress levels from becoming elevated.

In a similar way, Black Americans may have developed ways of handling the stress accompanying perceptions of negative treatment based on skin tone. When skin tone bias affecting the Black community is discussed, many individuals label it as "colorism." Colorism focuses on the negative ways in which Black Americans may treat one another because of the shade of their skin color. Conceiving of skin tone bias as colorism can raise awareness of the negative skin tone bias that Black people face but may not highlight positive discrimination to the same degree. Consequently, the emphasis on skin tone bias as colorism might lead Black people to develop ways of coping with perceptions of worse treatment because of their skin tone and keep distress levels from being especially high.

Not Perceiving Skin Tone Bias

Although some individuals indicated that they perceived skin tone bias operating in their lives, the majority of respondents disclosed that they were treated no differently because of skin tone. Considering the effect that skin tone can have on many aspects of Black American life, perception of skin tone bias may be underreported. Both psychological and social considerations may account for this underreporting. Psychologically, perceiving oneself to be the target of personal discrimination may be underreported because of difficulty in discerning situational cues indicating discrimination (Inman, Huerta, & Oh, 1998; Jackson et al., 1996). If Black Americans are unable to interpret a cue in a social situation as one involving skin tone bias, they will not report a perception of skin tone bias.

Socially, perceptions of skin tone bias may be underreported because of the taboo nature of skin tone bias (Breland, 1998; Russell, Wilson, & Hall, 1992). Black Americans may feel that disclosing their experiences with skin tone bias will reveal deep cleavages in the Black community that will hamper the cohesion necessary for attaining group goals. As it is often called, "airing dirty laundry" is something to be done in a private, controlled manner whereby individuals outside of the racial group will not be privy to divisions within the group. Black Americans subscribing to this belief may perceive skin tone bias but will refrain from reporting their perceptions by indicating that they have not been treated better or worse.

Conclusion

In both their early and later research, Kenneth and Mamie Clark showed an interest in how skin tone can affect Black Americans' lives. That initial interest focused on Black children and how they might construct their sense of racial identification in social environments denigrating their racial group (Clark & Clark, 1940). Subsequently, the Clarks undertook a large-scale survey of Black adults to ascertain the challenges that individuals had to overcome to maintain a positive sense of self and of their racial group (Clark & Clark, 1980). For both of these projects, information about participants' skin tone was collected. Particularly, in their early work the Clarks went beyond conceiving of skin tone as simply a status to which others would respond. They analyzed how individuals might respond to the status conveyed by their skin tone. Consequently, the Clarks highlighted the need to examine the perceptions associated with skin tone and how those perceptions might affect Black Americans.

Recent work has illustrated the need to consider not just the race but also the perceptions of individuals affected by racial bias (R. Clark et al., 1999). In the same manner, the research on skin tone bias needs to move beyond a simple interest in skin tone as a status to a perspective that assesses the perceptions of individuals who experience skin tone bias. When that shift to investigating perceptions occurs, then that initial work started by the Clarks more than 60 years ago relating skin tone bias to Black Americans' well-being will be more prominently included in the rich legacy that they have left for psychology.

References

Allen, W., Telles, E., & Hunter, M. (2000). Skin color, income and education: A comparison of African Americans and Mexican Americans. *National Journal of Sociology, 12,* 129–180.

Bond, S., & Cash, T. F. (1992). Black beauty: Skin color and body images among African-American college women. *Journal of Applied Social Psychology, 22,* 874–888.

Boyd-Franklin, N. (1991). Recurrent themes in the treatment of African-American women in group psychotherapy. *Women & Therapy, 11*(2), 25–40.

Branscombe, N. R., Schmitt, M. T., & Harvey, R. D. (1999). Perceiving pervasive discrimination among African Americans: Implications for group identification and well-being. *Journal of Personality and Social Psychology, 77,* 135–149.

Breland, A. M. (1998). A model for differential perceptions of competence based on skin tone among African Americans. *Journal of Multicultural Counseling and Development, 26,* 294–311.

Clark, K. B., & Clark, M. P. (1940). Skin color as a factor in racial identification of Negro preschool children. *Journal of Social Psychology, S.P.S.S.I. Bulletin, 11,* 159–169.

Clark, K. B., & Clark, M. P. (1947). Racial identification and preference in Negro children. In T. M. Newcomb & E. L. Hartley (Eds.), *Readings in social psychology* (pp. 169–178). New York: Holt.

Clark, K. B., & Clark, M. P. (1980, November). What do Blacks think of themselves? *Ebony,* 176–182.

Clark, R., Anderson, N. B., Clark, V. R., & Williams, D. R. (1999). Racism as a stressor for African Americans: A biopsychosocial model. *American Psychologist, 54,* 805–816.

Crocker, J., & Major, B. (1989). Social stigma and self-esteem: The self-protective properties of stigma. *Psychological Review, 96,* 608–630.

Crocker, J., Voelkl, K., Testa, M., & Major, B. (1991). Social stigma: The affective consequences of attributional ambiguity. *Journal of Personality and Social Psychology, 60,* 218–228.

Davis, F. J. (1991). *Who is Black?: One nation's definition.* University Park: Pennsylvania State Press.

Dressler, W. W. (1991). Social class, skin color, and arterial blood pressure in two societies. *Ethnicity and Disease, 1,* 60–77.

Harburg, E., Erfurt, J. C., Hauenstein, L. S., Chape, C., Schull, W. J., & Schork, M. A. (1973). Socio-ecological stress, suppressed hostility, skin color, and Black–White male blood pressure: Detroit. *Psychosomatic Medicine, 35,* 276–296.

Harvey, A. R. (1995). The issue of skin color in psychotherapy with African Americans. *Families in Society: The Journal of Contemporary Human Services, 76*(1), 3–10.

Hill, M. E. (2000). Color differences in the socioeconomic status of African American men: Results of a longitudinal study. *Social Forces, 78,* 1437–1460.

Hughes, M., & Hertel, B. R. (1990). The significance of color remains: A study of life chances, mate selection, and ethnic consciousness among Black Americans. *Social Forces, 68,* 1105–1120.

Hunter, M. L. (1998). Colorstruck: Skin color stratification in the lives of African American women. *Sociological Inquiry, 68,* 517–535.

Inman, M. J., Huerta, J., & Oh, S. (1998). Perceiving discrimination: The role of prototypes and norm violation. *Social Cognition, 16,* 418–450.

Jackson, J. S., Brown, T. N., Williams, D. R., Torres, M., Sellers, S. L., & Brown, K. (1996). Racism and the physical and mental health status of African Americans: A thirteen year national panel study. *Ethnicity & Disease, 6,* 132–147.

Keith, V. M., & Herring, C. (1991). Skin tone and stratification in the Black community. *American Journal of Sociology, 97,* 760–778.

Klonoff, E. A., & Landrine, H. (2000). Is skin color a marker for racial discrimination? Explaining the skin color–hypertension relationship. *Journal of Behavioral Medicine, 23,* 329–338.

Krieger, N., & Sidney, S. (1996). Racial discrimination and blood pressure: The CARDIA study. *American Journal of Public Health, 86,* 1370–1378.

Krieger, N., Sidney, S., & Coakley, E. (1998). Racial discrimination and skin color in the CARDIA study: Implications for public health research. *American Journal of Public Health, 88,* 1308–1313.

Landrine, H., & Klonoff, E. A. (1996). The schedule of racist events: A measure of racial discrimination and a study of its negative physical and mental health consequences. *Journal of Black Psychology, 22,* 144–168.

Lazarus, R. S., & Folkman, S. (1984). *Stress, appraisal, and coping.* New York: Springer.

Lee, S. (Producer/Writer/Director). (1988). *School daze* [Motion picture]. Los Angeles: Columbia Pictures.

Maddox, K. B., & Gray, S. A. (2002). Cognitive representations of Black Americans: Reexploring the role of skin tone. *Personality and Social Psychology Bulletin, 28,* 250–259.

Miller, C. T., & Kaiser, C. R. (2001). A theoretical perspective on coping with stigma. *Journal of Social Issues, 37,* 73–92.

Morrison, T. (1972). *The bluest eye.* New York: Washington Square Press.

Neal, A. M., & Wilson, M. L. (1989). The role of skin color and features in the Black community: Implications for Black women and therapy. *Clinical Psychology Review, 9,* 323–333.

Okazawa-Rey, M., Robinson, T., & Ward, J. V. (1987). Black women and the politics of skin color and hair. *Women & Therapy, 6,* 89–102.

Pearlin, L. I. (1999). Stress and mental health: A conceptual overview. In A. V. Horowitz & T. L. Scheid (Eds.), *A handbook for the study of mental health: Social contexts, theories, and systems* (pp. 161–175). New York: Cambridge University Press.

Robinson, T. L., & Ward, J. V. (1995). African American adolescents and skin color. *Journal of Black Psychology, 21,* 256–274.

Russell, K., Wilson, M., & Hall, R. (1992). *The color complex: The politics of skin color among African Americans.* New York: Anchor Books.

Sandler, K. (Producer/Writer/Director). (1992). *A question of color: Color consciousness in Black America* [Motion picture]. San Francisco: California Newsreel.

Scales-Trent, J. (1995). *Notes of a White Black woman.* University Park: Pennsylvania State Press.

Thompson, M. S., & Keith, V. M. (2001). The blacker the berry: Gender, skin tone, self-esteem, and self-efficacy. *Gender & Society, 15,* 336–357.

Thurman, W. (1929). *The blacker the berry.* New York: Macmillan.

Wade, T. J. (1996). The relationships between skin color and self-perceived global, physical, and sexual attractiveness, and self-esteem for African Americans. *Journal of Black Psychology, 22,* 358–373.

Williamson, J. (1980). *New people: Miscegenation and mulattoes in the United States.* New York: Free Press.

X, Malcolm. (1965). *The autobiography of Malcolm X.* New York: Ballantine Books.

8

"I *Can*, But Do I *Want* To?" Achievement Values in Ethnic Minority Children and Adolescents

Sandra Graham

Most of the contributors to this volume in honor of Kenneth B. Clark are social psychologists who are concerned with racial factors underlying the successful (or unsuccessful) adjustment of young adults. On the one hand, that is to be expected because social psychology has played a key role in advancing our understanding of how racism, prejudice, and discrimination can undermine successful adaptation, and social psychologists by and large study young adults. On the other hand, Kenneth Clark is largely remembered for what he had to say about *children* of color. His legacy is a stark reminder of how patterns of prejudice woven into society can be detrimental to the healthy development of all children, how the organization of public schools can undermine the self-esteem of Black children, and how teacher attitudes and expectations can interfere with achievement strivings of these same youths. A volume in honor of Clark's legacy is therefore an appropriate arena for considering the development of children of color in school settings and in the context of coping with the particular academic challenges that often accompany ethnic minority status.

In this chapter, I address development in children and adolescents of color. The research that I describe was conducted in public schools where my focus has been the development of academic motivation. I hope to make the case that the study of motivation provides a rich framework for addressing some of the most pressing issues about the school experiences of African American youths that were identified early on by Kenneth Clark and that continue to plague the educational system in the United States to this day. Those issues revolve around barriers to achievement such as low test scores, grade retention, early withdrawal, and various disciplinary practices like suspension and expulsion. By all indications, such barriers are disproportionately encountered by ethnic minority children, particularly African American youths. One might therefore hope that a motivational approach, which focuses on the *why* of achievement-related behavior rather than behavior itself, might offer fresh insights into the educational challenges faced by many African American students. In outlining a developmental perspective, I acknowledge my intellectual debt to Kenneth Clark, who so poignantly captured the struggles of children of color in American schools and who raised our consciousness about the role of psychology as a stimulus for social change.

Expectancy–Value Approaches to Motivation

Most contemporary approaches to motivation can broadly be cast within an expectancy–value framework. According to that framework, motivation is determined by some combination of the perceived likelihood that a goal will be attained (the expectancy component) and how much that goal is desired or wanted (the value component). Much of what we know about the motivational patterns of African Americans has focused on the expectancy component of expectancy–value theory. For example, it has been argued that a pattern of school failure can be linked to (predicted by) Black children's low expectations for future success and the perception of themselves as relatively incompetent.

Although motivation theory would suggest a strong relation between low expectancy and poor school performance, in truth the two constructs often are not correlated among African American youths. Some years ago I reviewed the empirical literature on motivation in Black students (Graham, 1994). That review found very little evidence that African Americans experienced either low expectancy for future success or low academic self-concept, even when they were doing poorly in school according to the standard indicators. If anything, the opposite—some would argue counterintuitive—pattern emerged. Compared with their higher achieving White classmates, African American students were found to be remarkably optimistic and to endorse positive self-views. There is much corroborating empirical evidence, both preceding and following that 1994 review, for high self-esteem among African Americans and for weak relations between self-esteem and performance (see, e.g., Crocker & Major, 1989; Gray-Little & Hafdahl, 2000).

A different kind of motivational explanation for Black underachievement that may hold more promise focuses on achievement values, the relatively more neglected part of expectancy–value approaches. Unlike achievement-related expectancies that largely center on beliefs about ability (*Can* I do it?), values have to do with desires and preferences (Do I *want* it?) and are more concerned with the perceived importance, attractiveness, or usefulness of achievement activities. Values also are rooted in the moral constructs of "ought" and "should" (Rokeach, 1973), as illustrated by the belief that one should try hard in school regardless of one's perceived abilities.

Because values have motivational properties, it might be argued that many Black students do poorly in school because they deny the importance, attractiveness, and utility of academic success, or because their own life experiences are discrepant with the notion that students ought to feel morally obligated to exert effort in school. In my work with urban teachers, I am struck with how often an implicit focus on values emerges in the teachers' lay theories about why so many Black adolescents are underachieving in school. For example, I hear comments such as "They can do the work but they just don't seem to *care*" or "The kids have not come to terms with the reality that you have to work hard in school to guarantee success in life."

As a motivation psychologist, there is little I can say to either support or refute these teachers' laments, for at present there is very little research that directly examines achievement values among African American youths from a motivational perspective. Values, in fact, have been relatively neglected in motivation research. The one notable exception is research by Eccles, Wigfield, and their colleagues on task-specific beliefs (e.g., Eccles & Wigfield, 1995; Eccles, Wigfield, & Schiefele, 1998). Those researchers defined tasks in terms of their *attainment* value (the perceived importance of doing well), *intrinsic* value (how much enjoyment the individual derives), *utility* value (how the task relates to future goals), and *costs* (the undesirable consequences of task engagement). Because that work has not been directly concerned with issues of race and task value, or the broader sociocultural context in which achievement values emerge, it does not shed light on the question of whether or why African American students devalue effort and whether this devaluing is related to disengagement from school. Motivation researchers concerned with relations between race and achievement values are therefore forced to look beyond their own disciplinary boundaries. And indeed, several analyses emerging from the disciplines of sociology, anthropology, and social psychology do offer new insights, each providing an explanation for the presumed devaluing of achievement strivings among African American youths.

Perspectives From Other Disciplines

Sociologists point to the opportunity structure in American society as they argue that economic and social disadvantage have led many Black students to believe that their efforts in school will have relatively little payoff in terms of economic and social mobility (e.g., Mickelson, 1990). That is, the perceived barriers imposed by a society that perpetuates inequality along race and class lines communicate to minority youngsters that there is little relationship between their efforts and eventual outcomes. The perception of barriers is likely to manifest itself as low educational and occupational aspirations (e.g., Cook et al., 1996) or as perceived discrimination by members of higher status groups (e.g., van Laar, 2000).

Anthropologists whose work is relevant focus on the historical circumstances and cultural forces that have shaped the experiences of African Americans. American Blacks are what John Ogbu called an *involuntary minority*— that is, a group who has become part of the American fabric not by choice, but as a result of slavery, conquest, or colonization (Fordham & Ogbu, 1986; Ogbu, 1997). One consequence of this history is that acceptance of mainstream values about working hard and school success may be perceived as threatening to one's social identity. Particularly during adolescence, African American youngsters may adopt oppositional identities whereby they show relative indifference, or even disdain toward achievement behaviors that are valued by the larger society. Fordham and Ogbu (1986) coined the term *acting White* to describe African American high school students' perceptions of their same-race peers who work hard to do well in school. Whereas scholars disagree about the level of empirical support for the acting-White construct (e.g., Cook & Ludwig, 1998; Foley, 1991), there is more consensus among researchers that many ethnic minority adolescents experience a particular kind of conflict between achievement strivings and their desire to be accepted by the general peer group (e.g., Arroyo & Zigler, 1995; Steinberg, Dornbusch, & Brown, 1992).

Yet a third disciplinary perspective is represented by social psychologists who focus on the relations between self-esteem and school achievement. Because those linkages appear to be weak in research on African Americans (e.g., Graham, 1994), social psychologists have argued that Black students often seek outlets other than achievement success to feel good about themselves or to avoid feeling bad. This esteem-protecting mechanism has been described with various labels, including disidentification with academic achievement (Osborne, 1997; Steele, 1997; see also Steele, chap. 4, this volume), disengagement (Major, Spencer, Schmader, Wolfe, & Crocker, 1997), and selectively devaluing those performance dimensions on which the self or one's group is perceived to do poorly (e.g., Crocker, Major, & Steele, 1998).

In summary, three processes reflective of three disciplinary perspectives can be enlisted as explanations for why African American students might devalue effort and high achievement in school. Sociologists focus on the perceived barriers to success, anthropologists highlight identity conflict, and social psychologists emphasize self-esteem maintenance. Although clearly capturing interrelated processes, the relevant literatures remain distinct and each has its own particular methodology. Sociologists primarily rely on survey methods, anthropologists tend to prefer ethnographic approaches, and social psychologists whose work is relevant use laboratory experimental paradigms as their primary research tools.

A New Empirical Approach to the Study of Achievement Values

In light of the cross-disciplinary literature that shaped our thinking, my colleagues and I set out to examine achievement values in African American adolescents. Given their position in the opportunity structure, their unique cultural and historical circumstances, and the possible disassociation of positive self-regard from achievement strivings, is there evidence that African American middle school students do indeed devalue the importance of trying hard and doing well in school? We focused on early adolescence because that is the developmental period during which attitudes toward school, including achievement values, take on heightened significance and may be particularly salient determinants of academic performance. Although our focus remains on African American youths, it will be seen that we have broadened our perspective to include multiethnic samples that share some of the same motivational beliefs and school achievement patterns as their African American counterparts.

Choosing a methodology for our research posed several challenges. We wanted an approach that was broader than targeting task-specific beliefs as in the Eccles and Wigfield research, yet one that was less daunting than the broad constructs and associated methodologies that emerged from the other disciplines discussed earlier. We also wanted to avoid the kind of direct probing that might be biased by social desirability and self-presentational concerns. For example, studies that directly ask adolescents whether they value school work, put forth effort, or think that getting a good education has long-term benefits generally reveal that all respondents, including African Americans, readily endorse these beliefs (e.g., Steinberg et al., 1992).

Our alternative was to use peer nomination procedures in which participants select classmates who fit various behavioral descriptions. Such procedures have a long history in the peer relations literature in which they have been successfully used with studies of children's social status, such as being popular versus rejected or aggressive versus victimized (see Coie, Dodge, & Coppotelli, 1982). In the present studies, we asked participants to nominate the classmates whom they most admired, respected, and wanted to be like. Our rationale for these questions was that if we can identify the characteristics of individuals whom an adolescent admires, respects, and wants to be like, this tells us something about the characteristics that the adolescent values.

Our method is not entirely unprecedented in motivation research. In early training studies to enhance the achievement motive, one popular technique was to have adolescents construct an "admiration ladder" in which they listed the names of individuals they most and least wanted to be like (Alschuler, Tabor, & McIntyre, 1971). That exercise then became the focus of discussions about "the qualities the students value in the people they most admire" (Alschuler et al., 1971, p. 142). Our peer nomination procedures can therefore be thought of as an adaptation of the admiration ladder.

Participants also nominated classmates who fit the descriptions of trying hard and getting good grades, not trying and receiving poor grades, following or not following school rules, dressing well, and being good at sports. Asking these additional questions permitted us to investigate relations between being "valued" (i.e., nominated as admired, respected, etc.) and other characteristics that are salient during adolescence. Finally, data were gathered on students' academic achievement level. That allowed us to examine whether classmates nominated as admired, respected, and someone others wanted to be like were those who were high or low in achievement as defined by more objective criteria.

We used this procedure in two studies (see Graham, Taylor, & Hudley, 1998, for further details about the method). The first study was conducted with about 300 low socioeconomic status (SES) African American sixth to eighth graders selected from 10 classrooms of a predominantly Black (99%) middle school in metropolitan Los Angeles. Located in an economically depressed community, the school qualified for Title I compensatory education funds, and a majority of the student body was eligible for the district free lunch program.

Nominations for "who do you (1) admire, (2) respect, and (3) want to be like" were highly correlated. That is, students who were nominated as admired also tended to be nominated as respected and as someone the nominator wanted to be like. Each student's number of nominations on the three questions was therefore summed to create a single index that was labeled *value* nominations. Our main goal in the analysis was to examine the choice patterns of male and female nominators as a function of gender and achievement level (high, average, or low) of the nominated student. In this way we were able to determine whether boys and girls preferentially valued same- or other-gender classmates and high versus average versus low achievers. Figure 8.1 displays these value nominations for girls (top) and boys (bottom).

It is evident here that girls overwhelmingly reported that they valued other girls rather than boys (92% vs. 8% of the nominations). Girls also nominated high-achieving girls more than average-achieving or low-achieving girls. Boys, on the other hand, were more likely to value male than female classmates (69% vs. 31%). As the bottom half of Figure 8.1 shows, boys tended to overnominate their low-achieving male classmates and undernominate their high-achieving peers (the percentages were significantly different from chance). That is, when nominating other boys, boys were *least* likely to select their high-achieving same-gender classmates as those they admired, respected, and wanted to be like.

Using the same analysis strategy, we next examined girls' and boys' nomination patterns in response to four of the remaining questions: who tries hard, follows school rules, does not try hard, and does not follow school rules. The pattern was quite clear for female and male nominators. Girls, particularly high-achieving girls, were overwhelmingly nominated for the positive characteristics of trying hard and following school rules. Hardly any boys, not even high-achieving boys, were nominated. For the more negative characteristics of not trying hard and not following school rules, the opposite pattern of nominations prevailed for both female and male nominators. Boys were greatly overnominated as not trying and not following school rules, particularly low-achieving boys. Hardly any girls, not even low-achieving girls, were selected for these more negative characteristics.

Let me now summarize these findings. Our methodology combined sociometric procedures from the peer relations literature and techniques first used by achievement motive theorists to study values. We were guided by the belief that asking students to nominate classmates whom they admire, respect, and want to be like tells something about the characteristics these students value. The findings therefore suggest that African American girls do indeed value academic effort and success. Girls consistently chose their high-achieving, same-gender classmates as those they admire, respect, and want to be like. These same high achievers were also consistently nominated as classmates who worked hard in school and followed school rules. Thus, girls' value nominations indicated preference for their female classmates who were not only high achieving by objective criteria (i.e., teacher ratings) but who also were perceived to be hard working and socially responsible.

In contrast, the data portray a more complex picture of achievement values among African American early adolescent boys. The majority of boys' nominations went to other boys, and the least valued among these nominees were high-achieving boys. The findings therefore suggest less valuing of academic achievement among African American boys than girls.

Although we emphasize differences between African American boys and girls in achievement values, there were two reasons why we felt the need to replicate the findings with a multiethnic sample. First, we could not be sure that the gender patterns are unique to African Americans. Other studies with

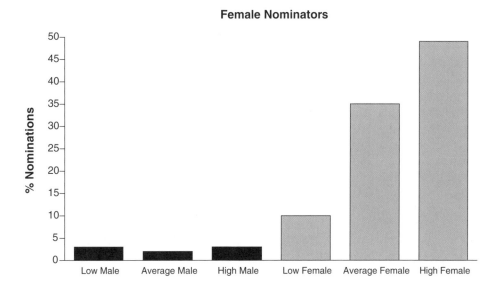

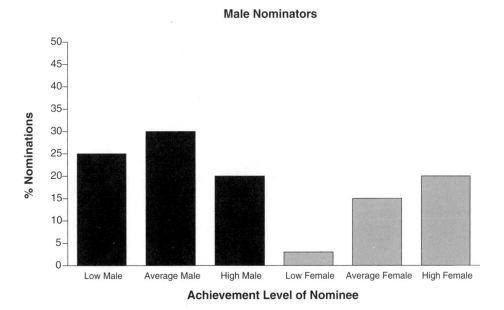

Figure 8.1. Classmates nominated as valued by African American females (top) and males (bottom) as a function of gender and achievement level of nominee (data from Graham et al., 1998, Study 1).

multiethnic samples and different assessment tools also report that adolescent boys seem to value academic success and hard work less than do girls (e.g., Berndt & Miller, 1990). Thus, the valuing of low achievers by male respondents may reflect more generalized gender preferences during adolescence rather than patterns that are unique to African American boys.

Second, there could be Gender × Ethnicity interactions in value preferences if there are other ethnic groups of adolescent males whose experiences are similar to those of African Americans. Latinos, for example, are the fastest growing ethnic group in the United States, yet as a group they experience much of the same kind of social and economic marginality as African Americans and similarly high rates of school failure (e.g., Suarez-Orozco & Suarez-Orozco, 1995). Furthermore, there is evidence that Latino male adolescents also endorse beliefs about barriers to social mobility, experience identity conflict, and display the same kinds of oppositional behaviors that Ogbu and others have attributed to African Americans (e.g., Matute-Bianchi, 1991). Thus as members of ethnic minority groups with marginalized status, it could be that Black and Latino male adolescents would tend to devalue academic achievement and trying hard more than their White male counterparts from the dominant group.

In the replication study (Graham et al., 1998, Experiment 2), participants were 400 low-SES African American, Latino, and White sixth to eighth graders recruited from an ethnically diverse middle school in metropolitan Los Angeles. As in the first study, nominations for being admired, respected, and someone others wanted to be like were highly intercorrelated and were summed to create a single value index. The analyses were more complex than in the first study because ethnicity of nominator and nominee were also relevant factors. Initial analyses showed that girls across all three ethnic groups overwhelmingly preferred other girls (90%) as someone they admired, respected, and wanted to be like, and boys across all ethnic groups strongly preferred other boys (71%) on these same questions. We therefore focused on within-gender analyses. That is, we examined girls' nominations of other girls and boys' nominations of other boys as a function of achievement level (high, average, low) and ethnicity (African American, Latino, White) of the nominee.

Figure 8.2 shows the data for the three groups of female nominators (African American, Latina, and White). The pattern to the nominations is quite similar across the three ethnic groups and conceptually replicates the results for African American female respondents reported in the first study. All three groups showed within-ethnicity preference in nominating other girls as someone they admired, respected, and wanted to be like. All three groups were also least likely to select low achievers (black bars) when compared with their nominations for average (diagonal) and high achievers (white bars).

When we turn to the nomination data for male respondents in the three ethnic groups, the pattern of findings is quite different. Figure 8.3 depicts the data for male respondents nominating other males as a function of ethnicity and achievement level of nominee. The first trend to note is that all three groups of boys also showed within-ethnicity preferences in whom they valued. For African American and Latino boys, the most highly valued peers within their ethnic group were low achievers. But notice the pattern for White male

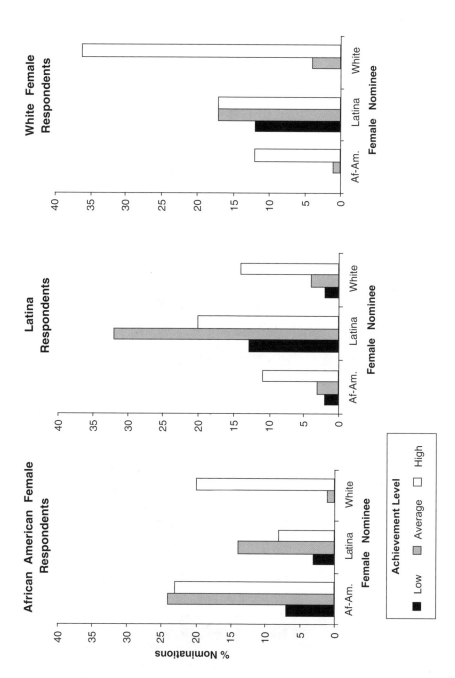

Figure 8.2. Female classmates nominated as valued by female nominators in three ethnic groups, as a function of ethnicity and achievement level of nominee (data from Graham et al., 1998, Study 2). Af-Am. = African American.

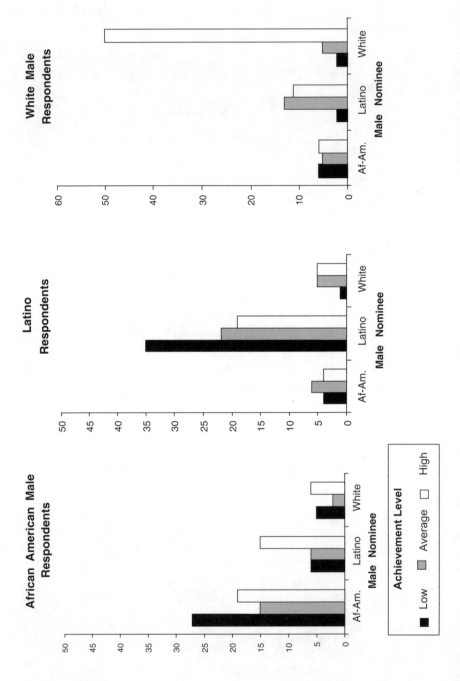

Figure 8.3. Male classmates nominated as valued by male nominators in three ethnic groups, as a function of ethnicity and achievement level of nominee (data from Graham et al., 1998, Study 2). Af-Am. = African American.

nominators. It is more similar to that for all groups of girls, in that White males were least likely to value low achievers over average and high achievers.

The remaining four questions asked respondents to nominate classmates who try hard, follow school rules, do not try hard, and do not follow school rules. For the positive characteristics of trying hard and following school rules, mostly girls of all three ethnic groups were nominated. For the two negative characteristics of not trying hard and not following school rules, male and female nominators were quite in agreement that these characteristics described male rather than female classmates (86% vs. 14% for not trying and 81% vs. 19% for not following school rules). The nomination patterns also varied by ethnicity and achievement level of male nominee. These data are displayed in Figure 8.4 for female and male nominators separately, but averaged across ethnicity of nominator. Two clear patterns are evident in Figure 8.4. First, both boys and girls nominated low-achieving boys over average and high-achieving boys as not trying and not following school rules. Second, these low achievers were predominantly African American and Latino rather than White male classmates. Thus, as in the first study, being male and a low achiever was associated with negative characteristics. But that was only the case when that low-achieving male was also an ethnic minority.

I believe these results underscore some of the problems faced by ethnic minority adolescent males when viewed from a values perspective. Minority males perform more poorly than their female counterparts on most indicators of school success. It is therefore not surprising that they might devalue behavioral domains in which they anticipate poor outcomes. But poor school performance as a possible antecedent to devaluing achievement is only part of the ethnic male's dilemma. In both of the studies, it was low-achieving minority males who were overwhelmingly nominated as not trying hard and not following school rules, suggesting that stereotypes, or shared beliefs, about Black and Latino males are largely negative. I suspect that the African American and Latino boys in our research are well aware of how they are seen in the eyes of others and that this awareness may have influenced what appeared to be their relative indifference to those who display achievement behaviors that are valued by the larger society. Claude Steele has written poignantly in this volume (see chap. 4) and elsewhere (Steele, 1997) about how coping with negative stereotypes about their academic competence has led many African American students to academically disengage and discount the importance of school success. Negative stereotypes can promote self-doubt and loss of confidence in one's environment, both of which foreshadow motivational decline.

A Further Exploration of Stereotypes

This issue of negative stereotypes about adolescent minority boys both intrigued my colleagues and me and encouraged us to pursue the topic further, using nomination procedures in a different experimental manipulation that more closely followed the stereotyping literature. In the 1920s the journalist Walter Lippman introduced stereotypes as scientific constructs when he defined them as "pictures in our heads" (Lippman, 1922). We elaborated on that

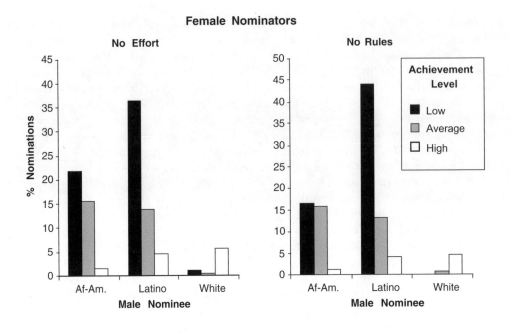

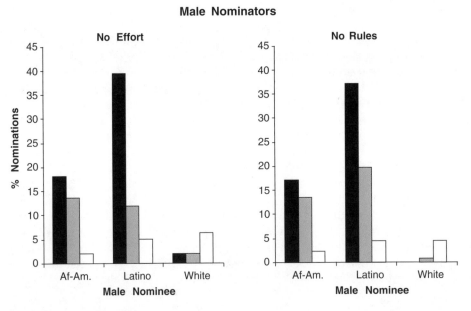

Figure 8.4. Male classmates nominated as not trying hard or following school rules, as a function of ethnicity and achievement level of nominee (data from Graham et al., 1998, Study 2). Af-Am. = African American.

metaphor in the next investigation, which we fondly labeled the "picture study" (Hudley & Graham, 2001).

Sixth- to eighth-grade students were asked to participate in a study of "first impressions." Each student was presented with large picture boards that contained 12 pictures randomly arranged. The pictures were high-quality color photographs of unknown middle school students who varied systematically by gender and ethnicity (Black, Latino, White). Thus there were two pictures of African American girls, two African American boys, two Latina girls, and so on. The color photos were arranged to resemble a year-book page.

Respondents had to pick one photo to match each of several descriptions. Two of the descriptions portrayed students who studied hard and did well in school, and two described students who did poorly and did not care much about school. For each question, the respondent had a different set of 12 photos from which to choose, but the photos always systematically varied the ethnicity and gender of the pictured student. Although still relying on nominations, notice how this procedure differs from that of our previous studies. In the earlier research, respondents nominated actual classmates from their homeroom whom they knew and interacted with on a regular basis. Thus one could argue that the nominations for positive or negative characteristics were unbiased (i.e., nonstereotypical) judgments of observed behavior. In the present studies, participants nominated unknown peers, and their preferences were based only on information about gender and ethnicity of the stimulus person. Any systematic pattern to the data on the basis of such cues could then be more revealing of bias or stereotypes about particular groups.

We conducted the picture study twice: once with a population of African American sixth to eighth graders who attended an all-Black middle school, and the second time with a multiethnic sample (African Americans, Latinos, and Whites) selected from two ethnically diverse middle schools (see Hudley & Graham, 2001, for details about the method). The findings in the two studies were virtually identical, and here I present the pattern of results for the multi-ethnic second study.

Figure 8.5 shows which pictures were selected for each question type as a function of the gender and ethnicity of the adolescent in the photo. The data are collapsed across gender and ethnicity of respondent (nominator) because all of the nominators were quite in agreement about which picture cues were associated with particular achievement descriptions. If no stereotypes or biases were operating, we would not expect any of the photo types to be selected at greater than chance levels. However, it is evident in the top two panels of Figure 8.5 that photos of unknown girls of all three ethnic groups were selected for the two high achievement descriptions and that hardly any photos of boys were chosen. In contrast, for descriptions of low achievement strivings (bottom half of Figure 8.5), the choices were mostly boys. But note that it was ethnic minority boys, more so than White boys, whose pictures were selected.

These data corroborate the argument I am advancing about negative stereotypes and being an ethnically minority boys, and how these two factors together relate to achievement values. I believe that minority boys, more than other adolescents, must cope with the dual stressors of academic challenge and negative stereotypes about their group, and that those stressors can undermine the endorsement of achievement values.

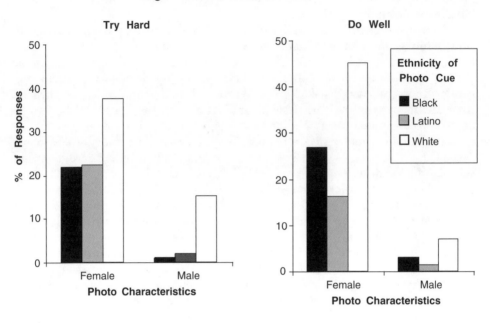

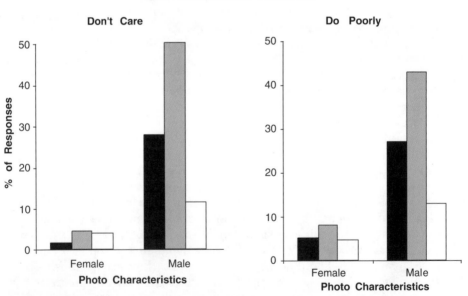

Figure 8.5.   Choice as a function of gender and ethnicity of photo cue in each of four achievement scenarios (data from Hudley & Graham, 2001).

The Development of Achievement Values

All of the analyses presented thus far have focused on adolescence. The next question concerned development. At what age or developmental period does one begin to see the kind of gender and ethnicity-related patterns of achievement values that were documented in the adolescent studies?

The relatively small literature on achievement task values that includes developmental analyses indicates that children value school subjects less as they get older, particularly as they approach the transition from elementary school to middle school (Wigfield & Eccles, 1992, 1994). Considering the developmental challenges of early adolescence, it is not surprising why achievement strivings might spiral downward. Changes in classroom reward structure over these years, such as increasing public evaluation, competition, and ability grouping, are known contributors to many students' declining interest in academic activities as they approach adolescence. At the same time children are developing a more "mature" understanding of the characteristics of low ability (i.e., that it may be stable and uncontrollable) and more realistic (performance-based) expectations for future success (see review in Stipek & MacIver, 1989). Lower expectancies have also been documented to depress achievement values (MacIver, Stipek, & Daniels, 1991). Finally, we also know that negative stereotypes about ethnic minority youths are especially popularized in the media consumed by adolescents (Blosser, 1988), that identity conflict is one of the hallmarks of adolescence (Erikson, 1968), and that perceptions of barriers to opportunity increase from the early elementary to middle school years (Cook et al., 1996). All of this related developmental research might therefore lead us to predict less valuing of high achievers and more valuing of low achievers among boys as they increase in grade level.

In the next study, my colleagues and I set out to replicate our methods for studying values with a sample of about 700 second, fourth, and seventh graders who were African American and Latino (Taylor, 2001). The seventh graders were recruited from one of two low-SES middle schools. One school was 90% African American, and the other school was about 90% Latino. Second and fourth graders were selected from a feeder elementary school for each middle school. These schools also were ethnically homogeneous. We used the same peer nomination questions that were used in the adolescent studies but with appropriate word changes where necessary. We also had objective measures of children's achievement levels based on teacher ratings.

The nominations for whom do the students admire, respect, and want to be like were again combined to create a single values index. As in the adolescent studies, girls across all grade levels nominated other girls rather than boys (75% vs. 25%), whereas boys were more likely to nominate other boys rather than girls (70% vs. 30%). Figure 8.6 shows the value nominations for African American girls and Latinas nominating other same-ethnicity girls as a function of grade level of nominator and achievement level of the female nominee. These data are entirely consistent with the adolescent studies (see Figure 8.2). Across all three grade levels in both ethnic groups, girls were least likely to nominate low achievers and most likely to nominate average or high achieving female classmates as those they admire, respect, and want to be like.

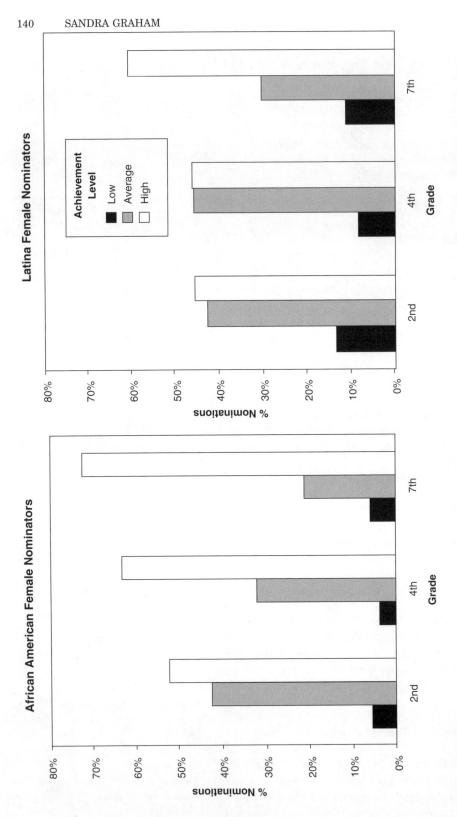

Figure 8.6. Female classmates nominated as valued by female nominators as a function of grade level of nominator and achievement level of nominee (data from Taylor, 2001).

Figure 8.7 shows the data for African American and Latino boys nominating other same-ethnicity boys across the three grade levels. Here the critical comparisons are the decreasing nominations of high achievers across grade and the increasing choice of low achievers as someone the nominator admired, respected, and wanted to be like. High or average achievers received the majority of value nominations from second- and fourth-grade boys (much like the girls' data). By seventh grade, however, the pattern reverts back to what we documented in the middle school studies.

Are value nominations related to (predicted by) factors other than gender and age? In addition to the peer nomination procedures, we included a series of questions adapted from Cook et al. (1996) to measure perceptions of educational and occupational barriers. For example, respondents were asked to think about the reasons why they might not be able to continue going to school or get the job they wanted. They then rated on 4-point scales their agreement with a number of perceived barriers. Among the environmental barriers to education were *bad teachers* and *no good schools in my neighborhood*. Among the occupational barriers were *no good jobs in my community* and *employment discrimination* (i.e., "they don't hire people like me"). Each barrier was accompanied by an illustration that was discussed with the second and fourth graders to ensure understanding.

There were gender and grade level effects for both barrier types. Boys perceived greater educational and occupational barriers than did girls, and the perceived obstacles increased across grade level for both boys and girls. Then we turned to the relationship between endorsement of barriers and value preferences. Our hypothesis was that high perceived barriers would be related to preference (more nominations) for low achievers. That would be consistent with a sociological perspective on the devaluing of achievement among groups who are economically and socially marginalized.

To test our hypothesis, we created a value index, which was the proportion of a respondent's total value nominations that went to low achievers. Multiple regression analysis was then used to predict that value preference. The predictors were gender, grade level, and combined educational/occupational barriers all entered as main effects, and the interactions between ethnicity, gender, and barriers. The three-way interaction was significant and it is displayed in Figure 8.8. The lines are regression slopes for each Gender × Age Group that predict valuing low achievers as a function of high and low perceived barriers. To simplify the presentation, the data for the two elementary grades were combined.

Figure 8.8 reveals that perceived barriers predicted the valuing of low achievers only for seventh-grade boys. To the degree that adolescent ethnic minority boys anticipate that factors outside of their control can negatively influence educational and occupational outcomes, they may be less likely to value effort and success in school.

As in the adolescent studies, we also had nomination data on the positive characteristics of trying hard and following school rules, as well as the negative characteristics of goofing off and not following school rules. Recall the adolescent findings: Girls were overwhelmingly nominated by both genders for positive traits, and ethnic minority boys were overwhelmingly selected for negative

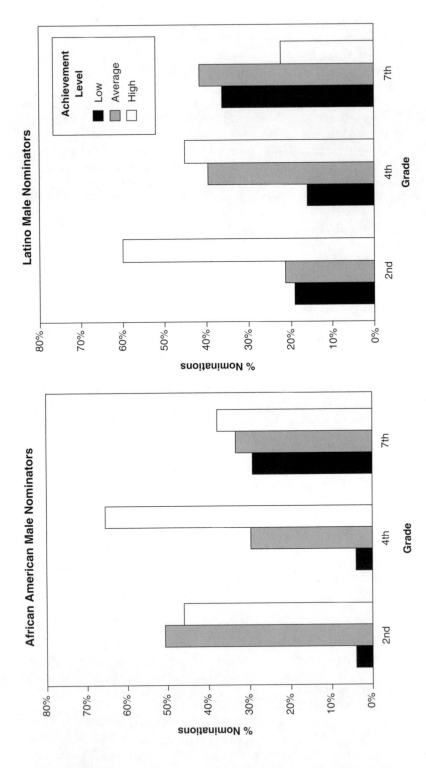

Figure 8.7. Male classmates nominated as valued by male nominators as a function of grade level of nominator and achievement level of nominee (data from Taylor, 2001).

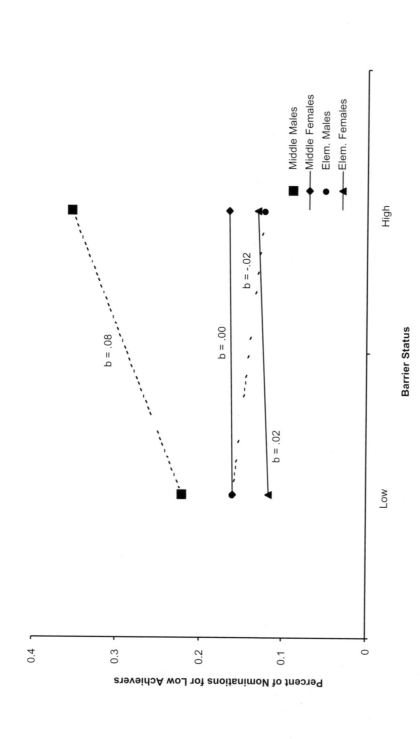

Figure 8.8. The relations between achievement values and perceived barriers to success, by gender and grade level (data from Taylor, 2001).

traits (see Figure 8.4). When we examined these data in the three grade levels of the developmental study, the pattern was quite different. High-achieving girls still received the majority of positive nominations, but a substantial number of high-achieving boys (29%) in both ethnic groups also were nominated by second and fourth graders as studying hard and being socially compliant. For the negative traits, boys continued to be overrepresented across all grade levels, but a substantial number of low-achieving girls (22%) also were nominated as goofing off and being socially noncompliant.

These developmental data tell us three things. First, in elementary school, ethnic minority boys are more like girls at all three grade levels in that they tend to value their high-achieving same-gender classmates. Second, being an ethnic minority male in elementary school is associated with desirable achievement-related characteristics, suggesting that the negative stereotypes about boys are not so pervasive before early adolescence. And third, at the same time that stereotypes become salient, the perceived barriers to opportunity also are increasing for ethnic minority boys.

Conclusions: Ethnicity, Gender, and Developing (Declining?) Achievement Values

My colleagues and I devised a new methodology for studying achievement values that yielded replicable findings across several studies. On the basis of our results, I believe that it would be a mistake to suggest that African American or Latino youngsters *as a group* devalue effort. Ethnic minority girls in all age groups that we studied showed a consistent pattern of admiring, respecting, and wanting to be like high achievers. Ethnic minority boys in the elementary grades displayed this same pattern of value preferences.

There are complex Ethnicity × Gender × Age interactions when studying achievement values, and those interactions highlight some of the problems faced by many adolescent minority boys. In comparative educational research that examines gender as well as ethnic differences between groups, it is clear that ethnic minority boys (i.e., African American and Latino) are faring more poorly than girls (e.g., Davis, 1994; Matute-Bianchi, 1991; Osborne, 1997; Simmons, Black, & Zhou, 1991). The ethnicity by gender differences increase across the school years and are particularly apparent when the measures are so-called markers of adolescent success (i.e., high school graduation) and young adult mobility (i.e., enrollment in and completion of college; see review in Sidanius & Pratto, 1999). Those differences persist into adulthood, as chapter 9 (this volume) by Hillary Haley, Jim Sidanius, and colleagues so clearly documents. Added to their academic challenges are the negative stereotypes about their group that adolescent boys confront. We found in our adolescent studies with multiethnic respondents that being a boy and an ethnic minority was associated with academic disengagement and social deviance. That is consistent with the larger stereotype literature, in which it has often been shown that the shared cultural beliefs about ethnic minorities are largely negative. The most prevalent stereotype about African American males, for example, is that they are unintelligent, unmotivated, and violent (e.g., Devine & Elliott, 1995; Niemann, Jennings, Rozelle, Baxter, & Sullivan, 1994).

As ethnic minority boys enter adolescence, their academic difficulties escalate and the negative images of their groups become more pervasive. It is not surprising that the perception of barriers to educational and occupational opportunity increased from elementary to middle school for boys in our research, which would be consistent with a heightened awareness of how one's group is viewed in the larger social context. Thus I argue that the multiple stressors of academic challenge, coping with negative stereotypes, and perceived barriers to opportunity can erode the endorsement of achievement values in some ethnic minority adolescent boys.

The findings presented in this chapter offer a developmental perspective on race and identity, the topic of this volume. They also have implications for the study of race and gender in motivation research. Individual differences have played a prominent role in motivation theory and research, whether conceptualized as motivational traits like the achievement motive, or as moderating influences like gender and age. Regarding gender, there is an empirical literature (albeit mixed) supporting the belief that girls are more vulnerable to motivational deficits than boys. For example, it has been argued that gender role socialization and stereotypes lead girls to question their academic competence more, particularly in math; display more maladaptive reactions to failure, including low ability attributions; perceive more barriers to success; and experience more conflict between individual achievement strivings and social conformity (see reviews in Eccles et al., 1998; Ruble & Martin, 1998). I suggest that taking ethnicity into account may require rethinking of these gender analyses showing motivational patterns that typically favor boys. In my own and related comparative research, it is ethnic minority boys who appear to be most at risk for motivational deficits. Particularly during adolescence, it is probably too limiting to study gender differences in motivation in the absence of Gender × Ethnicity interactions.

I have been emphasizing declining achievement values, but the methodology my colleagues and I used might also be helpful in uncovering the characteristics that adolescent boys *do* value in their male peers. Although not reported here, we found that minority boys in the adolescent studies admired, respected, and wanted to be like their male peers who were perceived to be good at sports. Like academics, sports is an achievement domain in which persistence and hard work are the hallmark of a good athlete, just as they are the markers of a good student. It could therefore be that adolescent minority boys do value achievement—but in an arena other than academics. What may be needed is attention to Ethnicity × Gender × *Context* interactions in the study of achievement values.

Kenneth Clark reminded us that psychology can have an impact on the well-being of children. In the spirit of that optimism, I believe that our research has implications for intervention. The methodology was adapted from procedures first used in the 1950s by David McClelland and colleagues (McClelland, Atkinson, Clark, & Lowell, 1953) in studies designed to enhance the achievement motive (Alschuler et al., 1971). Those researchers created the "admiration ladder" to stimulate discussion among children and adolescents about the characteristics in others that they valued. There is no reason why contemporary motivation enhancement programs could not incorporate similar techniques. Furthermore, if the goal is preventive intervention, then change efforts based on endorsing achievement values would need to be implemented before the critical transition to early adolescence when motivation begins to decline among all youths and when identity issues and negative stereotypes become so salient for ethnic minorities.

It is apparent to me that the study of achievement values and how they get expressed in the broader context of social and cultural influences might provide important clues for understanding the academic challenges faced by many ethnic minority youths. I hope that the approach presented here will stimulate new and creative ways to conceptualize values within a motivational framework and more awareness of the complex forces associated with ethnic minority status. That would be a good way for me to honor the legacy of Kenneth Clark.

References

Alschuler, A., Tabor, D., & McIntyre, J. (1971). *Teaching achievement motivation*. Middletown, CT: Education Ventures.

Arroyo, C., & Zigler, E. (1995). Racial identity, academic achievement, and the psychological well-being of economically disadvantaged adolescents. *Journal of Personality and Social Psychology, 69*, 903–914.

Berndt, T., & Miller, K. (1990). Expectancies, values, and achievement in junior high school. *Journal of Educational Psychology, 82*, 319–326.

Blosser, B. (1988). Ethnic differences in children's media use. *Journal of Broadcasting and Electronic Media, 32*, 453–470.

Coie, J., Dodge, K., & Coppotelli, H. (1982). Dimensions and types of social status: A cross-age perspective. *Developmental Psychology, 18*, 557–570.

Cook, P., & Ludwig, J. (1998). The burden of "acting White": Do Black adolescents disparage academic achievement? In C. Jencks & M. Phillips (Eds.), *The Black–White test score gap* (pp. 375–400). Washington, DC: Brookings Institution.

Cook, T., Church, M., Ajanaku, S., Shadish, W., Kim, J., & Cohen, R. (1996). The development of occupational aspirations and expectations among inner-city boys. *Child Development, 67*, 3368–3385.

Crocker, J., & Major, B. (1989). Social stigma and self-esteem: The self-protective properties of stigma. *Psychological Review, 96*, 608–630.

Crocker, J., Major, B., & Steele, C. (1998). Social stigma. In D. Gilbert, S. Fiske, & G. Lindzey (Eds.), *Handbook of social psychology* (4th ed., Vol. 2, pp. 504–533). New York: McGraw-Hill.

Davis, J. (1994). The effects of school context, structure, and experiences on African American males in middle and high school. *Journal of Negro Education, 63*, 570–587.

Devine, P., & Elliott, A. (1995). Are racial stereotypes really fading? The Princeton trilogy revisited. *Personality and Social Psychology Bulletin, 21*, 1139–1150.

Eccles, J., & Wigfield, A. (1995). In the mind of the actor: The structure of adolescents' achievement task values and expectancy-related beliefs. *Personality and Social Psychology Bulletin, 21*, 215–225.

Eccles, J., Wigfield, A., & Schiefele, U. (1998). Motivation to succeed. In N. Eisenberg (Ed.), *Handbook of child psychology* (5th ed., Vol. 3, pp. 1017–1095). New York: Wiley.

Erikson, E. (1968). *Identity: Youth and crisis*. New York: Norton.

Foley, D. (1991). Reconsidering anthropological explanations of ethnic school failure. *Anthropology & Education Quarterly, 22*, 61–86.

Fordham, S., & Ogbu, J. (1986). Black students' school success: Coping with the burden of acting White. *Urban Review, 18,* 176–206.

Graham, S. (1994). Motivation in African Americans. *Review of Educational Research, 64,* 55–118.

Graham, S., Taylor, A., & Hudley, C. (1998). Exploring achievement values among ethnic minority early adolescents. *Journal of Educational Psychology, 90,* 606–620.

Gray-Litttle, B., & Hafdahl, A. (2000). Factors influencing racial comparisons of self-esteem: A quantitative review. *Psychological Bulletin, 126,* 26–54.

Hudley, C., & Graham, S. (2001). Stereotypes of achievement strivings among early adolescents. *Social Psychology of Education, 5,* 201–224.

Lippman, W. (1922). *Public opinion.* New York: MacMillan Press.

MacIver, D., Stipek, D., & Daniels, D. (1991). Explaining within-semester changes in student effort in junior high school and senior high courses. *Journal of Educational Psychology, 83,* 201–211.

Major, B., Spencer, S., Schmader, T., Wolfe, C., & Crocker, J. (1997). Coping with negative stereotypes about intellectual performance: The role of psychological disengagement. *Personality and Social Psychology Bulletin, 24,* 34–50.

Matute-Bianchi, M. (1991). Situational ethnicity and patterns of school performance among immigrant and nonimmigrant Mexican-descent students. In M. Gibson & J. Ogbu (Eds.), *Minority status and schooling* (pp. 205–247). New York: Garland.

McClelland, D., Atkinson, J., Clark, R., & Lowell, E. (1953). *The achievement motive.* New York: Appleton-Century-Crofts.

Mickelson, R. (1990). The attitude-achievement paradox among Black adolescents. *Sociology of Education, 63,* 44–61.

Niemann, Y., Jennings, L., Rozelle, R., Baxter, J., & Sullivan, E. (1994). Use of free responses and cluster analysis to determine stereotypes of eight groups. *Personality and Social Psychology Bulletin, 20,* 379–390.

Ogbu, J. (1997). Understanding the school performance of urban Blacks: Some essential background knowledge. In H. Walberg, R. Reyes, & R. Weissberg (Eds.), *Children and youth: Interdisciplinary perspectives* (pp. 190–222). Thousand Oaks, CA: Sage.

Osborne, J. (1997). Race and academic disidentification. *Journal of Educational Psychology, 89,* 728–735.

Rokeach, M. (1973). *The nature of human values.* New York: Free Press.

Ruble, D., & Martin, C. (1998). Gender development. In N. Eisenberg (Ed.), *Handbook of child psychology* (5th ed., Vol. 3, pp. 933–1016). New York: Wiley.

Sidanius, J., & Pratto, F. (1999). *Social dominance.* New York: Cambridge University Press.

Simmons, R., Black, A., & Zhou, Y. (1991). African American versus White children and the transition into junior high school. *American Journal of Education, 99,* 481–520.

Steele, C. (1997). A threat in the air: How stereotypes shape intellectual identity and performance. *American Psychologist, 52,* 613–629.

Steinberg, L., Dornbusch, S., & Brown, B. (1992). Ethnic differences in adolescent achievement: An ecological perspective. *American Psychologist, 47,* 723–729.

Stipek, D., & MacIver, D. (1989). Developmental change in children's assessment of intellectual competence. *Child Development, 60,* 521–538.

Suarez-Orozco, C., & Suarez-Orozco, M. (1995). *Transformations: Migration, family life, and achievement motivation among Latino adolescents.* Stanford, CA: Stanford University Press.

Taylor, A. Z. (2001). *Writing off ambition: A developmental study of gender, ethnicity, and achievement values.* Unpublished doctoral dissertation, University of California, Los Angeles.

van Laar, C. (2000). The paradox of low academic achievement but high self-esteem in African American students: An attributional account. *Educational Psychology Review, 12,* 33–62.

Wigfield, A., & Eccles, J. (1992). The development of achievement task values: A theoretical analysis. *Developmental Review, 12,* 265–310.

Wigfield, A., & Eccles, J. (1994). Children's competence beliefs, achievement values, and general self-esteem: Change across elementary and middle school. *Journal of Early Adolescence, 14,* 104–138.

9

The Interactive Nature of Sex and Race Discrimination: A Social Dominance Perspective

Hillary Haley, Jim Sidanius, Brian Lowery, and Neil Malamuth

Social scientists have long assumed that all forms of discrimination are rooted in the same psychosocial processes, regardless of the types of groups targeted. Thus, discrimination against gender, ethnic, racial, class, national, and even minimal groups have all been understood as stemming from the same set of factors, whether these factors involve normal social comparison processes, realistic group conflicts, perceived group threats, existential anxiety, or an authoritarian personality (for reviews, see Mullen, Brown, & Smith, 1992; Sidanius & Pratto, 2001; see also Brewer, 1999). Within this standard approach, racism and sexism have therefore been viewed as psychologically equivalent forms of discrimination that differ only in terms of target groups involved.

In contrast to this standard approach, social dominance theory (e.g., Pratto, Sidanius, Stallworth, & Malle, 1994; Sidanius, 1993; Sidanius & Pratto, 2001) argues that different psychosocial processes underlie discrimination against different types of targets. In particular, the theory posits that there are important distinctions between discrimination based on sex (i.e., patriarchy) and discrimination based on more socially constructed group differences such as race, ethnicity, class, or caste (i.e., arbitrary-set discrimination).

Patriarchy and Arbitrary-Set Discrimination

Sidanius and Pratto's (2001) review of the discrimination literature suggests that patriarchy is essentially an attempt by men to *control* women's sexual, economic, political, and social prerogatives, whereas arbitrary-set discrimination is instead a more aggressive endeavor designed to exploit and *debilitate* outgroup members. While patriarchy will therefore involve social control and a certain degree of instrumental violence, it will on average involve far less

149

aggression than arbitrary-set discrimination. In line with this view, a number of researchers (e.g., Glick & Fiske, 2001; Jackman, 1994) have argued that patriarchy can be largely characterized as a "paternalistic" rather than "debilitative" or hostile enterprise. This is to say that patriarchy, in contrast to arbitrary-set discrimination, is comprised of both a desire to control women's prerogatives and positive affect toward women.

Social dominance theory posits several reasons why patriarchy and arbitrary-set discrimination differ in terms of aggression, one of which is particularly relevant here (see Sidanius & Pratto, 2001, for a detailed discussion). This is the simple fact that men and women are existentially symbiotic to a degree that arbitrary-set groups generally are not. In other words, while one can easily imagine the wholesale slaughter of the members of one arbitrary-set group by members of another arbitrary-set group (e.g., "ethnic cleansing" in Rwanda, Nazi Germany, Croatia, East Timor), a society that engaged in the mass slaughter of women by men would soon find itself confronting oblivion. The symbiotic relationship between men and women therefore offers a straightforward reason why one should expect patriarchy to involve far less aggression than arbitrary-set discrimination.

The Interaction Between Partriarchy and Arbitrary-Set Discrimination

It is a broadly observed fact that most, if not all, arbitrary-set groups are patriarchically structured (e.g., Goldberg, 1994). Within virtually every race, ethnicity, class, and caste, men enjoy disproportionate amounts of economic, political, and social power as compared with women.

Given this patriarchal structure, social dominance theorists posit certain cognitive and behavioral consequences. First, arbitrary-set groups should be viewed as male-gendered social categories. Relevant research in social cognition generally supports this view. For example, Zarate and Smith (1990) found that men are more readily perceived in terms of their race as compared with women. Similarly, Eagley and Kite (1987) found that national and ethnic stereotypes are more strongly linked to stereotypes of men than to stereotypes of women.

Second, social dominance theorists expect that when efforts are made by one arbitrary-set group to exploit or debilitate another arbitrary-set group, those efforts will be targeted primarily at males rather than females. This is precisely because men are more physically aggressive than females (e.g., Maccoby, 1998) and should therefore be more likely to effectively oppose attack. In other words, we should expect arbitrary-set group attacks to be targeted primarily at males because males constitute a core opposition. This reasoning implies that in the case of arbitrary-set discrimination, aggression and *aggressive intent* should be primarily directed against out-group men rather than out-group women. Social dominance theory has referred to this idea as the *subordinate-male-target hypothesis,* or the SMTH (see Sidanius & Pratto, 2001; Sidanius & Veniegas, 2000).

Evidence in Support of the SMTH

Careful inspection of the discrimination literature shows survey and archival evidence that is fairly congruent with the SMTH across several domains, including the labor market, the educational system, the health care system, and the criminal justice system. In original analyses of public opinion surveys, Sidanius and Pratto (2001) found that men reported more racial and ethnic discrimination than did women across each and every ethnic and racial group examined. This pattern was found among a national probability sample of Black American adults; among Black, Latino, and White American college students; among representative samples of West Indian, Pakistani, Indian Asian, and African Asian immigrants to Great Britain; and among African, Arab, and Yugoslavian immigrants to Sweden.

Evidence for the SMTH is apparent not just in studies of perceived discrimination but also in archival studies of more objective discrimination. For example, examination of U.S. census data from 1994 shows that after controlling for critical human capital differences (e.g., education level), there are substantial wage differences among White, Latino, and Black men but essentially no such differences among White, Latino, and Black women (see Sidanius & Pratto, 2001, p. 159). A similar situation is found even among those educated at the most prestigious American colleges and universities. For example, in an examination of the mean earnings of 1997 White and Black graduates from a sample of America's most prestigious colleges and universities, Bowen and Bok (1998) found that even after controlling for demographic, educational, and professional differences between White and Black men (e.g., SATs, grade point average, field of study, socioeconomic status, advanced degrees attained, sector of employment, selectivity of college or university attended), White men still earned substantially higher yearly incomes than did Black men ($98,000 vs. $89,500 per year). At the same time, however, they found no difference between the mean annual salaries of White and Black women. Along similar lines, Farley and Allen (1987) examined U.S. census data from 1960 and 1980 to assess the economic return on educational investment. While women received a smaller average rate of return than men, there was no evidence that White women received a higher rate of return than Black women. Quite the contrary, in both 1960 and 1980, White women received a slightly lower rate of return on educational investment in hourly salary than did Black women ($.59 vs. $.62 in 1960, and $.64 vs. $.79 in 1980, respectively). In contrast, White men consistently enjoyed a substantially higher rate of return for every additional year of higher education than did Black men (i.e., $.78 vs. $.56 in 1960; $.96 vs. $.69 in 1980, respectively).

Evidence for the SMTH also extends to the realm of authority within the workplace. When ethnic minorities are given authority in the workplace, they are typically given authority over other minorities, and only rarely given authority over Whites (e.g., Zegers de Beijl, 1990). This authority gap is apparently far smaller between White and Black women than it is between White and Black men. In addition, the net authority gap between White and Black women has shown a greater degree of attenuation over time than has the gap between White and Black men (Smith, 1997).

Evidence for this asymmetrical racial discrimination can also be found within the criminal justice system. For example, in one of the very few studies of its kind, Hood and Cordovil (1992) examined the effects of sex discrimination and racial discrimination within the English criminal justice system. After examining some 2,884 criminal cases adjudicated by the Crown Court Centres in 1989, these researchers found that Blacks and Asians tended to be imprisoned at significantly higher rates than Whites. However, the degree to which Black and Asian women were disproportionately imprisoned was completely accounted for by legally relevant factors (e.g., previous criminal record, nature of pleas, seriousness of crime). In contrast, regardless of the legally relevant factors considered, Black and Asian men were still imprisoned at significantly higher rates than White men.

Although there is fairly extensive archival evidence consistent with the SMTH, there has been essentially no experimental work testing the hypothesis. An exception is research by Ayres (1995) that reports incidental experimental support for the SMTH. In this research, teams of male and female White and Black auditors went to the same Chicago car dealerships to negotiate the best deals they could for new cars. Naturally, care was taken to ensure that the auditors were as equivalent as possible in all respects other than their sex and race. Consistent with much of the other discrimination literature, results showed that White auditors were generally offered better deals for these new cars than were Black auditors. However, in line with the SMTH, there was also clear evidence of an interaction between the sex and race of the auditor. Whereas the difference between the mean offers made to White women and Black women was relatively small ($231), Black men were asked to pay a staggering $1,133 more than were White men. Furthermore, by use of a game-theoretical approach, Ayes concluded that the higher prices demanded of Black men did not simply result from economic motives on the part of the dealers but from aggressive motives as well.

While all of this evidence is strongly consistent with the SMTH, the thesis is clearly in need of more experimental support. The study reported here represents the first attempt to explicitly test the validity of the SMTH using an experimental design. We decided to explore the SMTH by the use of random sample, survey-based experimental methodology. This type of methodology has the advantage of exploiting probability sampling within the broader population rather than restricting itself to non-probability samples of college students. At the same time, it allows for rigorous experimental control of extraneous and potentially confounding variables.

Method

The data were taken from the 2000 and 2001 samples of the Los Angeles County Social Survey (LACSS) conducted by the Institute for Social Science Research at the University of California, Los Angeles. The LACSS is a large omnibus telephone survey of residents of Los Angeles County selected by use of random digit dialing. The survey assesses approximately 200 variables, including standard demographics, feeling thermometers concerning numerous social groups, general ethnicity attitudes, support for policies targeted toward various social groups, and political ideology.

Participants

The 2000 and 2001 samples consisted of 596 and 866 adults, respectively. Only the responses of White and Black participants were analyzed, leaving an effective combined sample of 581 respondents (289 Whites and 292 Blacks). This sample comprised 247 male and 334 female respondents, with an average age of approximately 42 years.

Procedure

PRIMING CONDITION. An experimental, split-ballot design was used in which respondents were randomly assigned to one of four experimental priming conditions, each of which described a convicted drug felon. Respondents were each presented with one of the four following primes: (a) "Malik Richards, a 32-year-old Black male and third-time drug felon, has been convicted of drug cocaine possession"; (b) "Ralph Richards, a 32-year-old White male and third-time drug felon, has been convicted of drug cocaine possession"; (c) "Taneshia Richards, a 32-year-old Black female and third-time drug felon, has been convicted of drug cocaine possession;" or (d) "Margaret Richards, a 32-year-old White female and third-time drug felon, has been convicted of drug cocaine possession." Respondents were then asked how much prison time the convicted felon should be sentenced to. The sentencing categories were as follows: 1 = *no prison time at all, but drug treatment instead*; 2 = *2 years in prison*; 3 = *10 years in prison*; 4 = *25 years in prison*; 5 = *life in prison without the possibility of parole*; 6 = *don't know*; and 7 = *refused to answer*. The number of respondents assigned to each of the four primes was as follows: (a) Malik Richards (n = 155), (b) Ralph Richards (n = 135), (c) Taneshia Richards (n = 135), and (d) Margaret Richards (n = 156).

DEPENDENT VARIABLE. Immediately after being primed with one of the four criminals, respondents were asked to give their opinions about the leniency of the current American criminal justice system. It is important to note that this question was constructed to be quite general and made no mention of either the criminals' sex or criminals' race. We were therefore able to detect the presence of bias in an unobtrusive fashion. The specific question read: "In general, what do you think about the length of prison sentences in the USA?" The response categories were that prison sentences are *much too lenient, somewhat lenient, about the right length, somewhat severe,* or *much too severe*. The responses were coded such that the higher the number, the more lenient prison sentences were perceived to be.

Results

Our primary analysis examined whether participants' race, along with the sex and race of the prime, interacted—as predicted by the SMTH—to predict judgments of the criminal justice system. As a secondary analysis, we also examined whether there was any evidence for this same three-way interaction in predicting responses to the prime question itself, regarding judgments about the appropriate prison sentence for the named criminal.

Judgments About the Criminal Justice System

We submitted the data to a 2 (Sex of Criminal) × 2 (Race of Criminal) × 2 (Race of Respondent) analysis of variance. This analysis revealed a significant main effect for respondents' race; in general, White respondents ($M = 3.44$, $SD = 1.21$) were more likely to see the criminal justice system as too lenient as compared with Black respondents ($M = 2.77$, $SD = 1.36$), $F(1, 573) = 39.24$, $p < .01$, $\eta = .25$. The analysis revealed no other significant main effects and no significant two-way interactions. Notably, respondents' sex did not moderate any of the main effects, the two-way interactions, or the three-way interaction, although female respondents as a whole were generally more likely to see the system as too lenient ($M = 3.25$, $SD = 1.34$) than were male respondents ($M = 2$. $F(1, 573) = 9.53$, $p < .01$, $\eta = .13.91$, $SD = 1.29$).

Our main interest was, however, in the pattern of the three-way interaction. We expected that neither Black respondents nor White respondents would show in-group bias (bias in favor of the in-group) in their judgments about the criminal justice system following the female primes. Instead, we expected that for both groups, bias would emerge only following the male primes. Specifically, we expected that Blacks would be more likely to judge the system as too lenient when primed with the White male criminal rather than the Black male criminal. And we expected that Whites, conversely, would be more likely to judge the system as too lenient when primed with the Black male criminal rather than the White male criminal. Consistent with our expectations, there was indeed a significant three-way (Sex of Criminal × Race of Criminal × Race of Respondent) interaction, $F(1, 573) = 6.66$, $p = .01$, $\eta = .11$. As shown in Figure 9.1, the pattern of this interaction conformed to theoretical expectations.

As anticipated, when Black respondents were primed with the female criminals, they showed no evidence of in-group bias in their subsequent judgments about the criminal justice system. Rather, Blacks judged the system nearly identically regardless of whether they were primed with a White female criminal ($M = 2.72$, $SD = 1.39$) or a Black female criminal ($M = 2.75$, $SD = 1.41$), $F(1, 150) < 1$, ns. When Black respondents were primed with male criminals, however, their judgments about the criminal justice system sharply diverged. As expected, Blacks were more likely to view the system as too lenient when primed with the White male criminal ($M = 3.14$, $SD = 1.29$) rather than the Black male criminal ($M = 2.52$, $SD = 1.32$), $F(1, 140) = 7.84$, $p = .01$, $\eta = .23$. In other words, Black respondents showed in-group bias when primed with male criminals but not when primed with female criminals.

An analogous but somewhat more complex pattern was found for White respondents. Like the Black respondents, White respondents showed no evidence of in-group bias when primed with the female criminals; in fact, Whites showed a slight tendency to judge the system as *less* lenient when primed with

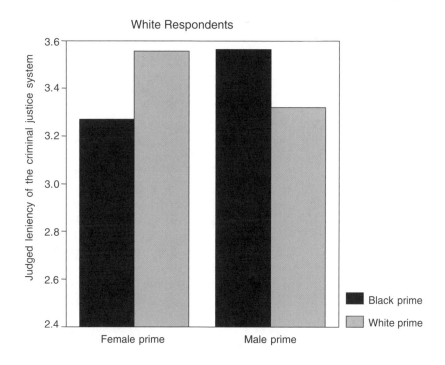

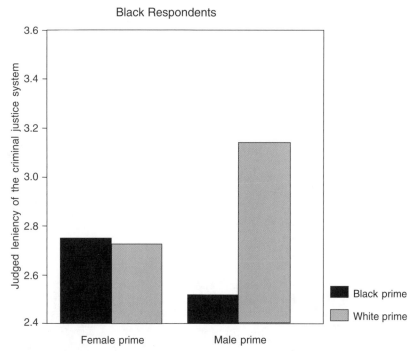

Figure 9.1. Judged leniency of the American criminal justice system as a function of the sex and race of the primed criminal, by respondent race.

the Black female criminal (M = 3.27, SD = 1.23) rather than the White female criminal (M = 3.56, SD = 1.12), $F(1, 139)$ = 2.10, ns. However, when primed with male criminals, a different pattern emerged. In this case, as expected, Whites were more likely to judge the system as too lenient when primed with the Black male criminal (M = 3.56, SD = 1.23) rather than the White male criminal (M = 3.32, SD = 1.24), though this trend did not reach statistical significance, $F(1, 148)$ = 1.44, ns.

Closer examination of the data revealed one reason for this relatively weak effect among Whites. This was the fact that White male and female respondents judged the system quite differently as a function of the sex and race of the prime. In fact, for White respondents there was a significant three-way (Sex of Criminal × Race of Criminal × Sex of Respondent) interaction, $F(1, 281)$ = 3.94, $p < .05$, η = .12. Notably, White male respondents showed a relatively strong pattern of in-group bias vis-à-vis the male primes (for the Black male prime, M = 3.50, SD = 1.26; for the White male prime, M = 3.00, SD = 1.16) consistent with our predictions. But contrary to our predictions, White female respondents showed essentially no in-group bias vis-à-vis the male primes (for the Black male prime, M = 3.62, SD = 1.21; for the White male prime, M = 3.59, SD = 1.26). Thus, White respondents' overall tendency to show in-group bias vis-à-vis the male primes was apparently much diluted by the unexpected lack of bias among White female respondents.

Recommended Prison Sentences

It is worth observing that Black and White respondents largely showed the same patterns as above when we examined their responses to the prime question itself. Here respondents were asked to recommend a prison sentence for one of the four named felons ("Malik," "Ralph," "Taneshia," or "Margaret") ranging from no time to life in prison (with higher numbers indicating harsher sentences). Because the named criminals acted as direct, conspicuous targets in this question, we might well have expected that respondents would modify their answers in an effort to appear "nondiscriminatory," thereby masking effects (e.g., Fazio, Jackson, Dunton, & Williams, 1995). Nonetheless, we did find evidence for the same Sex of Criminal × Race of Criminal × Race of Respondent interaction as with our less obtrusive measure, $F(1, 580)$ = 6.54, $p < .05$, η = .10 (see Figure 9.2).

Black respondents again showed no in-group bias in criminal justice perceptions when faced with female criminals (for the White female prime, M = 1.90, SD = 1.67; for the Black female prime, M = 1.99, SD = 1.04), $F(1, 150)$ < 1, ns. However, Blacks did show such bias when faced with male criminals, recommending a longer sentence for Ralph, the White male felon (M = 2.58, SD = 1.14), than for Malik, the Black male felon (M = 1.92, SD = 1.00), $F(1, 140)$ = 13.31, $p < .01$, η = .30. White respondents, however, did not show significant levels of in-group bias when faced with the female primes (for the White female prime, M = 2.04, SD = 1.06; for the Black female prime, M = 1.89, SD = 0.93), $F(1, 139)$ < 1, ns, or when faced with the male primes (for the White male prime, M = 2.07, SD = 1.10; for the Black male

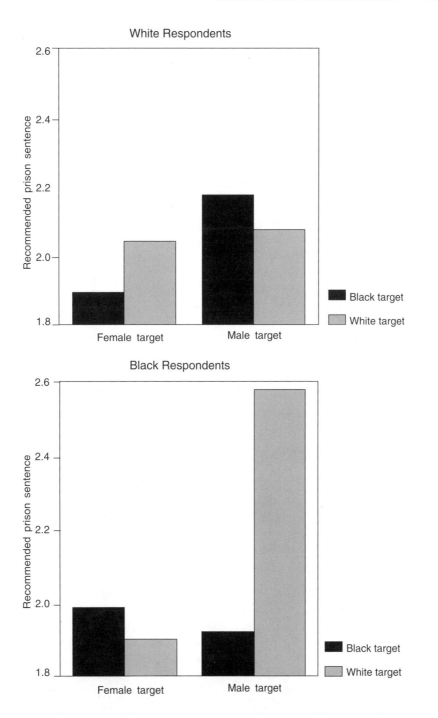

Figure 9.2. Recommended prison sentence as a function of the sex and race of the targeted criminal, by respondent race.

prime, $M = 2.17$, $SD = 1.22$), $F(1, 148) < 1$, *ns*, very probably due to the conspicuous nature of the question.

Discussion

Taken together, our results provide moderate support for the SMTH, the argument that discrimination against arbitrary-set groups (e.g., ethnic groups,
national groups) will be primarily directed at the men rather than the women
within those groups (Sidanius & Pratto, 2001). We tested this hypothesis using
a relatively unobtrusive measure that asked respondents to judge the leniency
of the current criminal justice system after being primed with a specific criminal, and we obtained the expected three-way interaction among the sex of the
criminal, the race of the criminal, and the race of the respondent. Consistent
with the SMTH, neither Black respondents nor White respondents showed in-
group bias following the female primes. Instead, bias emerged only following
the male primes. Specifically, Blacks were more likely to judge the system as
too lenient when primed with the White male criminal rather than the Black
male criminal. Conversely, Whites showed a tendency to judge the system as
too lenient when primed with the Black male criminal rather than the White
male criminal, though this tendency was not statistically significant. It is
interesting to note that we also obtained the expected three-way interaction
with the prime question itself, in which bias was measured relatively conspicu-
ously. Thus, although we found the expected three-way interaction with both
the relatively unobtrusive measure and the more conspicuous measure, our
results were unexpectedly weak for White participants.

The fact that White male and White female participants responded to the
primes quite differently helps to explain why, overall, Whites' tendency for
racial bias following male primes was relatively muted. This tendency was
much more pronounced among White male respondents than among White
female respondents, with White female respondents showing essentially no
bias at all. It should be noted that although Black male and female respondents
answered more similarly to one another, Black male respondents also showed
slightly more in-group bias vis-à-vis the male primes than did Black female
respondents. This male–female asymmetry is consistent with existing research
showing that males endorse group-based inequalities more than do females
(e.g., Kravitz & Platinia, 1993; Pratto, Stallworth, & Sidanius, 1997). It remains
puzzling, however, that respondent sex exerted a somewhat stronger effect
among Whites than among Blacks, and future research on the SMTH would
do well to closely examine this male-female asymmetry across groups.

We suspect that a second reason why Blacks but not Whites showed a
strong pattern of racial bias involves our choice of domain. In particular, Blacks'
greater sensitivity to issues of discrimination within the criminal justice system
may well have played a part in their greater expression of in-group bias in
this research. It is worth observing that Black–White disparities within the
criminal justice system have been growing since the 1950s (e.g., The California
Commission on the Status of African-American Males, 1992; National Research
Council, 1989) and have been particularly pronounced since America declared

a "war on drugs" in the mid-1980s and began exercising increasingly severe criminal policies. For example, just after the war on drugs was initiated, Black youths were arrested at nearly five times the rate of White youths, even though their levels of substance abuse were identical. Tougher criminal justice practices within the past several years have therefore had a disproportionately tough effect on Blacks, making it quite plausible that our Black respondents had more direct experience with the criminal justice system than our White respondents, and were more cognizant of racial disparities within the system. We suspect that these differences may have contributed to Blacks' greater expression of in-group bias relative to Whites.

Conclusion

The research reported here should be regarded as a "first cut" at experimental confirmation of the SMTH hypothesis, as it suggests at least two important directions for future research. First, future research should directly test whether the SMTH entails male–female asymmetry among those engaging in discrimination. Second, future work needs to determine whether the SMTH holds true across different groups and across different social domains. In particular, research will need to determine whether the hypothesis holds true for both *positive allocations,* or allocations of "good things" such as scholarships, prizes, and promotions, and *negative allocations,* or allocations of "bad things" such as salary decreases, demotions, and death sentences. While existing archival evidence supports domain generalizability (e.g., across the criminal justice system, the labor market, the retail market, and the educational system; see Sidanius & Veniegas, 2000), future work must be able to demonstrate this generalizability experimentally.

References

Ayres, I. (1995). Further evidence of discrimination in new car negotiations and estimates of its cause. *Michigan Law Review, 94,* 109–147.

Bowen, W. G., & Bok, D. (1998). *The shape of the river: Long-term consequences of considering race in college and university admissions.* Princeton, NJ: Princeton University Press.

Brewer, M. B. (1999). The psychology of prejudice: Ingroup love or outgroup hate? *Journal of Social Issues, 55,* 429–444.

California Commission on the Status of African-American Males. (1992). *African-American males: The struggle for equality.* Sacramento, CA: Author.

Eagley, A. H., & Kite, M. (1987). Are stereotypes of nationalities applied to both women and men? *Journal of Personality and Social Psychology, 53,* 451–462.

Farley, R., & Allen, W. R. (1987). *The color line and the quality and life in America.* New York: Russell Sage Foundation.

Fazio, R. H., Jackson, J. R., Dunton, B. C., & Williams, C. J. (1995). Variability in automatic activation as an unobtrusive measure of racial attitudes: A bona fide pipeline? *Journal of Personality and Social Psychology, 69,* 1013–1027.

Glick, P., & Fiske, S. T. (2001). An ambivalent alliance: Hostile and benevolent sexism as complementary justifications for gender inequality. *American Psychologist, 56,* 109–118.

Goldberg, S. (1994). *Why men rule: A theory of male dominance.* Chicago: Open Court.

Hood, R., & Cordovil, G. (1992). *Race and sentencing: A study in the Crown Court: A report for the Commission for Racial Equality.* Oxford, England: Clarendon Press.

Jackman, M. (1994). *The velvet glove: Paternalism and conflict in gender, class and race relations.* Berkeley: University of California Press.

Kravitz, D. A., & Platinia, J. (1993). Attitudes and beliefs about affirmative action: Effects of target and of respondent sex and ethnicity. *Journal of Applied Psychology, 78,* 928–938.

Maccoby, E. E. (1998). *The two sexes: Growing up apart, coming together.* Cambridge, MA: Belknap Press/Harvard University Press.

Mullen, B., Brown, R., & Smith, C. (1992). Ingroup bias as a function of salience, relevance, and status: An integration. *European Journal of Social Psychology, 22,* 103–122.

National Research Council. (1989). *A common destiny: Blacks and American society.* Washington, DC: National Academy Press.

Pratto, F., Sidanius, J., Stallworth, L., & Malle, B. (1994). Social dominance orientation: A personality variable predicting social and political attitudes. *Journal of Personality and Social Psychology, 67,* 741–763.

Pratto, F., Stallworth, L. M., & Sidanius, J. (1997). The gender gap: Differences in political attitudes and social dominance orientation. *British Journal of Social Psychology, 36,* 49–68.

Sidanius, J. (1993). The psychology of group conflict and the dynamics of oppression: A social dominance perspective. In S. Iyengar & W. McGuire (Eds.), *Explorations in political psychology* (pp. 183–219). Durham, NC: Duke University Press.

Sidanius, J., & Pratto, F. (2001). *Social dominance: An intergroup theory of social hierarchy and oppression.* New York: Cambridge University Press.

Sidanius, J., & Veniegas, R. C. (2000). Gender and race discrimination: The interactive nature of disadvantage. In S. Oskamp (Ed.), *Reducing prejudice and discrimination: The Claremont symposium on applied social psychology* (pp. 47–69). Mahwah, NJ: Erlbaum.

Smith, R. A. (1997). *Race and job authority: An analysis of men and women, 1972–1994.* New Brunswick, NJ: Rutgers University, School of Management and Labor Relations.

Zarate, M. A., & Smith, E. R. (1990). Person categorization and stereotyping. *Social Cognition, 8,* 161–185.

Zegers de Beijl, R. (1990). *Discrimination of migrant workers in Western Europe.* Geneva, Switzerland: International Labour Office.

10

TRIOS: A Model for Coping With the Universal Context of Racism

James M. Jones

Kenneth B. Clark is a passionate activist and advocate for social justice. As an immigrant from Panama, Clark believed fervently in the American Dream and has worked his entire life to extend its reach to all United States citizens of all colors. His distinguished career, including presidencies of the Society for the Psychological Study of Social Issues and the American Psychological Association, counselor to community and national leaders, scientist, scholar, and teacher, will forever be best captured by the elegantly powerful studies he did with his wife Mamie Phipps Clark on the psychological consequences of racial apartheid for young Negro children in the 1940s (Clark & Clark, 1947).

The question the Clarks posed is how does the knowledge and self-aware-ness of one's membership in a stigmatized racial group affect their ego develop-ment? That is, given that children are aware of their group membership (racial identification) and aware of the stigma attached to their group (manifested by racial segregation and social mores), will they internalize that stigma in the form of negative views of themselves (low personal self-esteem) and their group (low racial identity or racial preferences)? The doll choice methodology was quite simple and, by contemporary standards, somewhat unsophisticated (cf. Banks, 1976, Cross, 1991). Nevertheless, at that time and place in our history, the doll studies made an empirical claim that supplanted the sophistry of racist rhetoric.

In *Brown v. Board of Education,* the United States Supreme Court rejected the flawed reasoning in *Plessy v. Ferguson* that led to the so-called "separate but equal" doctrine that statutory racial segregation (maintained with perfunctory efforts at equality) did *not* abridge the rights of Negro citizens guaranteed by the 14th Amendment to the United States Constitution. Rather, the Court argued in *Brown* that modern social science trumped and invalidated the flawed reasoning of *Plessy* and provided empirical evidence that racial segregation was *inherently* unequal.

The modern social science argument was contained in a brief to the Court and was cited in Footnote 11 of the *Brown* decision. It featured in its analysis, among others, the Clarks's findings that Negro children could identify their race by selecting a doll whose skin tone and hair color corresponded to white

(94% accuracy) and "colored" (93% accuracy) but "preferred" white dolls to play with (35% differential—60% to 25%—in preference for the white doll over the colored doll) as the nice doll (31% preference), as the nice doll (22% preference), and as the doll that did *not* look bad (42% preference). The conclusion was that Negro children could identify their own racial group membership but tended to reject it as a source of positive personal or racial identity. This, the conclusion ran, was the legacy of racial apartheid in America, and *Brown* argued that it should be dismantled.

The *self-hatred* thesis was a standard of analysis in the 1940s and 1950s. The argument was made by, among others, Kardiner and Ovesy in their book *Mark of Oppression* (1951), and is reflected in the views of Kurt Lewin (1946/ 1997), who noted:

> One of the most severe obstacles in the way of improvement seems to be the notorious lack of confidence and self-esteem of most minority groups. Minority groups tend to accept the implicit judgment of those who have status even where the judgment is directed against themselves. There are many forces which tend to develop in the children, adolescents, and adults of minorities deep-seated antagonisms to their own group. . . . The discrimination which these individuals experience is not directed against them as individuals, but as group members, and only by raising their self-esteem as group members to the normal level can a remedy be produced. (p. 151)

While the damaging psychological effects of racial oppression were no doubt real and significant, there can also be no doubt that psychological resilience was an equally powerful factor in the mental and emotional life of African Americans. The evidence of the damaging effects was marshaled to make the case for the extension of basic civil and human rights to Negroes. But from a social and behavioral science point of view, the story of survival and resilience was not adequately conceptualized, studied, or told.

What is that story? The story tells of a people who were uprooted, transplanted, enslaved, dehumanized, oppressed, yet over centuries survived and have achieved a central and productive status in America. Rather than the theme of self-hatred, the more interesting plotline is resilience of a people. The roots of Black life in America began in Africa. The long saga of dehumanization and truncated individual liberties and freedom began with the commerce in Black bodies and continued through the middle passage to various points in the Americas. Racial oppression was sewn with intricate stitches into the fabric of American society and culture by the hands of political, economical, educational, judicial, and social institutions. Institutionalization of racial oppression is a cultural legacy as well as an enduring and pervasive element of our psychological consciousness. The ability of Africans in America to survive oppression in all its permutations and progress over four centuries raises a basic question: What psychological and cultural resources enabled African-descended people in America to survive?

In this chapter, I propose a theory of TRIOS as one story of this resilience. TRIOS is an acronym for the psychological elements of a cultural system and consists of five dimensions: Time, Rhythm, Improvisation, Orality, and Spirituality. It is proposed that each TRIOS dimension represents an important element of collective African experiences. It is further proposed each element can be represented in the psychology of individuals. In addition to each element influencing behavior on its own, the theory suggests that the five elements combine to create an integrated collective and individual-level worldview.

The TRIOSic worldview is extrapolated from multiple African societies and melded into a localized pattern of coping, communication, and group process. The structure of each element as well as the coherence of their intersection will depend on the ecocultural context in which it unfolds in the African diaspora. Convergence of people from different African societies takes place through the common circumstance of slavery and oppression, and the responses to these circumstances will be influenced by the cultural capital brought to the situation. To the extent that these Africans share a common fate and circumstance, it is incumbent on them to use whatever means is available to protect them from the most adverse circumstance. So while TRIOS is predicated on a common ethos in 15th and 16th century Africa, it becomes a theory of contemporary African American psychoculture as we trace its emergence and unfolding through the particulars of that historical experience.

The psychohistorical account is important because if we pick up the story in the 1940s or 1950s, it seems that the adverse effects of oppression and dehumanization have only one "rational" outcome—self-loathing, guilt, or pity.[1] The psychological issues of self-esteem, individual and collective identity, and how they mediate psychological well-being and performance cannot be understood wholly *within* the context of the events leading up to and encompassing the civil rights movement of the 1960s.

Furthermore, the crucible of African American experience may offer insight into a broader set of psychologically meaningful principles that apply to the experience of and responses to oppression more generally. That is, individuals who belong to stigmatized or oppressed groups must chart a psychological course that addresses both the collective stigma and the generalization of that stigma to the self, and find ways to diminish their adverse effects in the service of their psychological well-being.

The formula for ultimate social justice and opportunity must be a bilateral understanding of the dynamic interplay within and between cultural groups. Further, TRIOS examines the intergenerational dynamics of the predicament (defined as a *situation* in which a person's psychological or physical well-being is threatened) of African Americans. As Lewin (1943/1997) conceived it, a situation is represented psychologically by all of the experiences one has had, is having, or can imagine having and one's cognitive representations at a moment in time. This leads to a recurring situation that reflects the predicament faced by African Americans as cognitive representations of membership in a socially significant oppressed group that stretches back in time, includes

---

[1] D. M. Scott (1997) argued the pertinence of DuBois's (1903) famous line regarding the double-consciousness of African Americans who struggled with this double-consciousness while the world looks on with amused contempt and pity. The "damaged imagery" of the Negro has persisted whether one is identified as a liberal and seeks to ameliorate the racial problem or a conservative and wishes to confirm the infirmities of Negroes. The idea that there are resiliencies that survive the well-documented hardships and disadvantages needs another analytical angle.

continuing elements of stigmatization, and casts the shadow of an uncertain future on the present. The life space of individuals is hereby expanded for members of oppressed groups to include the life space of their group. The more one identifies with one's group, the more that collective history is an important part of one's construal of the situation. By this reasoning, the history of African Americans is not simply the stories of what happened during slavery but the cognitive representation of those events in the present.

In this chapter, I first elaborate on the dynamics of TRIOS by providing general observations about the origins and nature of the specific elements and their representation in African societies and across the diaspora. I then offer more specific ideas about how TRIOS may serve adaptive and coping functions for African Americans within an environment that is by degrees oppressive and racist. I speculate on contemporary manifestations of TRIOS, including early attempts to measure it, and show connections to psychological processes. Finally, I return to the self-hatred thesis and assess how this view needs to be modified in light of the TRIOS analysis.

TRIOS: Origins and Characteristics

I argue that African American culture is continuous with its African origins. Contemporary African American culture is represented psychologically by dual processes of *reactionary* and *evolutionary* mechanisms (see Jones, 1988). Reactionary mechanisms consist of adaptation-coping sequences that emerge over time to address the ecological challenges faced by members of the cultural group. These challenges require a variety of psychological and social means of coping with two fundamental aspects of an oppressed status: loss of freedom and dehumanization. Evolutionary mechanisms consist of those expressions of psyche that reflect the core cultural ethos of a people. I propose that TRIOS can be used instrumentally as a means of recovering certain forms of physical and psychological freedom and that can frame the foundation of a humanized existence in a hostile environment. I also suggest that TRIOS reflects the core African cultural ethos.

Slavery is defined by the loss of individual freedoms and liberties for those who are its victims (for an excellent general overview of slavery and its influences, see Franklin & Moss, 1994, chaps. 3–8). The abject loss of freedom resulting from enslavement generated a primary psychocultural motivational system designed to gain control over one's body and over one's life. As a result, claiming psychological freedom in any and every form possible can be seen as a consistent pattern of psychological adaptation and a cardinal goal of social psychological development. Although slavery was officially abolished in 1865, the truncated rights and informal systems of constraint and other forms of race-based denigration and dehumanization were quickly established and have remained in effect for years after (see Woodward, 1951).

Physical dehumanization was related to cultural and psychological dehumanization. African civilization was judged to be primitive and its inhabitants barely human. Persons of African decent in America were dehumanized and marginalized for more than 400 years.[2] It is not surprising that self-esteem, self-worth, and individual and collective identities emerged as issues at the forefront of psychological analysis of African Americans. One can reasonably expect that the ongoing quest for freedom and dignity is not just a civil rights agenda but a psychological motivation that organizes and energizes the dual-process mechanisms of self-protection and self-enhancement.

This dynamic process has unfolded over centuries with psychological conse-quence. The foundation for psychological mechanisms and adaptation capaci-ties followed from the cultural conditioning that preceded the arrival of Africans in America. Faced with a new and challenging situation, Africans in America used the cultural patterns they knew to cope with and adapt to these dangerous and threatening contexts. These prior culturally conditioned attributes and capacities make up the evolutionary mechanisms—those cultural dynamics that emerged in the ecological context of Africa and evolved and were articu-lated in a variety of ecological niches throughout the African diaspora. The reactionary mechanisms were those specific adaptations and strategies that resulted from the specifics of the experiences in America and were essential to survival both individually and collectively. African American psychological culture has been forming and evolving over centuries and was not invented out of whole cloth on the spot of the first conflict on a slave ship or at a Jamestown plantation in 1619. Rather, they constitute the cumulative conse-quences of the evolutionary tendencies (here I am suggesting they can be summarized by TRIOS) and the specific articulation via reactionary mecha-nisms to ensure African American adaptation and survival.

DuBois (1903) captured the duality of the African American psychological state when he articulated his concept of "double-consciousness" as

> a peculiar sensation this double-consciousness, this sense of always looking at one's self through the eyes of others, of measuring one's soul by the tape of a world that looks on in amused contempt and pity. One ever feels his two-ness,—an American, A Negro; two warring ideals in one dark body, whose dogged strength alone keeps it from being torn asunder. (pp. 214–215)

Over time, the dynamics of these processes expand from simple physical and psychological *survival* to physical and psychological *well-being*. Progress in rights and opportunities, however much qualified, opens up new possibilities and expands the range of goals to which the reactionary and evolutionary mechanisms may be directed. As individual rights and statutory protections have progressed, the contexts for constraint and dehumanization become more subtle. The psychological mechanisms that mediate appropriate adaptation to these perhaps more ambiguous contexts are importantly transformed over time

---

[2] I acknowledge that slavery did not rise full blown with the first slave ship from Africa but emerged over time as the economic, social, and political needs created the slavery solution. Further, slavery was not a monolithic institution but varied in important ways across states and plantations, and changed over time. Similarly, it is likely that group identification of Africans rose in proportion to their collective representations as a human group defined by their legal, social, and putative scientific status.

by the subtle necessities of coping with threats that are more veiled but not necessarily less pernicious.

Through this dynamic interaction, the conditioning or evolutionary mechanisms are modified and transformed by the reactionary adaptation-coping sequences. As a result, a dynamic process of continuity and change connects contemporary African American psychological culture to its historical roots. I propose that TRIOS comprises one version of those psychologically meaningful historically derived mechanisms. I further argue that TRIOS provided the repertoire of skills, perspectives, beliefs, and values that informed the initial means of adapting to and coping with the horrific experiences of slavery. Over time, TRIOS elements were modified by the exigencies of ecological challenges and underwent transformations that established their relevance and utility as modes of adaptation for survival in the new world.

African Associations With TRIOS

Contemporary writings about African culture, society, and psyche point fairly clearly to the multiple central psychocultural elements that correspond to TRIOS. The plausibility of the centrality of TRIOS elements to the broad view of African culture(s) is here assumed, and the brief overview of the points merely illustrates ways in which they are conceived. Like any set of theoretical assumptions they are not proven facts but have merit to the degree that making them allows one to test ideas or hypotheses that would not otherwise come into view. In the following summaries, I have used the writings of contemporary scholars who are historians, anthropologists, philosophers, and linguists (e.g., Asante, 1987; Chernoff, 1979; Jahn, 1961; Mbiti, 1970; Senghor, 1956; Sobel, 1987).

Time is typically parted into past, present, and future. Cultures around the world have come to value different aspects of these time zones, and characteristic cultural and personality differences have emerged. On one side is event or social time (Hall, 1983). Time is reckoned by the events that it accompanies, particularly social events. It is also reckoned by the movement of nature (harvesting crops, setting of sun, rainy season) and thus is patterned around the relevance of events for one's life. For Africans, time was slow moving and practical, *deriving from* tasks and behaviors, *not prescribing them.* By contrast, clock time imposes a linear, ordinal, and unitary understanding of time to which human events must conform (McGrath, 1988). Time is valued in its own right (McGrath, 1988, called this valuing of time *temponomics*). By distinguishing event time from clock time (Levine, 1997), one is contrasting worldviews and ways of life. Mbiti (1970) suggested that in Swahili no word for the future exists, only for the past (*Zamani*) and present (*Sasa*). Variations in conceptions of time and their implications for the structure of society, and behavior within it, strongly suggest that this one dimension may be pivotal in explaining characteristics of early African cultural systems.

With respect to *rhythm,* Chernoff (1979) commented that

one of the most notable features of African cultures is that many activities—
paddling a canoe, chopping a tree, pounding grain, or simply moving—seem
set in a rhythmic framework . . . the African dancer may pick up and respond
to the rhythms of one or more drums; the dancer, like the drummer, adds
another rhythm, [one that is not being played by the drummer but which
the dancer invents to provide syncopated movement and greater emotional
and physical tension and expression]. He tunes his ear to hidden rhythms
and he dances to gaps in the music. (p. 144)

I argue that rhythm is recurring patterns of behavior set in time that gives
shape, energy, and meaning to psychological experience. It is complex and is
a means of attaching psychological structure to the external world. For example,
the patterns of behavior that correspond to life in a large urban environment
diverge from those found on a small dairy farm in the Midwest. Behaviors are
entrained to the necessities and affordances of the environment. The match
between them invokes rhythm. Levine (1997) wrote eloquently and provoca-
tively about pace of life as an extension of time. The TRIOS idea views pace
of life as a manifestation of rhythm, which is marked and set off by time. It
is also an internal response to the rhythmic patterns of the external world,
including one's own behavior. Individuals' internal rhythms are "entrained" to
their external environment so that they "correspond" to and come under the
control of the external environmental rhythms. Losing control of one's environment is also losing internal control of one's rhythmic center.

Spencer (1995) has argued that rhythm is the central carrying agent of
African culture. African rhythm represents the commonalities found in the
rhythmic world of Africans and includes multirhythms, cross-rhythms, and
asymmetrical patterning, all of which are expressed percussive, expressed in
dance, and involve some form of call and response. With the drum as the
organizing energy, and the ring shout as the collective manifestation of community, rhythm is the core element of the connection between Continental Africans
and the African diaspora. The summary concept of *rhythmic confidence* expresses this centrality and is manifested as *soul,* to which African Americans
return regularly in a normative way much as others cultures may perform
rituals to sustain historical connections.

Improvisation, like rhythm, is a way of connecting the internal and the
external worlds. Improvisation is a means of control and a way to structure
interactions among people. With respect to music, Chernoff (1979) noted:

Improvisation is not so much in the genesis of new rhythms as in the
organization and form given to the already existing rhythms, and a musi-
cian's style of organizing his playing will indicate the way he approaches
from his own mind the responsibility of his role toward making the occasion
a success. (p. 112)

Improvisation then serves both a social integrative function and a personally expressive one. Improvisation is an organizational principle that is goal
oriented and expressive. Improvisation enables creative solutions to problems

that arise in a given situation. Moreover, the expression of one's soul and spirit is an improvisational action.

Orality is a broad concept, which includes storytelling, naming, singing, drumming, and the important lessons of socialization and cultural transmission. Asante (1987) used the word *orature* to represent the many aspects of the oral tradition. Orality is used here as a more psychologically oriented term, reflecting the great tendency of people to value and use the variety of oral expressions referred to above in their everyday life. The *Word* (*Nommo*) is the life force, and as Jahn (1961) suggested, "all activities of men and all movement in nature rest on the word . . . a newborn child becomes human only when his father gives him name and pronounces it" (p. 125). This tradition was shown to dramatic effect when Kunta Kinte was named in a ceremony in the 1977 television miniseries, *Roots*. The important meanings and values of culture are spoken or sung, not written down. The organizing principles and values of culture are handed down through stories and parables. The oral tradition connects the present to the past. Orality gives meaning to life and binds people together in common understandings and humanity. The Griot in the African cultural tradition is a professional storyteller. The life of a people is told in stories that chronicle major events, parables or truths to live by, and important values and tell the life lessons that serve as guides for living.

Orality presupposes a socially centered society in which the words and the nonverbal accompaniments carry and define the meaning of things. Orality is the cement of relationships and the means by which one's essential nature is conveyed. The call-and-response systems create local communities in a moment of time and manifest the individual and collective life force.

Spirituality may be the most central aspect of African origins. According to Jahn (1961), all things can be assigned to one of four categories: *Muntu*—god, spirits, and human beings; *Kintu*—all forces that do not act on their own but under the control of Muntu; *Hantu*—time and space; and *Kuntu*—qualities such as beauty, laughter. The importance of this taxonomy is that all categories are *forces,* which means they affect the world. The universal force comes from the stem *ntu*. Spirituality in this conception is the idea that forces beyond human beings act with effect in the world of human beings. In a field force sense, causality is multiply determined, and not all causes are material or knowable. At the heart of spirituality is the sense that it pervades the essence of humanity, and individuals cannot live outside of its sphere of influence.

Spirituality is also conceived more closely allied with religiousness or religiosity (Kim & Seidlitz, 2002). Spirituality is conceived in some ways as a search for the sacred, and thus is at its heart an alternative to the profane world of everyday (see Larson, Swyers, & McCullough, 1998). However, in many indigenous cultures there is no principal distinction between the sacred and the profane, and spirituality is integral to everyday life (D. T. Parades, personal communication, June 3, 2003). Spirituality in the TRIOS context is functional and binds the world of spirits with the world of the living in a functional symbiosis that must be taken into account.

TRIOS, then, is a worldview that summarizes several core principles of African culture. There is always a danger that reducing the complexity and variability of a continent of people to five characteristics may imply a uniformity that is unwarranted or overgeneralized. TRIOS does not argue that all Africans can be equally characterized by these five elements, or that the elements are equally important across African societies, or that there are not other characteristics that could be considered. Nor does it argue equal involvement of each TRIOS element in the adaptations of Africans in America, nor that over time, there is substantial variability among African Americans in their possession of these TRIOSic tendencies.

It is, however, clear that the cultural foundation of Africans who arrived in America diverged from the core cultural principles, beliefs, and their manifestations in British colonial America. To survive and thrive in that colonial world of servitude, slavery, denigration, oppression, and dehumanization, both individual and collective strategies had to be developed. Upon what would Africans draw to forge these adaptive responses? I argue that the core of their cultural heritages was sufficiently similar, that they could draw on common philosophies and human tendencies when their circumstance forced them into a socially, legally, and economically defined category of persons. Over time, Africans became African Americans, which meant that the African foundation was intertwined with the ecological challenge of a European-centered worldview and the realities of oppression. TRIOS played an important role in this evolution and, I argue, continues to define aspects of the essence of contemporary African American psyche.

Ecological Challenges in the New World

The ecological challenges of slavery engaged the patterns of TRIOS in adapting–coping sequences. In this oppressive environment, the opportunities for expression, social organization, and control demanded each of the TRIOS elements. Creole or pidgin languages emerged to enable oral communication among people who may have spoken somewhat different languages or dialects (Morgan, 1998). Improvisation was a means of creating linguistic meanings that were privileged among the native speakers and thus shielded the speaker from adverse consequences when speech was heard by a person hostile to his or her well-being. Expression of the human spirit was made possible through music, song, and dance. Social organization was necessarily improvised, as were strategies for control of self-protective collective actions. The cultural patterns became practical means of coping, adapting, and surviving. Thus humanity was preserved through using known and deep cultural principles and practices.

TRIOS Dynamics in a Culture of Racism

"Race" is a relatively recent concept emerging in the 18th century to make sense of the growing awareness of the diversity of peoples in the world and to rationalize the hierarchical and oppressive relationships among Europeans and others (Smedley, 1993). Racism emerged over time as a summary of the systematic patterns of relationships that were oppressive and dehumanizing and organized around the hierarchical principles of race (cf. Appiah, 1990; Jones, 1997; Smedley, 1993).

I have proposed a three-part model of racism by which individual, institutional, and cultural levels combine to create and reflect social structures and, in so doing, influence the development of individual cognitive structures (see Jones, 1997, Figure 17.1). Racism presupposes both the superiority of one's own racial group and the inferiority of others; it rationalizes privilege based on the superiority presumption and provides a rationale that makes privileged dominance both rational and normative (cf. Jones, 1997; Sidanius & Pratto, 1999; Smedley, 1993). These principles of racism not only operate at the individual level and function much like race prejudice but also operate at aggregate organizational levels by which institutional policy, practice, organization, and outcomes are manifestly linked to racial disparities. This edifice of racism suffuses American culture in prevailing ideologies and worldviews, including values, beliefs, symbols and myths, language, aesthetics, and so on.

Racism has implications for both perpetrators and their targets. There are both commonalities and differences in racial socialization of people from privileged and stigmatized groups. Traditional psychological research on racism has focused on the effects of race on members of privileged groups. TRIOS focuses more on the psychological processes that characterize stigmatized groups, in this case, African Americans. While we as researchers represent these macrolevel elements in our theories, specific theoretical propositions occur at the level of the individual, as do, of course, all of our measurements. If culture and psyche make each other up, we need to formally represent culture in our theoretical formulations. TRIOS is an attempt to do that.

The starting point is the *universal context of racism*. Targets of racism live daily with the possibility of threat, bias, denigration, denial, and truncated opportunity. Individual and collective histories of targets are psychologically available at any given moment, and thus are part of the situation that influences behavior. This leads to two assumptions. The first assumption is that *racism is an accessible, explanatory construct with motivational consequences*. Belonging to a group that is socially salient and historically stigmatized renders the possibility of race-bias highly accessible as an influence on one's interpretations of one's experiences. Although every negative experience is not attributed to or interpreted by racism, it is often a plausible explanation whether applied to the self or to others in one's group.

There are two types of motivational consequences of the universal context of racism: (a) *self-protective motivations* by which one is oriented to detecting the occurrence of, protecting oneself from, avoiding if anticipated, and conquering if confronted with racism—needless to say, these mechanisms occupy valuable cognitive and emotional resources; and (b) *self-enhancing motivations* by which one is oriented to expressing, defending, and enhancing one's self-worth and humanity. I argue that both of these motivational tendencies are triggered by the universal context of racism. The self-protective, more than the self-enhancing motives, however, have been the subject of theory and research on race. TRIOS is a theory that combines them both in the service of promoting psychological as well as physical well-being among African Americans.

This model of adaptation and psychological health shares certain features with an ego-resiliency approach (Block & Kremen, 1996). When the threatening qualities of a context are perceptually, cognitively, or emotionally salient, self-protective motives and mechanisms are aroused (e.g., stereotype threat; Steele, 1997). In the ego-resiliency model, self-enhancing motives are released when the context is perceived to be secure. Thus, in general, perceived threat will increase the likelihood that self-protective motives will be aroused and decrease the likelihood of self-enhancing motives.

However, I propose that self-enhancing motives may be used in threatening situations in two ways. The first is to alter the negative elements of a threatening environment so that one's personal sense of security is enhanced. Creating micro-contexts in which one feels comfortable is one way to enable self-enhancing motives to emerge (see, e.g., Tatum's, 1999, book *Why Are All the Black Kids Sitting Together in the Cafeteria?*). The second is to convert a threatening environment to a nonthreatening one by adhering to core individual or collective principles. For example, "keeping it real" can be a core principle that slices through the threat a given context may impose. Or one may align with others in the group to alter the values attached to certain behaviors so that matching an other-group standard is replaced by a standard endorsed by the in-group.

This dual-process model, then, provides an understanding of how a racially threatening context can elicit adaptive mechanisms that are both self-protective and self-enhancing. Self-protective and self-enhancing processes may occur at either the individual level (an action a person might take) or in concert with others in the stigmatized group (collective action).

Another feature of this model is that while self-protective processes are more likely individually based, a psychological community of others whose positive responses affirm self-worth aids the self-enhancing mechanisms. This dual-process model may help explain the strong tendency toward individualism among African Americans (cf. Oyserman, Coon, & Kimmelmeier, 2002; L. D. Scott, 2003) but also suggests that traditional notions of collectivism (e.g., Triandis, 1994) may need to be modified to capture the psychological dynamics of self-enhancement through collectivism (or communalism) suggested here (cf. Boykin & Ellison, 1995; Jones, 1999). Further, this dual model is consistent with a distinction between stereotype *threat* (evoking self-protective mechanisms) and stereotype *obligation* (evoking collective affirmation mechanisms; B. Marks, personal communication, March 10, 2002).

The second assumption is that *psychological tensions result from individual versus group level dynamics.* I propose three sets of conflicted force fields: (a) Personal identity versus reference group orientation captures the relative importance of personal uniqueness versus group belonging needs at a moment in time (Brewer, 1991); (b) racial identity versus superordinate identity reflects the relative importance of in-group distinctiveness versus superordinate group identity; and (c) instrumentality versus expressivity pits the desire for self-expression against the perceived self-constraint that may be required for mainstream success.

Belonging to a marginalized minority group creates the potential for conflicts and tensions in each of these domains. How targets resolve these psychological tensions or conflicts substantially influences their range of behavioral and attitudinal options in a universal racism context.

The self-hatred thesis presupposes that targets in general experience devalued collective self-esteem (see Luhtanen & Crocker, 1992) and that it "leaks" over to individual self-esteem (Kardiner & Ovesy, 1951). However, research on racial identity suggests that racial identity for Black people is based in part on a high regard for Black as their reference group (Cross, 1995; Sellers, Rowley, Chavous, Shelton, & Smith, 1997). At the individual level, Crocker and Wolfe (2001) found no support for diminished self-esteem of Black people. If anything, Black self-esteem is demonstrably higher than other ethnic/racial groups including Whites. One mechanism by which Black self-esteem can be maintained is by decoupling self-worth from outcomes in domains perceived to offer low probabilities of self-affirmation (Steele, 1988). Crocker and Wolfe (2001) argued that contingencies of self-worth may be selectively chosen to reflect self-protective or self-enhancing needs.

Osborne (1995) used a protective disidentification analysis to explain the observation that the correlation between self-esteem and grade point average declined substantially for Black boys between 8th (.22) and 10th (.08) grades but not for White boys (.25 and .26, respectively). What matters, I believe, is the perceptual context in which one's experience is set and the motivational systems that provide meaning and understanding to it. The psychological dynamics and normative cultural influences will affect a host of interpretations of phenomena related to psychological well-being.

As noted earlier, Lewin (1946) proposed that minorities developed deep-seated antagonisms toward their own group and that their self-esteem suffered by virtue of their group membership. The Osborne (1995) data suggest that embracing one's own group and disidentifying with the broader social context in which adverse outcomes are widely expected may actually strengthen self-esteem. Rather than being a source of antagonism, the in-group can be a source of self-esteem maintenance and enhancement (Jones & Morris, 1993). This possibility requires a more complex cultural theory of African Americans. It is certainly true that minority groups are aware of the implicit judgments of high status groups and do take them into account. However, it does not necessarily follow that *awareness* of those judgments leads, as Lewin suggested, to deep-seated antagonisms to their own group. Nor does acceptance of this status quo as normative lead to false consciousness that what is normative is correct (Jost & Banaji, 1994).

I propose that TRIOS provides a way of conceptualizing a basis for positive regard at both individual and collective levels. Further, TRIOS proposes a worldview that organizes the meaning of behavior and charts strategies for navigating the universal context of racism toward positive psychological well-being. Let me now turn to assumptions underlying these theoretical possibilities.

TRIOS: Its Psychological Properties in a Contemporary World

As a cultural worldview, each TRIOS dimension reflects human capacity developed from the fabric of experience, necessity, belief, and evolutionary success.

Psychological concepts derive from a particular cultural history and the problems and issues it defines. Mainstream psychology is inspired by European American cultural concerns and worldviews that celebrate individual initiative and success. TRIOS offers an alternative origination of basic psychological ideas, situated in the context of African psychological culture and its elaboration in the African diaspora. In this context, psychology is inspired by African American cultural concerns and worldviews that emphasize the human life force, living in the now, and the universal spirit that sustains the individual.

TRIOS rests on three related organizing principles: (a) TRIOS concepts are driven by and responsive to context; (b) contexts are meaning-generating systems that define the local meaning of things, validate or confirm one's self-conception, or construal, and provide a framework for interpreting the flow of behavior; and (c) TRIOS elements are distinctive as well as synergistic in combination. As a result, TRIOS as a whole should be taken as a worldview, instantiated over time, and expressed by individuals who have been enculturated to it. Let us examine each of these principles in turn.

TRIOS and Context

TRIOS presumes that a large percentage of meaningful events occur within a context. Context describes a moment in time but contains cognitive, emotional, and attitudinal representations of people, places, things, and events that are not only psychologically or physically extant in the immediate context but may exist outside of that moment. This approach reflects Lewin's idea of the situation as it can be objectively portrayed and as it is construed by a person at a particular moment in time. From the outside looking in, one speculates on a person's construal of the situation and its impact on behavior.

Another way of looking at context is as an object of regard with goal-relevant properties. Goals that can be achieved in a context include self-presentation, social influence, hedonic intentions, desires, and social control. Each of these context-driven goals can be achieved through the elements of TRIOS. Further, these goals can also be linked to motivations triggered by historically derived responses to loss of freedom and dehumanization.

If value, knowledge, and meaning are imposed from without and their source is the adversarial system of racism, then one is at a disadvantage that the imported standards will reinforce the stigmatized status they seek to avoid. But if one can interpret relevant information and values from the context itself, then one may have more control. Thus this theory of context is a theory of personal control. TRIOS elements function in an online manner so are optimally suited to confer this sort of control in context.

TRIOS and Meaning

Encounters in the moment derive meaning from the relevance of ongoing behaviors and their interpretation. Simply put, context is dynamic. For example, from a contextual viewpoint language is not dependent on semantic meaning so much as its paralinguistic features, inflections, body language, facial cues, and so on. Conventional meanings of words are replaced by colloquial or neologistic meanings that privilege the speaker over the audience. In Trinidad, "mamaguy" describes verbal utterances whose meaning is opposite to its semantic content. "Your hair looks very nice today," means just the opposite when a person is "mamaguying" you. More commonly, we are culturally aware, now, that "bad" can mean "good, as can "stupid" or "dope." Understanding is not just cognitive ("I understand") or perceptual ("I see what you're saying" or "I hear you") but emotional ("I feel you"). By strategic use of inflection, a simple affirmation ("uh-huh" with a rising inflection and head nod) can become a negation ("uh-huh" with a falling inflection and head shake). Alternative linguistic conventions in this contextual arsenal include the diminutive alternative (home equals "crib"), the graphically illustrated action (to leave is to "bounce"), to show appreciation is to "love," to be an exemplar of the group or geographical area is to "represent."

Language provides a compelling argument for power "in" the situation. In each of these cases, the language captures the interpersonal, intragroup, and the intrapsychic meaning of things, and links the speaker and the audience in a union fortified against the outsider who, absent cultural understanding, is marginalized and stripped of power to harm. What an utterance means or an actor intends is defined by the parameters in the context itself. The anthropologist E. T. Hall (1983) made a similar point in his distinction between *context-rich* and *context-poor* communications. Context-rich communications are semantically sparse, and thus their meaning is derived by locating the utterances in a rich web of cultural nuance and meaning. Context-poor communications, on the other hand, are of necessity semantically dense and rely on the literal meaning of words that are both explicit and durable over time and place.

The community of perceivers who know the culture-symbols get it, and outsiders do not. Thus one gains a measure of control when meaning is context dependent. Conversely, imposed meanings that are instantiated and defined in a hostile culture impose external controls and reduce one's flexibility at self-definition. It is reasonable then to perceive this reliance on context as a means of gaining personal control in the situation and, ultimately, control of one's self-worth.

The resurgence of culture in psychology (Fiske, Kitayama, Markus, & Nisbett, 1998; Markus & Kitayama, 1991) has focused attention on the context as a variable in human behavior. One aspect of culture-as-context is the way in which the self is implicated in the construal of the meanings of things. The broadest distinction of self-relevant variables is independence from or interdependence with others (Markus & Kitayama, 1991). A similar distinction is made by individualism and collectivism (see Triandis, 1994). The TRIOS analysis, though, conceives the collective and individualistic self-contruals as complementary, not oppositional.[3]

---

[3] It is not clear that collectivism is the best way to represent the interdependencies that members of oppressed groups endorse. Most of the literature presumes that collectivism serves as a defining quality of a cultural expression. However, when interdependencies serve self-protective functions

Collectivism can be expressed at the level of the individual (Jones, 1999). Psychologically, meaning is defined in this context, at this time. What a person means is determined by parameters of the immediate context itself. Who I am is also defined in that context. My creative improvisational performance, if accepted by the audience, defines the qualities of character I possess and to which I lay claim. My audience is crucial to who I am as a result. My authentic self is not imposed on me but defined by my actions, speech, and dress. It makes a self-defining statement of who I am. As we will see, the vital elements of TRIOS are jointly affected in this contextual analysis.

I have suggested elsewhere that the collective affirms the self, *and* the individual expression of TRIOSic attributes also affirms the collective (Jones, 1999). Rather than choosing between an individualistic or collective orientation, TRIOS joins them. A recent meta-analysis examined a large number of published studies of individualism and collectivism (Oyserman et al., 2002). The authors identified specific concepts commonly measured as part of the individualism construct and those measured by the collectivism construct. The meta-analysis showed that overall African Americans were more individualistic than and not different from in collectivism. However, these results showed important variability when one considers which of the individualism and collectivism concepts were being measured.

When individualism was measured by directness of communication with others, privacy of self-thoughts, competition with others, and personal uniqueness, African Americans were more individualistic than Whites. But when individualism was measured by self-knowledge, they were not. Although African Americans were not different in collectivism from Whites overall, when the measure of collectivism *excluded* seeking advice from others, moderating one's behavior to fit the context, or accepting authority, African Americans were more collective. However, when measures of collectivism *included* group harmony, a preference for group-based work, or belonging to groups, African Americans were quite similar to Whites. In sum, the TRIOS perspective emphasizes strong individualistic orientations to adaptation, coping, and well-being but within a group-centered context. The data on individualism–collectivism seem to support this general tendency. However, the story is more complex than that.

Centuries of oppression, dehumanization, and discrimination require one to seek and secure sources of self-worth that are not routinely available in the broader society. Further, the community of others who can validate one's self-worth must be carefully chosen in a generally hostile context. It is possible that being individualistic means something different for a person in an oppressed situation than it does for one who is in a relatively secure context. Individualism in the service of survival and establishing self-worth may be of a different quality than individualism that serves personal achievement and enculturated self-representations. Similarly, collectivism for marginalized and oppressed

---

in a hostile environment, they may take on different properties. Communalism may be a concept better suited to this circumstance (cf. Boykin & Ellison, 1995; Moemeka, 1998).

groups may be quite different from what is expressed by groups who define the values of worth and have ready access to them.

Further, collectivism may have less to do with duty and obligation, which can themselves impose significant restrictions on individual freedoms, than with establishing a self-protective community (meta-culture) whose symbolic representations and privileged understandings help to establish support for individualistic expression and well-being. Collectivism, like individualism, serves survival and self-worth needs and goals for individuals. The ability of a group to validate one's self-worth is not specifically reflected in the collectivism concept, and duty to others in one's group is not the same thing.

TRIOS as Worldview

TRIOS is well suited to a context-driven worldview because each of its dimensions either reflect or provide a means of controlling aspects of a given context. People often consider goals, expectations, plans, and intentions in an extended time frame. That is, the basic motives in psychology seem to rest on connecting the present to a distant future that is typically desirable and presumed to be attainable (McGrath, 1988; Zaleski, 1994, Zimbardo & Boyd, 1999). Specific motives consist of figuring out where one wants to be in the future and establishing means-end sequences that help one reach one's goals.

As a cultural syndrome, TRIOS reflects the psychological realism of being-in-the-world. Being-in-the-world is not only a present-time focus but also a spiritual focus in which living status (being) is shared with others in the broad lexicon of spirituality related to *Muntu* (Jahn, 1961). It is improvisational because one is successful by virtue of continued life (being), not by life's products (doing). It is oral because it is only now that one meets face to face and defines and redefines, expresses, and reveals one's essential nature. The language of being-in-the-world is immediacy (the durative "be" in linguistics, "I be going"; see Smitherman, 1977). Being-in-the-world, then, is defined as a focus on the fundamental challenges of living and the acceptance of a place in a universe in which all things matter. More practically, being-in-the-world is a self-system that does not take the future for granted and lets go of the past.

What might one expect from such a theory? First, TRIOS elements may formulate themselves in a coherent way that is structurally integrated. Second, African Americans who are relatively more TRIOSic should have a higher level of psychological well-being. Third, to the extent that other groups may also experience dehumanization, restricted freedom, and marginalization, they may also be inclined toward TRIOSic qualities. Now let us turn to some initial attempts to organize these ideas into empirically measurable and conceptually testable hypotheses.

TRIOS: Its Measurement, Structure, and Function

I have argued that TRIOS represents a worldview that has psychological correlates in the attitudes, cognitions, values, and behaviors of African Americans.

I have further proposed that the structure of this worldview plays a moderating or mediating role in important behavioral outcomes. The following discussion addresses initial evidence about the measurement and structure of TRIOS, ethnic/racial differences in endorsement of TRIOS elements, and evidence that TRIOS level is related to the relationship between stress and psychological well-being.

Measuring TRIOS

First, students from my graduate seminar on the Cultural Psychology of African Americans and I wrote 100 questionnaire items constructed to tap the five TRIOS dimensions. Table 10.1 describes the underlying characteristic of each TRIOS dimension and a sample item.

Using a 7-point Likert scale for responses with a range of −3 = *not at all true of me* to 3 = *very true of me* and 0 = *not relevant to me,* we obtained responses from 200 people, including students in classes at the University of Delaware, Howard University, friends, relatives, and neighbors. We created nonempirically derived subscales based on the TRIOS dimensions the items were written to assess and computed item–subscale correlations. We eliminated those items with a poor correlation, along with those that we judged to be poorly worded or confusing. This left us with 60 items, which we augmented, with 17 additional items to assess aspects of the TRIOS concept that were missing in the original item set.

We then administered this expanded set of 77 items to a larger convenience sample derived from several sources, including a private university in California, a city college in Los Angeles, a private predominantly Black university on the East Coast, a public university on the East Coast, Delaware, a predominantly Black high school in Philadelphia, a public university in South Florida, and others notable by their convenience. The final sample consisted of 1,415 respondents of whom two thirds were women and one third men, a little over 40% were White, 21% were Black, 19% were Latino, and 11% were Asian. The age range was 14 to 62 years, with the average age for each group between 20 and 21 years.

The Structures of TRIOS

We conducted an exploratory principal-components factor analysis (EFA) on the entire sample of respondents for the 77 items, setting an eigenvalue cutoff at 2.0. This produced six factors. We then removed all items whose commonalities were less than .30 and reran the EFA, setting a five-factor criterion and using an oblique rotation. The five factors that emerged accounted for 43% of the common variance. I summarize the factor structure in order of the TRIOS model rather than the order in which the factors were extracted.

Spirituality is defined by a belief in a higher power as a functional element of one's daily life. Spirituality was the first factor extracted, consisting of nine items, and had the highest reliability (α = .88). This view of spirituality is consistent with the conceptualization of spirituality in the TRIOS model. The

Table 10.1. TRIOS Domains and Assessment

Dimension name	Description	Sample item
Time	Focuses attention on the present; immediacy of goals or behavior	I try to live one day at a time.
	Setting goals and planning for the future	I make extensive plans for the future.
	Emotion-laden thoughts about the past	I think about the past a lot.
Rhythm	An internal rhythmic processes with external dynamic properties—flow, entrainment	I always try to get in synch with surroundings.
	Importance of and preference for physical expression	Music and dance are important forms of personal expression.
Improvisation	Creative problem solving in conflicted contexts	When something disrupts my goals, I often figure out how to achieve them anyway.
	Personally characteristic expressiveness or style	I have a personal style that is all my own.
Orality	Preference for verbal exchange that is face to face	I always try to deal with people straight up and face to face.
	Words, speech, and humor are fundamental modes of personal expression	I often feel that my experiences are not real until I tell someone about them.
	Means of creating and maintaining social bonds	In my social group, laughter often holds us together.
	Means of communicating cultural values, knowledge, and expectations	The most important things I know come more from stories I have heard than things I have read.
Spirituality	Belief in a higher power or force	Belief in God or a greater power helps me deal with the circumstances of my life.
	Control and responsibility is shared with this Force	There are forces that influence my life that I cannot explain.

eight items that create the Spirituality subscale were the first factors extracted and had the highest reliability coefficient (α =.88). Four representative items follow:

1. Belief in God or a greater power helps me deal with the circumstances of my life.
2. In most every aspect of my life, I am strengthened by my spiritual beliefs.
3. I believe that the world is full of powerful and unknowable forces.

4. There are reasons beyond our understanding for everything that happens.

There are two aspects to this Spirituality subscale. First is the everyday functionality of spirituality. Six of the items capture the idea that spiritual beliefs and priorities help one cope with everyday life. An additional three items portray spirituality as the powerful and unknown forces that intervene to determine life events. It is often suggested that spirituality is related to an external locus of control or is a reflection of religiosity. These spirituality items acknowledge that one may not be in control of everything that happens but do not imply a passive, pawnlike relationship to one's circumstances, or simply a surrogate of churchgoing or formal religious beliefs. Rather, spirituality can serve an important function in taking control of one's life on a daily basis. Like improvisation, spirituality provides a sense of confidence that living and doing one's best is what one has a responsibility to do. There are greater forces that set out one's purpose to which one must work to achieve. This may be a very healthy attitude for a person who in fact faces a challenging circumstance that contains many obstacles that are unscripted and must be managed.

Improvisation is a reflection of the belief that one can successfully overcome unforeseen obstacles, that one can achieve in spite of external barriers to success, and that one's manner of accomplishing this is heavily based on personal qualities that are self-defining. Improvisation was the second factor extracted consisting of six items with decent reliability ($\alpha = .72$). Four representative items follow:

1. When a situation arises, I usually know two to three different ways to handle it.
2. When things do not go as planned, it is easy for me to devise another plan right on the spot.
3. I can figure my way out of almost any situation.
4. When something disrupts my goals, I often figure out how to achieve them anyway.

Improvisation is captured by creative and effective problem solving in a challenging context. Uncertainty of expectations is countered by the belief that one will handle whatever arises. In this belief resides a feeling of control. This form of control is different from the kind based on control of events external to the self. Improvisation holds the self capable of controlling outcomes even when the circumstances are unpredictable, controlled by others, or perhaps even relatively likely to produce adverse outcomes. Belief in one's ability to handle whatever comes along is a comforting feeling and provides the person with a sense of optimism about the future. The addition of personal style to Improvisation reflects the individuality of improvisation and its self-defining quality. Further, handling issues "face-to-face" implies the directness of the improvisational approach. Like the other dimensions, the Improvisation subscale is context dependent and conveys both the self-protective motives through problem solving and the self-enhancement motives through personal style and expression.

Orality was conceived principally as the oral expression of meaning through words and song in a social context. Orality conveys meanings handed down over time through stories but also establishes social bonds through the privileged meanings, styles of speech, and preferences for in-group relations. Orality emerged as the third factor extracted, consisted of six items, and was reasonably reliable (α =.69). Four representative items follow:

1. It is important to be yourself at all times.
2. It is important for me to be comfortable in a situation in order to be successful.
3. In my social group, laughter often holds us together.
4. It is important for me to maintain harmony in my group.

Orality presupposes a high-context social environment (Hall, 1983). Orality is characterized by a generalized sensitivity to interpersonal relationships in a social context. Relations with friends and in-group harmony reflect the use of orality to maintain social boundaries and promote in-group cohesion. The socially constructed self is reflected by the need for a personal social identity defined by personal properties and invariance across settings. Further, feeling comfort in the social context may be a precondition for psychological well-being. The implication of being in a comfortable social setting, tied to others through humor and social sharing, while maintaining positive personal identity supports the idea that personal distinctiveness and group belonging are highly related (Brewer, 1991). It also makes plausible the connections between individualism and collectivism as suggested earlier in this chapter and elsewhere (Jones, 1999). Interestingly, the independent item ("be yourself at all times") and the interdependent item ("valuing harmony in my group") from Singelis (1994) *both* loaded on this factor. This suggests that the Orality subscale may tap both individually oriented and more collectively oriented sentiments. Orality also suggests that social context can be both a source of self-protective motives (Tatum, 1999), and a means of self- and collective expression and self-enhancement. Sitting together in one's group may convert an uncertain and uncomfortable environment into one that is more secure. The resulting psychological comfort then enables one to perform successfully in other settings.

Time, in the TRIOS model, is represented broadly as a present-time orientation—living-in-the-now. Time emerged as the fourth factor extracted consisted of six items and was moderately reliable (α = .61). Four illustrative items are as follows:

1. Preparing for what might happen in the future is often a waste of time.
2. It's better to live the present moment to the fullest than to plan for the future.
3. When I try to envision the future, I draw a blank.
4. I have made extensive plans for the future.

The character of this factor is as much a rejection of the importance or utility of thinking about the future as it is a focus on the present. It is important to note that this version of present orientation is neither hedonistic/pleasure seeking nor a fatalistic view of an uncontrollable future as other scales have found (Zimbardo & Boyd, 1999). It is simply an expression of living-in-the-now uninfluenced by future possibilities, and a *preference* for this approach to life.

Rhythm does not emerge clearly as a factor in this TRIOS structure. Rhythm was the fifth factor extracted, consisted of only three items, and was unreliable ($\alpha = .35$). The three items are as follows:

1. I often feel anxiety when I am late for a scheduled event.
2. If I feel someone is attacking me, I sometimes struggle not knowing what to do.
3. I often feel that my experiences are not "real" until I tell someone about them.

The three items that form this factor were actually written to tap time, improvisation, and orality, respectively. Although they do not reflect the original ideas of the Rhythm dimension, they do seem to reflect an asynchrony in relationships between a person and his or her surroundings. By reverse scoring each item, we still use the concept of rhythm as conceptually described. Thus those who score low on this factor are considered to be higher on the Rhythm dimensions. The low reliability of the Rhythm subscale may be because of the limited number of items composing the subscale, because rhythm is particularly difficult to capture in a paper-and-pencil measure, or because we have not selected the best items to assess it.

Holistic TRIOS

Taken as a whole, then, these measures of TRIOS fit the overall concept of TRIOS as a context-driven focus on being-in-the-world and a five-dimensional structure reasonably well. One recurring question concerns whether the five TRIOS dimensions function as separate factors or can be combined into a single TRIOS index. We calculated the reliability index of all 29 items (reverse scoring for the 3 Rhythm items and 2 Present Orientation items as noted) and obtained an alpha of .69. This suggests that the items constituting the five factors can be combined as a single TRIOS index. We combined these 29 items into a composite index of TRIOS and labeled it TRIOS-C. TRIOS-C scores may be used as an estimate of an individual's overall level of TRIOSity. In addition, their individual subfactor scores could be used independently as predictors of attitudes and behaviors more relevant to specific dimensions. For example, present orientation is often linked to a variety of negative behaviors such as unhealthy risk-taking and poor academic performance. But when present orientation is part of the TRIOS-C structure, it is tempered and buffered by the other TRIOS dimensions that may be related to more positive outcomes. The higher order TRIOS-C and the second-order present orientation would thus make differential predictions about behavioral outcomes. Determining the validity and utility of these hierarchical relationships between TRIOS-C and the subscales remains for future research.

Table 10.2. Mean TRIOS Scores by Race and Gender Total Sample Factor

	Spiri-tuality	Improvi-sation	Orality	Time (Present)	Rhythm	TRIOS-C
Race/Ethnicity						
White (N=603)	.41a	1.36a	2.18a	.05a	0.35a	.72a
Black (N=293)	1.52b	1.44a	2.37b	.29c	0.63b	1.09b
Hispanic (N=295)	1.06c	1.49a,b	2.03c	.24b	0.47a,b,c	.90c
Asian American (N=150)	.87c	1.23a,c	2.17a,c	.08a	0.19a,c	.75a
Gender						
Males (N=408)	.70	1.49	2.15	0.17	0.58	.88
Females (N=804)	1.00	1.36	2.22	0.15	0.31	.85
Significance						
Race/Ethnicity	.000	.05	.000	.000	.023	.000
Sex	.000	.06	.018	.022	.000	ns
Race/Ethnicity × Sex	ns	ns	ns	.06	ns	ns
Cronbach Alpha	.88	.72	.69	.61	.35	.70

Note. Values within columns with different subscripts are significantly different from each
other based on Tukey post hoc HSD statistic. TRIOS-C is the average of scores on Spirituality, Improvisation, Orality, Time (Present), and Rhythm.

Ethnic Racial Differences in TRIOS

The derivation of the TRIOS concept would suggest that the items used to
assess it would be endorsed to a greater extent by African Americans than by
other groups. To test this idea, mean scores for each empirically derived TRIOS
factor including TRIOS-C served as dependent variables in a 4 (race/ethnicity)
× 2 (sex) multivariate analysis of variance (MANOVA). Tukey's honestly significance difference (HSD) statistics were computed for post hoc comparisons
of racial/ethnic and gender differences. Table 10.2 presents the mean factor
scores for Whites, African Americans, Hispanics, and Asian Americans for each
of the five factors and TRIOS-C. There were significant race/ethnicity main
effects on each of the five dimensions and significant sex main effects on all but
the Improvisation dimension. There were no reliable Race × Sex interactions on
any of the dimensions.

In summary, African Americans scored significantly higher than all
other groups on TRIOS-C. In addition, they scored significantly higher than
or as high as any of the other racial/ethnic groups on all of the TRIOS
dimensions. Latinos scored higher than Whites and Asian Americans on
TRIOS-C, and Asian Americans and Whites did not differ. Latinos also
scored higher than Whites on the Spirituality and Present Orientation
dimensions. These results support the idea that dimensions of TRIOS have
greater representation among persons of African descent as reflected in
scores on the TRIOS scale.

Is TRIOS Related to Better Coping?

I have argued that TRIOS processes facilitate coping with adverse circumstances characterized by restricted freedom and dehumanization. That African Americans scored higher on TRIOS is one piece of evidence that this idea may have merit. It would be further important to know that one's level of TRIOS played a positive role in their psychological well-being. My colleagues and I tested this idea in a pilot study in which African American and White college students were asked to describe either a very positive event or a very negative event that occurred in the past year. After describing the event, they rated how well they thought they had coped with it. For positive events, participants were asked how well they were able to make the positive effects last, for negative events, how well they were able to diminish the negative events. We also asked participants to evaluate their responses using the COPE measure (Carver, Scheier, & Weintraub, 1989), as well as the Positive and Negative Affect Schedule (PANAS) to describe their level of positive and negative affect during the event.

There were no differences between African Americans and Whites in self-reported coping. However, there were significant differences between African Americans and Whites in the affect associated with the events. African Americans tended to rate positive events more positively and negative events more negatively than Whites, and this difference was greatest for those high in TRIOS. TRIOS level seems to matter more for African Americans than Whites and to expand the affective experiences associated with life events.

The COPE measure allows respondents to identify the degree to which each of several types of coping responses characterized how they responded to the positive or negative event they described. COPE consists of 13 subscales that reflect generally problem- or emotion-focused coping styles. We computed each of the subscales, then conducted an EFA on all 13. Four factors emerged, which we labeled Socioemotional Support, Denial, Spirituality (positive growth, acceptance, disengagement, and religion), and Planning.

The two most interesting results concerned the use of the Spirituality and Planning factors as coping styles. African American participants used spirituality coping styles more than Whites did, and those high in TRIOS used spirituality more than those low in TROIS. But there was no TRIOS × Race interaction. Because African American participants tend to be higher in TRIOS than White participants, the race effect could be attributed to the relative greater representation of TRIOSity in the African American sample. But the absence of a TRIOS × Race interaction also suggests that TRIOS effects may not be limited to African Americans. Results also showed that African American participants used the Planning factor more than White participants, but this was qualified by a Race × Event Condition interaction. African American participants used planning coping styles more than White participants in positive than in negative events. This was most true when African American participants were high in TRIOS.

The positive event condition was included as a control condition, but it emerges as an important distinguishing factor for both race and TRIOS level effects. There is an overall positivity bias in TRIOS such that more focus is paid to positive than negative events, even for the processes of planning. It is possible that this positive orientation reflects the self-enhancement aspect of the theory. As further support for this positivity tendency, we found that participants higher in TRIOS level reported higher current positive affect but no differences in current negative affect. Again, although African American participants also showed marginally higher current positive affect, the absence of a Race × TRIOS interaction suggests a more general phenomenon.

Does TRIOS Moderate the Relationship Between Stress and Psychological Well-Being?

If TRIOS is source of resilience, adaptation, and coping, one would expect that endorsing TRIOS should be associated with greater psychological well-being. This should be true over and above the level of stress a person reports. Further, one might expect that TRIOS is more central to the well-being of African Americans than Whites. Another study assessed these ideas.

College students at a public predominantly White university ($n = 124$), a private historically Black university ($n = 87$), and a community college serving predominantly African Americans ($n = 79$), all on the East Coast, as well as from a university in the African country of Ghana ($n = 436$) completed the TRIOS scale and measures of stress and well-being. Stress was measured in two ways: the Inventory of College Student's Recent Life Experiences (ICSRE; Kohn, Lafreniere, & Gurevich, 1990) and the Perceived Stress Scale (PSS; Cohen, Kamarck, & Mermelstein, 1983). ICSRE assesses the degree to which a person has experienced a variety of "hassles" during the past month (*not at all a part of my life* to *very much a part of my life* on a 1–4 scale). The PSS asks participants to indicate the extent to which they have experienced several sources of stress in the past month (*never* to *very often* on a 0–4 point scale). Psychological well-being was also measured in two ways: Depression was assessed using the Center for Epidemiological Studies—Depression Scale (CES–D; Radloff, 1977), which asks participants to indicate how often they have felt certain ways from fearful to happy (*rarely* to *most of the time* on a 1–4 scale), and positive/negative affect was assessed using the PANAS (Watson, Clark, & Tellegen, 1988), which asks respondents to indicate to what extent they have felt hostile, excited, scared, strong, and so on over the past week (1 = *very slightly* to 5 = *extremely*).

An EFA was conducted on the combined items for the two stress measures and produced three factors. The first consisted of five items, all of which came from the ICSRE, and was labeled Social Conflict (e.g., being let down or disappointed by friends, being taken for granted, having your trust betrayed by a friend, being taken advantage of, and conflicts with friends). A second factor consisted of five items, again all from the ICSRE, and was labeled Stress. It reflected the experience of stress resulting from time pressures (e.g., not enough time to meet your obligations, not enough time for sleep, too many things to do at once, not enough leisure time, and a lot of responsibilities). The third factor consisted of six items, all of which came from the PSS, and was labeled Positive Coping (e.g., dealt successfully with irritating life hassles, felt that you were effectively coping with important changes that were occurring in your life, felt confident about your ability to handle your personal problems, felt that things were going your way, were able to control irritations in your life, and felt like you were on top of things). A composite Stress score was created by combining the three subscales so that a higher score indicated greater perceived stress.

Another EFA was conducted on the two psychological well-being measures and produced two factors. The first consisted of six items, all from the CES–D, and was labeled Depression (e.g., I felt that I could not shake off the blues even with help from my family or friends, I felt depressed, I talked less than usual, I felt lonely, I had crying spells, and I felt sad). The second factor came from the PANAS and consisted of six items and was labeled Ego Activation (e.g., I felt . . . attentive, strong, alert, active, determined). These two subscales were combined so that the higher the score the more positive psychological well-being.

The sample was subdivided into three "racial" groups: Whites, African Americans, and Africans. We first standardized all scores and conducted a MANOVA on the five TRIOS dimensions, plus the composite TRIOS-C and composite stress and psychological well-being variables. The results showed significant race main effects on each variable. Tukey's HSD post hoc tests confirmed that Africans were significantly higher in overall well-being than both African Americans and Whites (.18 vs. –.28 for African Americans and –.32 for Whites) and lower on stress (–.38 vs. .76 for African Americans and .38 for Whites). In addition, African Americans were significantly higher in stress than Whites.

With respect to TRIOS, Africans and African Americans were higher in TRIOS-C, Improvisation, and Spirituality than Whites and not different from each other. Africans were lower in Rhythm than African Americans, who were no different from Whites. Thus we have good support for the continuing distinctions between Whites and Africans and African Americans on TRIOS. This is consistent with previously reported results (Jones, 2003), although the finding that Whites were higher in Present-Time Orientation is somewhat surprising. These race main effect differences in endorsement of the content of TRIOS suggest stable racial differences in worldview.

To determine if TRIOS level played the same or a different role across racial groups in the relationship between self-reported stress and psychological well-being, we conducted multiple regression analyses with well-being as the dependent variable and stress, TRIOS, and the Stress × TRIOS-C interaction as independent variables. We conducted these regression analyses on the entire sample and separately for Africans, African Americans, and Whites. Results for the entire sample showed that both stress and TRIOS-C were significant predictors of TRIOS level with standardized coefficients of –.52 and .13, respectively ($p = .000$). The interaction term was not significant suggesting that TRIOS did not play a moderating role in the stress and well-being relationship. For Africans, both TRIOS-C and stress were significant predictors of well-being, and the interaction between them was marginally significant ($\beta = .29$, $p = .08$). The interaction showed that TRIOS level made little difference in psychological well-being when reported stress was low. But when stress reported was high, well-being was significantly lower for low TRIOS-C than for high TRIOS-C scoring Africans. Thus for Africans, TRIOS level moderated the relationship between stress and well-being.

The same pattern was found for the improvisation for the entire sample. Again, both improvisation (β = .28, p = .000) and stress (β = $-$.40, p = .000) predicted well-being, and their interaction did as well (β = .07, p = .038). In this case, high improvisation was more positively related to well-being under low stress; and low improvisation was more negatively related to well-being under high stress. The improvisation and stress main effects applied to all race groups, but the moderation effect applied to Africans only. We also found a similar moderation effect for rhythm for the entire sample, for spirituality for Africans only, and for orality for Whites only but in a direction opposite to what we found above.

These preliminary results suggest a number of things. One, simply knowing that one group differs from another in overall TRIOS level does not mean that TRIOS is more important in a functional way. African Americans score higher than Whites on most TRIOS dimensions, but they do not show differential effects of TRIOS in the domains of stress and well-being. African Americans and Africans do not differ in overall TRIOS level, but TRIOS seems to play a far greater role for Africans than African Americans. Whites systematically score lower than both African Americans and Africans on TRIOS domains, but the effects of TRIOS are quite similar. More work needs to be done to tease out the individual difference effects from the culture/race effects.

Conclusion

TRIOS is conceptualized as a worldview reflecting a cultural ethos of African origins and expressed by individual motivations for self-protection and self-enhancement in a universal context of racism. It is proposed that TRIOS is psychologically adaptive because it represents self-relevant beliefs and values that foster ego-resilience and optimism. TRIOS is an effective approach to living because it presupposes individual capacity, skill, and successful functioning in challenging circumstances. A TRIOSic worldview is also supported by the value of others and the assistance that a spiritual life can provide.

It would follow from the outline of origins and character of TRIOS that African Americans internalize its elements to a greater degree than other ethnic/racial groups, particularly Whites. Further, it could be argued that a high level of TRIOSity would moderate psychological well-being in challenging psychosocial contexts. The empirically derived psychometric structure supports the underlying assumptions about its organization and coherence. The comparative analyses show that African Americans could be described as more TRIOSic than other racial/ethnic groups. This is a promising extension of the descriptive hypothesis about the TRIOS concept, to an empirically validated measure of it.

However, when we look deeper we find a mixed pattern of effects. Results of the self-reported coping study suggest that people who are TRIOSic tend to report more active coping in positive than in negative circumstances. Further, they report significantly greater use of spirituality as a coping mechanism overall, including the positive events. It seems possible that TRIOS encompasses the self-enhancement aspects of the universal racism response.

Data from the stress and well-being study support this finding in that relationships of TRIOS and all of its dimensions were consistently more highly related to psychological well-being than to stress. That is, one's level of TRIOS was not predicted by self-reported stress, but the level of well-being was reliably predicted by TRIOS level, even when stress was accounted for.

We consistently find a race main effect in endorsement of TRIOS. But the data reported above suggest that TRIOS functions in a similar way for Whites, African Americans, and Africans. African Americans, though, reported a higher level of stress in their lives than either Whites or Africans. It could be that the universal context of racism is a salient factor in their experience, but that a more sensitive research approach that embeds TRIOS in the everyday context of stress and well-being is needed to detect some of these effects.

Furthermore, in some preliminary research we find that high scores on TRIOS-C were related to the values (Schwartz, 1992) of achievement, self-direction, stimulation, benevolence, and universalism and to self-worth contingent on virtuous living (Crocker & Wolfe, 2001). By contrast, spirituality was related to self-worth contingent on God's love (Crocker & Wolfe, 2001), and improvisation was related to ego-resilience (Block & Kremen, 1996). These relationships were found with White participants. This sort of validity research will help direct us to domains in which we might expect TRIOS level to matter, and to allow us to contrast the first-order TRIOS-C with the second-order individual TRIOS dimensions.

The possibility that self-enhancement is an important correlate of TRIOS is an important balance to the self-hatred that dominated the psychological literature on racial oppression. The presumption that systematic racial oppression necessarily erodes psychological well-being is overstated. Well-being is a strong motivational goal, and one's personal and cultural capital is recruited to sustain it. My colleagues and I will continue to explore the dynamics of TRIOS effects with the promise that it will not only illuminate the resilience of African Americans, the cultural foundations of Africans, but a positive spirit of humanity. Kenneth Clark believed strongly in the common humanity of all people, and the universal value of equality and social justice for all. The concept of TRIOS may advance us closer to that reality in the years ahead.

References

Appiah, K. A. (1990). Racisms. In D. T. Goldberg (Ed.), *Anatomy of racism* (pp. 3–17). Minneapolis: University of Minnesota Press.

Asante, M. K. (1987). *The Afrocentric idea.* Philadelphia: Temple University Press.

Banks, W. C. (1976). White preference in Blacks: A paradigm in search of a phenomenon. *Psychological Bulletin, 83,* 1179–1186.

Block, J., & Kremen, A. (1996). IQ and resilience: Conceptual and empirical connections and separateness. *Journal of Personality and Social Psychology, 70,* 349–361.

Boykin, A. W., & Ellison, C. M. (1995). The multiple ecologies of Black youth socialization: An Afrographic analysis. In R. L. Taylor (Ed.), *African American youth: Their social and economic status in the United States* (pp. 93–128). Westport, CT: Praeger.

Brewer, M. B. (1991). The social self: On being the same and different at the same time. *Personality and Social Psychology Bulletin, 17,* 475–482.

Brown v. Board of Education of Topeka, 347 U.S. 494 (1954).

Carver, C. S., Scheier, M. F., & Weintraub, J. K. (1989). Assessing coping strategies: A theoretically based approach. *Journal of Personality and Asocial Psychology, 56,* 267–283.

Chernoff, J. M. (1979). *African rhythm and African sensibility: Aesthetics and social action in African musical idioms.* Chicago: University of Chicago Press.

Clark, K. B., & Clark, M. P. (1947). Racial identification and preference in Negro children. In T. M. Newcomb & E. L. Hartley (Eds.), *Readings in social psychology* (pp. 602–611). New York: Holt.

Cohen, S., Kamarck, T., & Mermelstein, R. (1983). A global measure of perceived stress. *Journal of Health and Social Behavior, 24,* 385–396.

Crocker, J., & Wolfe, C. T. (2001). Contingencies of self worth. *Psychological Review, 108,* 593–623.

Cross, W. E. (1991). *Shades of Black: Diversity in African American identity.* Philadelphia: Temple University Press.

Cross, W. E. (1995). The psychology of nigrescence: Revising the Cross model. In J. G. Ponterotto, J. M. Casas, L. A. Suzuki, & C. M. Alexander (Eds.), *Handbook of multicultural counseling* (pp. 93–122). Thousand Oaks, CA: Sage.

DuBois, W. E. B. (1903). *The souls of Black folk.* Chicago: McClurg.

Fiske, A., Kitayama, S., Markus, H. R., & Nisbett, R. E. (1998). The cultural matrix of social psychology. In D. T. Gilbert, S. T. Fiske, & G. Lindzey (Eds.), *Handbook of social psychology* (Vol. 4, pp. 915–981). New York: McGraw Hill.

Franklin, J. H., & Moss, A. A. (1994). *From slavery to freedom: A history of African Americans* (7th ed.). New York: McGraw Hill.

Hall, E. T. (1983). *The dance of life: The other dimension of time.* Garden City, NY: Anchor Press/Doubleday.

Jahn, J. (1961). *Muntu: An outline of the new African culture.* New York: Grove Press.

Jones, J. M. (1979). Conceptual and strategic issues in the relationship of Black psychology to American social science. In A. W. Boykin, A. J. Franklin, & J. F. Yates (Eds.), *Research directions for Black psychologists* (pp. 390–432). New York: Russell Sage Foundation.

Jones, J. M. (1988). Racism in Black and White: A bicultural model of reaction and evolution. In P. A. Katz & D. A. Taylor (Eds.), *Eliminating racism: Profiles in controversy* (pp. 117–158). New York: Plenum Press.

Jones, J. M. (1997). *Prejudice and racism* (2nd ed.). New York: McGraw Hill.

Jones, J. M. (1999). Cultural racism: The intersection of race and culture in intergroup conflict. In D. A. Prentice & D. T. Miller (Eds.), *Cultural divides: Understanding and overcoming group conflict* (pp. 465–490). New York: Russell Sage Foundation.

Jones, J. M. (2003). TRIOS: A psychological theory of African legacy in American culture. *Journal of Social Issues, 59,* 217–241.

Jones, J. M., & Morris, K. T. (1993). Individual versus group identification as a factor in intergroup racial conflict. In J. Simpson & W. Wood (Eds.), *Conflict between people and peoples* (pp. 170–189). Chicago: Nelson Hall.

Jost, J. T., & Banaji, M. R. (1994). The role of stereotyping in system-justification and the production of false consciousness. *British Journal of Social Psychology, 33,* 1–17.

Kardiner, A., & Ovesey, L. (1951). *The mark of oppression.* New York: Norton.

Kim, Y., & Seidlitz, L. (2002). Spirituality moderates the effect of stress on emotional and physical adjustment. *Personality and Individual Differences, 32,* 1377–1390.

Kohn, P. M., Lafreniere, K., & Gurevich, M. (1990). The inventory of college students' recent life experiences: A decontaminated hassles scale for a special population. *Journal of Behavior Medicine, 13,* 619–630.

Larson, D. B., Swyers, J. P., & McCullough, M. E. (1998). *Scientific research on spirituality and health: A consensus report.* Bethesda, MD: National Institute for Healthcare Research.

Levine, R. E. (1997). *A geography of time.* New York: Basic Books.

Lewin, K. (1943). Defining the "field at a given time." *Psychological Review, 50,* 292–310. (Reprinted in *Field theory in social science: Selected theoretical papers,* pp. 200–211, by D. Cartwright, Ed., 1997, Washington, DC: American Psychological Association)

Lewin, K. (1946). Action research and minority problems. *Journal of Social Issues, 2,* 34–46. (Reprinted in *Resolving social conflicts: Selected papers on group dynamics,* pp. 143–152, G. W. Lewin, Ed., 1997, Washington, DC: American Psychological Association)

Luhtanen, R., & Crocker, J. (1992). A collective self-esteem scale: Self-evaluation of one's social identity. *Personality and Social Psychology Bulletin, 18,* 302–318.

Markus, H. R., & Kitayama, S. (1991). Culture and the self: Implications for cognition, emotion, and motivation. *Psychological Review, 98,* 224–253.

Mbiti, J. S. (1970). *African religions and philosophy.* Garden City, NY: Anchor Doubleday Books.

McGrath, J. E. (Ed.). (1988). *The social psychology of time.* Newbury Park, CA: Sage.

Moemeka, A. A. (1998). Communalism as a fundamental dimension of culture. *Journal of Communication, 48,* 118–141.

Morgan, P. D. (1998). *Slave counterpoint: Black culture in the eighteenth-century Chesapeake and Lowcountry.* Chapel Hill: University of North Carolina Press.

Osborne, J. W. (1995). Academics, self-esteem, and race: A look at the underlying assumptions of the disidentification hypothesis. *Personality and Social Psychology Bulletin, 21,* 449–455.

Oyserman, D., Coon, H. M., & Kimmelmeier, M. (2002). Rethinking individualism and collectivism: Evaluation of theoretical assumptions and meta-analyses. *Psychological Bulletin, 128,* 3–72.

Plessy v. Ferguson. 163 U.S. 537 (1896).

Radloff, L. S. (1977). The CES–D Scale: A self-report depression scale for research in the general population. *Applied Psychological Measurement, 11,* 385–401.

Schwartz, S. H. (1992). Universals in the content and structure of values: Theoretical advances and empirical tests in 20 countries. In M. P. Zanna (Ed.), *Advances in experimental social psychology* (Vol. 24, pp. 1–65). San Diego, CA: Academic Press.

Scott, D. M. (1997). *Contempt and pity: Social policy and the image of the damaged Black psyche, 1880–1996.* Chapel Hill: University of North Carolina Press.

Scott, L. D. (2003). Cultural orientation and coping with perceived discrimination among African American youth. *Journal of Black Psychology, 29,* 235–256.

Sellers, R. M., Rowley, S. A. J., Chavous, T. M., Shelton, J. N., & Smith, M. A. (1997). Multidimensional inventory of Black identity: A preliminary investigation of reliability and construct validity. *Journal of Personality and Social Psychology, 73,* 805–815.

Senghor, L. (1956). *L'esprit de la civilisation ou les lois de la culture Negro-africaine* [The laws of civilization or the laws of Nego–African culture]. Paris: Presence Africaine.

Sidanius, J., & Pratto, F. (1999). *Social dominance: An intergroup theory of social hierarchy and oppression.* New York: Cambridge University Press.

Singelis, T. M. (1994). The measurement of independent and interdependent self-construals. *Personality and Social Psychology Bulletin, 20,* 580–591.

Smedley, A. (1993). *Race in North America: Origin and evolution of a worldview.* Boulder, CO: Westview Press.

Smitherman, G. (1977). *Talkin' and testifyin': The language of Black America.* Detroit, MI: Wayne State University Press.

Sobel, M. (1987). *The world they made together: Black and White values in eighteenth-century Virginia.* Princeton, NJ: Princeton University Press.

Spencer, J. M. (1995). *The rhythms of black folk: Race, religion and Pan-Africanism.* Trenton, NJ: Africa World Press.

Steele, C. M. (1988). The psychology of self-affirmation: Sustaining the integrity of the self. In L. Berkowitz (Ed.), *Advances in experimental social psychology* (Vol. 21, pp. 261–346). San Diego, CA: Academic Press.

Steele, C. M. (1997). A burden of suspicion: How stereotypes shape the intellectual identities and performance of women and African-Americans. *American Psychologist, 52,* 613–629.

Tatum, B. D. (1999). *Why are all the black kids sitting together in the cafeteria.* New York: Basic.

Triandis, H. C. (1994). *Culture and behavior.* New York: McGraw-Hill.

Watson, D., Clark, L. A., & Tellegen, A. (1988). Development and validation of brief measures of positive and negative affect. *Journal of Personality and Social Psychology, 54,* 1063–1070.

Woodward, C. V. (1951). *Origins of the new South, 1877–1913.* Baton Rouge: Louisiana State University Press.

Zaleski, Z. (1994). *Psychology of future time orientation.* Lublin, Poland: Towarzystwo Naukowekul.

Zimbardo, P. G., & Boyd, J. N. (1999). Putting time in perspective: A valid, reliable individual-differences metric. *Journal of Personality and Social Psychology, 77,* 1271–1288.

Part IV

Our Common Destiny

Introduction:
The Context of Culture

Barbara Schecter

The grounds for considering a common destiny are many; the arenas in which a sense of shared purpose needs to be forged are innumerable. For instance, it is still the case that most psychology courses being taught on issues of race and ethnicity are separated from other standard courses in a curriculum, and that this content is often isolated within a course to consist of a special "unit on race." Many academic psychologists, as well as those practicing in clinical and educational settings, still find it difficult to integrate cultural approaches into their ongoing work. This resistance derives from a number of sources, arising both from disciplinary commitments that we hold on to and from confusion and uncertainty about the social and moral implications of some of the claims for a cultural psychology. From a theoretical point of view, the newer cultural psychology (as opposed to the older "cross-cultural" psychology) poses fundamental challenges to some still cherished assumptions at the heart of our discipline. It is very difficult to let go of deeply rooted claims for the individual (isolated from context) as the unit of analysis, for the goal of finding broad underlying principles of behavior, and for conceptualizing development in terms of stages and hierarchies. The challenge of cultural relativism to these widespread, but often unexamined, assumptions has tended in the history of psychology to polarize arguments on various sides of the classic debate over universalism and particularism. In the recent context of psychology, these issues have unfolded in a historical and political context in which a liberal White ideology of ignoring differences (everyone is the same) in the service of goals of political equality has been pitted against an identity politics of difference. These theoretical issues have epistemological and methodological implications. They pose a crisis of interpretation because they raise fundamental questions about the relationship between experience and knowing, and the role of the standpoint of the observer. They point to the need for more ethnographic methods of doing research, as well as the challenge to move beyond "populations of convenience" that reproduce sameness of background.

It is in this context that I, as a developmental psychologist, have come to see the critical importance of teaching a cultural developmental psychology. This requires the integrating of developmental theory with the experiences of children from different cultural backgrounds. The challenge is neither to abandon theory nor to continue to isolate classical theories from cultural concerns in separate academic courses. Students need to be exposed to the idea that all theory is interpretive from the beginning, to the critical view that theories are lenses for understanding human experience, with strengths and weaknesses. Otherwise students reject the role of theoretical knowledge; they see it as irrelevant to their lives.

The pedagogical approach that I have evolved from these concerns is to teach theories of development in dialogue with research, ethnographies, and narrative accounts of children's experiences in different cultural contexts that challenge the theoretical approaches. What does it mean to critique developmental psychology from a multicultural perspective? It means not only to critique the opposition of biology and culture, universal and particular, but more fundamentally to affirm the very notion that we as teachers and researchers have different standpoints. This shifts the critique to the role of subjectivity in all theorizing, to the cultural context of knowledge claims—whose children, which families—or as Delpit (1995) cautioned White psychologists and educators, to reflect on our assumptions about *Other People's Children*. We need to understand the thorough integration of culture and development, that psychological notions of recognition, self-esteem, and identity are cultural issues; or conversely, as Spencer (1990) said, "minority status is an identity issue as well as a societal one" (p. 268).

A critical approach entails asking more differentiated kinds of questions. Sometimes the question that needs to be asked is this: Given the cultural context in which a theory originated, to whom does it apply? For example, when considering psychoanalytic theories, how do these themes apply outside of nuclear, heterosexual, middle-class families? How can the theory be expanded, reinterpreted, revised, to shed light on other family and cultural experiences? Sometimes it is not the professional psychologists who are doing this kind of thinking. Consider Steedman's (1987) reconfiguration of psychoanalytic theory to articulate a psychological subjectivity to working-class life, or Spillers's (1987) application of psychoanalysis to understand aspects of African American experience. Other times, the challenge is to see the question the theorist is asking in a new light, as in the way Ramsey (1998) returned to Piaget's early questions about how children develop their ideas to analyze children's awareness of racial concepts.

We need to be willing to ask the difficult questions of value in which the needs of children may conflict with cultural practices, or to paraphrase Okin's (1999) book: Is multiculturalism always good for children? There may be tensions between the multicultural value of validating diverse cultural practices and the domination of patriarchal or repressive child-rearing practices. How can we discuss these, while being mindful of what Delpit (1995) has called the "benevolent domination of liberal pedagogies?"

The imperative seems great to me to find a way to address these concerns both among ourselves, as psychologists, and with our students of all ages. The risk of continuing not to do so is captured by the comment of the young Haitian niece of a friend of mine on her feelings about school: "I wish they would wake me when they get to me." We need a new kind of theorizing that addresses the challenges discussed above—theorizing that responds to the critiques without abandoning the lives of children in the process, theory that is responsive to a differentiated conception of what "real needs" or "real lives" can mean in different cultural contexts.

References

Delpit, L. (1995). *Other people's children: Cultural conflict in the classroom.* New York: New Press.

Okin, S. M. (1999). *Is multiculturalism bad for women?* Princeton, NJ: Princeton University Press.

Ramsey, P. (1998). *Teaching and learning in a diverse world* (2nd ed.). New York: Teachers College Press.

Spencer, M. B. (1990). Development of minority children: An introduction. *Child Development, 61,* 267–269.

Spillers, H. J. (1987). Mama's baby, Papa's maybe: An American grammar book. *Diacritics, 17*(2), 65–81.

Steedman, C. (1987). *Landscape for a good woman.* New Brunswick, NJ: Rutgers University Press.

11

Immigration and the Color Line

Kay Deaux

The story of immigration in the United States has always been, to a significant measure, a story of color. From the forced migration of slaves in the 17th and 18th centuries to the governmental policies of the 20th century, constructions of race have been both explicit and implicit in defining what this society is and will be. The choice of *line* in my title (acknowledging my debt to DuBois, 1903/ 1976) is a case of "thick" definition. In one sense, line refers to a basis of categorization and demarcation—a boundary, an outline, a limit. From another perspective, *line* suggests procedures, rules, a plan of action, or the party line. All of these meanings are part of the story that I want to tell about immigration.

This chapter focuses on three issues related to immigration and color. First, I review the legislative history and demographics of immigration, with particular attention to the role that race has played. Second, I consider the social construction of race in the United States and how social representations of immigration, most notably the "melting pot," are shaped by ideas about race. Finally, I describe the preliminary results of an empirical project that explores ethnic identification and performance among first- and second-generation Afro-Caribbean immigrants in the United States.

Immigration to the United States: A Historical Overview

The movement of large numbers of Blacks to the United States had its obvious beginning in the slave trade. From the beginning of the slave trade in 1619 until its federal prohibition in 1807, an estimated 8–10 million Africans were shipped to the Americas against their will. The exact number of Africans forcibly brought to the United States can probably never be known; but with two centuries of slave trade and subsequent births, Black persons became a significant minority in the U.S. demographic picture.

By 1751, Benjamin Franklin was already expressing concern that "the number of purely white people in the world is proportionably very small"

This chapter was prepared while the author was a visiting scholar at the Russell Sage Foundation, New York City. The support of the Foundation is gratefully acknowledged.

(quoted in Jacobson, 1998, p. 40). His palette was restricted—even Germans were viewed as "swarthy"—but his preferred balance was clear, wishing that the numbers of Whites be increased. Franklin's hopes were reflected in the 1790 naturalization law, in which the U.S. Congress stipulated that "all free White persons" were entitled to the rights of citizenship, provided they satisfied residency requirements and gave an oath of allegiance, thus excluding Blacks and members of other "non-White" groups (Jacobson, 1998). The definition of Whiteness itself was increasingly questioned during the 19th century, as increased immigration from Southern and Eastern Europe altered the previous conception of White as implying Anglo Saxon origin. In the aftermath of the Civil War, in 1870, Senator Charles Sumner introduced an amendment to strike the word *White* from naturalization policies. His intentions were only partially realized: While people "of the African race or of African descent" were added to the category of those eligible for citizenship, strong anti-Asian sentiments precluded a totally nondiscriminatory bill from passage (Jacobson, 1998).

The beginning of the 20th century marked the beginning of a new migration of Blacks to the United States, this one voluntary and almost entirely from the Caribbean. This is, in fact, the period in which Kenneth Clark migrated with his mother to the United States from the Panama Canal Zone (in 1914). By the early 1920s, somewhere between 5,000 and 8,000 immigrants were arriving each year, and by 1930 the proportion of first- and second-generation Black immigrants to the total population of Blacks in the United States was approximately 1.5% (Kasinitz, 1992). In New York City at this time, West Indians accounted for 25% of the city's Black population (Kasinitz, 2001).

Black immigration rose much more slowly in the period between 1930 and 1965, as did immigration overall, and the percentage of foreign-born Blacks in the United States remained stationery during this time (Kasinitz, 1992). One reason for the general slowdown was the Immigration Act of 1924, which created a quota system, based on national origins and representation in the U.S. population (and conveniently backdated to a reference point of 1890 so that Western European immigrants would be favored). Subsequently, the economic depression made the United States a less attractive destination, and in fact during the period from 1932 to 1937, more West Indian immigrants returned to the Caribbean than entered the United States (Kasinitz, 1992; Massey, 1995). Some West Indians continued to migrate to the United States in subsequent decades, many using British passports to allow them to come in under the British quota. Subsequent legislation in 1952 cut out this colonial loophole, and at the same time retained national quotas, basing them on 1920 proportions (DeLaet, 2000), thus further dampening Afro-Caribbean immigration. But in general, the color of the country changed during the period between 1924 and 1965, proportionately tilting toward Whiteness.

This balance shifted again with the 1965 amendments to the Immigration and Nationality Act. Instigated by President John F. Kennedy prior to his death (Kennedy, 1964), the new amendments eliminated immigration quotas based on national origins that had been in place for more than 40 years, and also removed the ban on Asians. Immigration was not made completely open: There were still caps on total immigration and established preferences for families and for certain occupational categories. Nonetheless, the racial and ethnic biases that were the foundation of the 1924 law were now eliminated (DeLaet, 2000).

The impact of the 1965 policy has been dramatic. In the first decade following implementation of the new policies, immigration to the United States increased by 60% (DeLaet, 2000). Perhaps more significantly, the ethnic distribution changed markedly. In contrast to the European-dominated immigration of the previous decades, Latin America and Asia are the major source of immigrants now. As just one point of comparison, between 1931 and 1940, 66% of immigrants to the United States came from Europe, and only 33% came from Central and South America and from Asia combined. Between 1984 and 1993, in contrast, Europeans accounted for only 10% of immigrants, compared with 54% from the Americas and 33% from Asia (Massey, 1995).

Black immigration, which had been relatively low and steady until 1970, began to rise rapidly following the changes in immigration policy. Between 1970 and 1980, the foreign-born (i.e., first generation) population in the United States more than tripled, from approximately 250,000 in 1970 to more than 800,000 in 1980 (Kasinitz, 1992). By the year 2000, the number of Americans whose immediate ancestry was either Afro-Caribbean or African numbered more than 2 million, accounting for more than 6% of the total Black population in the United States (Logan & Deane, 2003). In New York City, nearly one-third of the Black population was foreign-born in 1998 (Foner, 2001). Although the majority of Black immigrants are from the countries of the Caribbean, the immigration rate from Africa has increased dramatically in recent years, thus further diversifying the nature of the U.S. Black population.

Social Representations of Immigration and Social Constructions of Race

Governmental policies and demographic realities are two elements of the immigration picture. Were these the only elements of importance, there would be little reason for social psychologists to enter the immigration arena. But while important, policies and demography need to take their place alongside other key aspects of the process—aspects that are fundamentally social psychological in nature. I consider two of these social aspects here: first, the social representation of the melting pot and reactions to the use of that representation; and second, more general issues in the social construction of race as related to immigration.

The United States as a Melting Pot

The image of the *melting pot,* a metaphor that dominated discussions of immigration for much of the 20th century (Gleason, 1964), traces its origin to a play by Israel Zangwill first performed in Washington, DC, in October 1908 and published in 1909. Zangwill, though a British citizen himself, dedicated *The Melting Pot* to Theodore Roosevelt, for what he saw as the President's "strenuous struggle against the forces that threaten to shipwreck the great republic" (1909/1994). In symbiotic spirit, President Roosevelt accompanied Zangwill to the Washington opening and enthusiastically declared it a "great play."

The somewhat flowery dedication to Roosevelt reflects the text of the play itself, in which the spirit of music and lofty goals confront the scourge of discrimination and anti-Semitism. Zangwill's hero, a young Russian immigrant who seeks to compose the great symphony, sees music as the transcendent force in a country where "all the races of Europe are melting and re-forming" (p. 33). "America is God's Crucible," he states, as he envisions "the coming superman" that will represent a "fusion of all races" (pp. 33–34).

Zangwill himself was neither an American nor a first-generation immigrant. His parents had emigrated to Britain in the mid-19th century—his father, from Russia, coming to avoid being conscripted into the tsar's army, and his mother arriving from Poland with a cousin, aspiring for a better life—and Zangwill was born in London. Zangwill's dreams of an ideal society seem less driven by the experience of being a second-generation immigrant than by the role that Judaism played in his life. Indeed, the fusion that he most clearly articulated was one between Judaic and Gentile, the evolution of a "new Hebraic man" (Udelson, 1990). At the same time, he believed that similar possibilities existed for people of color: "Even upon the negro the 'Melting Pot' of America will not fail to act in a measure as it has acted on the Red Indian" (Udelson, 1990, p. 289, Footnote 22). Whatever the particular mix, Zangwill viewed America, not Europe, as the site in which a multiethnic, multiracial civilization could emerge (Udelson, 1990).

Zangwill wrote his paean to the spirit of America at the height of immigration to the United States. In the first two decades of the 20th century, immigration increased rapidly and was responsible for something between a third and a half of the total population growth in the United States (Carter & Sutch, 1999). For many, the arrival of hundreds of thousands of (primarily European) immigrants epitomized the Zangwillian dream and the fulfillment of American democratic ideals. For others, however, the rapid influx was seen as a threat to the American way of life, a sentiment that precipitated the passage of the Johnson-Reed Act in 1924.

Political opponents of immigration had their counterparts in academic critics of the melting pot image. The sociologist Henry Pratt Fairchild (1926) was one such voice. Fairchild described a pre-Zangwill era in which the appearance of "tolerant indifference" to immigration masked that fact that "it was not actually welcome" (p. 9). Then, he caustically observed, "came the symbol, like a portent in the heavens" of America as a melting pot (p. 10). The flaw in this symbol, from Fairchild's vantage point, was that it "did not take account of the true nature of group unity"—a unity that in his view is "primarily racial" (p. 21). Although Fairchild allowed that a common nationality might be acquired through common group experience (if socialization is begun early enough), he argued that the hereditary basis of race precluded such a merger. "Racial dissimilarity always constitutes an element of weakness in group life" (p. 79), he proclaimed. For the United States "to remain a stable nation, it must continue to be a white man's country for an indefinite period to come"

(p. 240). Thus, where Zangwill saw the melting pot as an ideal to be achieved, Fairchild regarded it as a "molten mass" that had little to commend it.

The growing influence of the eugenics movement was another counterforce. The argument was made that genetic defects—stereotypically associated with non-White, nonmiddle class—could proliferate and contaminate the good. As stated by Charles Davenport, the first director of the Cold Spring Harbor research station established for the experimental study of evolution, "The idea of a 'melting pot' belongs to a pre-Mendelian age" (Kevles, 1985, p. 47). Madison Grant, then chairman of the New York Zoological Society, chimed in with similar arguments, pointing to Mexico as evidence of the fallacy of the melting pot (Grant, 1921). By blending the blood of Spanish conquerors and native Indian populations, Mexicans evolved as a racial mixture that Grant saw as "now engaged in demonstrating its incapacity for self-government" (p. 17).

Not all objections to the melting pot as a dominant metaphor for immigration were based on racism. Some critiques of the concept came from liberals as well, who questioned the assumptions of homogeneity and the implied abandonment of one's native culture that the term implied. More recently, some writers have suggested that other images are more appropriate to a diverse society, offering terms such as *multicolor mosaic, rainbow coalition,* and *salad bowl* as alternative conceptions. These images are worth study in their own right, but are somewhat tangential to the arguments that I am developing here.

Constructions in Black and White

Just as conceptions of race served as the basis for challenging the desirability of a melting pot, so did they color the views that Americans had of specific immigrant groups. Throughout the 19th and 20th centuries, constructions of Black and of White emerged and framed discussions and actions toward members of various ethnic groups.

Attitudes toward the Irish immigrant is a case in point. During the 19th century, Irish immigration was substantial: approximately 1 million in the first four or five decades and 1.8 million between 1845 and 1855 (Ignatiev, 1995). In his informative volume *How the Irish Became White,* Ignatiev (1995) described how Irish immigrants and Black Americans were often "thrown together," restricted to the same poor neighborhoods and competing for the same low-paying jobs. In the latter endeavors, the Irish were often more successful. In the North, for example, Ignatiev (1995) suggested that Irish immigrants were often willing to work for less money than were free Blacks, an argument consistent with statistics showing that unskilled laboring jobs in New York in 1855 were overwhelmingly held by the Irish (87%), with minor (3%) Black occupation (Ignatiev, 1995). Hiring preferences in the South were sometimes justified in other terms. Frederick Law Olmsted (reported by Ignatiev) cited a stevedore official who favored Irish over Blacks in dangerous dockworker positions: "The niggers are worth too much to be risked here; if the Paddies are knocked overboard, or get their backs broke, nobody loses anything" (Ignatiev, p. 109).

Although the economic realities often favored the Irish, stereotypical images of the two groups frequently merged. The Irish were called "niggers turned inside out" (Ignatiev, 1995, p. 41); Celtic characteristics were said to include "the black tint of the skin" (Jacobson, 1998, p. 48). Blacks in turn were called "smoked Irish" (Ignatiev, 1995, p. 41). Frederick Douglas saw the Irish as doing the "black man's work": "If they cannot rise to the dignity of white men, they show that they can not fall to the degradation of black men" (Ignatiev, 1995, p. 111).

Although the Irish were sometimes viewed as more similar to Black than White in the early years of their U.S. residence, they became, as did Italian and Jewish immigrants, what some have termed "probationary Whites" (Foner, 2000). As the doors of immigration closed to many with the passage of the Johnson-Reed act, references to separate European nationalities or ethnicities became replaced with what Jacobson (1998) called "the ascent of monolithic whiteness" (p. 93). Previously ethnic groups had been measured against a standard of Anglo-Saxon (whereby Italians, Slovaks, and other groups were found wanting); now Caucasian became the White standard.

The language of social science reified distinctions between what were termed the Negroid, Caucasoid, and Mongoloid races—groupings which the late anthropologist Melville Herskovits (1935) said were derived "from common-sense observation as well as from the scientist's classification" (p. 207). The popularity of race as a means of categorization is reflected in the 1935 *Handbook of Social Psychology* (Murchison, 1935), in which chapters are devoted to the social histories of, in order, the Negro, the Red Man, the White Man, and the Yellow Man. In large part, the dominant paradigm shifted, from an emphasis on ethnicity (as exemplified in the work of the Chicago school, perhaps best known through *The Polish Peasant in Europe and America*) to categorization by race. In the race-based scheme, a White-at-the-top hierarchy was evident. In some cases, categorization boiled down to its simplest, dichotomous form, as evidenced in the following comment by a Baptist minister, recounting a history of Chinese Americans in Mississippi (Loewen, 1971):

> "You're either a white man or a nigger, here. Now, that's the whole story. When I first came to the Delta, the Chinese were classed as nigras. And now they are called whites?"
> "That's right!"

As Sidanius and Pratto (1999) have shown, this hierarchy of color continues to the present day, with Whites accorded the highest status, Blacks and Latinos lowest, and Asians in between. It is these constructions of race, then, that form the background into which contemporary immigrants enter the United States.

Afro-Caribbean Immigration

As noted earlier, immigration from the countries of the Caribbean region has been substantial, beginning early in the 20th century, leveling off during the middle decades of the century, and increasing sharply with the 1965 changes in immigration policy. These population shifts have forced a new way of thinking about immigration, away from traditional assimilation models to more nuanced explanations. Whereas previous analyses of immigration assumed a static host culture and a gradual assimilation of immigrants into the dominant society (what Sanchez, 2000, termed "a bipolar model of opposing cultures"), the hierarchical culture of race in the United States has made those models problematic as a description of the course of new immigrants. Black immigrants from the Caribbean regions could not become White, as generations of European immigrants did before. Thus we see the introduction of new terms, such as *segmented assimilation,* to describe differing courses of assimilation and confrontation with the U.S. culture (Zhou, 1999).

The segmented assimilation hypothesis describes two trajectories that may be alternatives to the traditional path of upward mobility and assimilation. One of these is an oppositional mode, in which the immigrant identifies with the urban underclass. A second is the retention of the culture of origin. It is these two different paths that have framed much of the recent discussion of Afro-Caribbean immigration to the United States.

Many scholars have pointed to the West Indians as a success story in immigration, typically contrasting their success with the allegedly less successful outcomes of native-born African Americans (rather than against other immigrant groups). Witness this statement of Glazer and Moynihan (1964): "The ethos of the West Indians, in contrast to that of the Southern Negro, emphasized saving, hard work, investment and education" (p. 35). And: "But the West Indians' most striking difference from the Southern Negroes was their greater application to business, education, buying homes, and in general advancing themselves" (p. 35). Chiswick (1979) concluded that foreign-born Blacks who had been in the United States for at least 10 years had higher annual earnings than native-born Blacks. Model's (1995) examination of first- and second-generation English-speaking West Indians in New York, using census data from 1970, 1980, and 1990, found that West Indian men and women have higher labor force participation rates than native-born African Americans. Similarly, Kalmijn (1996) found that Black immigrants and their descendants from English-speaking Caribbean countries (e.g., Barbados, Jamaica, and Trinidad-Tobago) were more educated, had higher prestige occupations, and earned more than Black Americans. While there continues to be some debate as to whether West Indians have an earnings advantage over Black Americans, the employment and occupational advantage of West Indians appear to be reliable (Waters, 1999b).

Numerous sociological theories have been proposed to account for these differences, invoking possible causes such as the selectivity effects of immigration (Portes & Rumbaut, 1992), employer discrimination that favors foreign-born Blacks (Kasinitz & Rosenberg, 1999; Waters, 1999b), and cultural differences between West Indians and Black Americans (Reid, 1939). Although some or all of these explanations may be partially valid, they leave untouched a number of more social psychological questions. One key issue concerns ethnic identification: How do Afro-Caribbean immigrants think about themselves, and how do they negotiate their ethnic identities in the context of the representations of color that are prominent in the United States?

Sociologist Milton Vickerman (2001) suggested that prior to the 1960s, most Black immigrants from the Caribbean saw their primary choice as one of becoming African American. More recently, with a larger population of West Indians in areas such as New York City, he argued that it is easier for West Indians to maintain their ethnic identity. This difference may be one of emphasis rather than kind. For example, in his oral history Kenneth Clark (1976) himself referred to tensions between African Americans and West Indians in the 1920s and 1930s. Similarly Paula Marshall's 1959 *Brown Girl, Brownstones* account of Barbadian immigrants in Brooklyn in the early part of the 20th century suggests a strongly maintained Caribbean-based identity among some members of the neighborhood (Marshall, 1959/1981).

Whatever the past condition, there is ample evidence today that immigrants from the Caribbean vary in their subjective ethnic identification. Mary Waters (1994, 1999a, 2001) has documented three identity paths among West Indian adolescents in New York City: (a) to identify as an (Afro)American; (b) to identify as an ethnic American, for example, a Jamaican American; and (c) to identify more generally as an immigrant, not dealing specifically with racial and ethnic categories. Approximately equal proportions of adolescents in her Brooklyn sample chose the first and second options. Somewhat fewer teenagers chose the third option, and these were primarily quite recent immigrants.

Ethnic Identification and Stereotype Threat

These potential variations in subjective identification, as well as possible differences between generations, led my colleagues and I (Deaux, Steele, Eberhardt, Waters, & Thomas, 1999) to speculate on the impact that stereotype threat, as documented by Steele and his colleagues in earlier work (Steele, 1997; Steele & Aronson, 1995), might have on West Indian immigrants of different generations and different subjective identifications. Would it be the case, we speculated, that maintaining an ethnic identification as a West Indian would protect or buffer the immigrant from the climate of negative stereotypes that associate Black Americans with inferior academic performance? On the other side, would subjective identification as an African American make the immigrant susceptible to the same effects previously demonstrated among native-born American Blacks? I should clarify that knowledge of the stereotype is not the issue here—indeed, we assume that both groups are aware of the stereotypes that exist in the United States linking color to expected performance. Rather, the difference lies in the degree to which those stereotypes are believed to be applicable to oneself, a function of one's subjectively determined ethnic identification.

The sample we selected for testing our hypotheses were first- and second-generation West Indian college students enrolled in public colleges in New York City. As might be expected, subjective identification and generation are associated: First-generation students (who, on the average, had come to the United States when they were 13 years old, but who in our sample were approximately the same in age and presumably similar in socioeconomic class to the second-generation students) are more likely to define themselves as West Indian than are second-generation students. Similarly, time spent in the United States and subjective identification are also related ($r = .41, p < .001, N = 243$), such that longer time in the United States is associated with a greater tendency to identify, at least in part, as African American.

I use the term "in part" because ethnic identification does not always have sharp boundaries. On an open-ended question about ethnic identity, respondents often provided two or more labels, including nationality of origin, Afro-Caribbean, African American, and/or Black. In the quantitative scale measure that we used, respondents were asked to place themselves on a dimension varying from "definitely West Indian" to "definitely African American," with "equally West Indian and African American" as a midpoint. On this measure, the overall mean indicated a tendency to label as West Indian, though with many respondents moving toward an incorporation of African American. Specifically, 63% of our sample identified as "definitely" or "more" West Indian; 25% considered themselves equally West Indian and African American, and only 12% said that they were "more" or "definitely" African American. These proportions, it should be noted, show fewer shifting toward African American identification than Waters found in her sample of adolescents. It suggests that the differences in ethnic labeling may be associated with different academic pathways, possibly linked to differences in educational opportunity and socio-economic status that Waters (1994) reported.

In addition to assessing a variety of demographic and attitudinal measures in an initial questionnaire phase, we brought back a subset of the students to participate in a standard stereotype threat experiment. In brief, the major experimental condition involved describing the test that the participants were asked to perform as either diagnostic of their ability or as nondiagnostic. According to the model of stereotype threat, designating a test as diagnostic will trigger stereotypes related to performance in that domain (in this case, an exam based on items from the GRE verbal test), and performance will, as a consequence, be worse for those who believe the stereotype to be relevant to them. In contrast, if the stereotype is not relevant or if the test is not believed to be diagnostic of ability, performance will not be affected (and in some cases, will be superior to a control group). Thus, it was our prediction that students who were second-generation immigrants and who identified more strongly as African American would be more likely to show the negative effects of stereotype threat, performing worse when the test was considered diagnostic than when it was nondiagnostic. In contrast, first-generation immigrants and those who identified primarily as West Indian would be less likely to have their performance hampered and should show no decrement when a test was described as diagnostic.

Figure 11.1 shows the findings, in terms of the number of correct answers on the GRE-like test of verbal skills, of first- and second-generation students in the two conditions. The interaction between generation and diagnostic condition is significant, $F(1, 67) = 4.59$, $p < .05$. When we categorized participants solely on the basis of ethnic identification, the pattern was the same although not statistically significant at conventional levels (the consequence of having considerably less power in the latter analysis). Thus, as the means suggest, first-generation West Indian immigrants are protected in some way from the impact of stereotype threat, even though they are no less aware of the stereotypes than are second-generation immigrants. And indeed, when faced with a

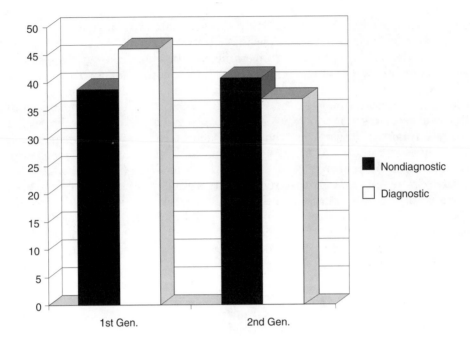

Figure 11.1. Performance of first-generation (1st Gen.) and second-generation (2nd Gen.) West Indian students under diagnostic and nondiagnostic conditions (percentage correct).

challenge that the diagnostic instructions seem to provide, they do better than in the neutral condition. In contrast, second-generation immigrants (though still vacillating between identification as African American and West Indian in our sample) show the pattern of stereotype threat effects that Steele and his colleagues have observed previously in samples of African Americans.

What do these results tell us? First, there is a first-generation story here, one that may be true of any immigrant group that feels stigmatized or challenged by attitudes in the host country. When confronted with a diagnostic challenge, first-generation students perform noticeably better than in more neutral conditions. The second-generation West Indian story is a different one. In moving more closely toward identification with native-born African Americans, West Indian immigrants appear to now be susceptible to the negative images that associate Blacks with decreased performance. Although in the United States only 13 years longer than the first-generation immigrants (the years from birth to age 13, on the average), these second-generation students have already begun to show the behaviors previously associated with African Americans and the culture of low expectations.

Questions remain as to exactly what accounts for the generational difference. Although we found similar but nonsignificant results for the effect of ethnic identification on performance, covarying identification did not substantially weaken the generation effect. Other differences between first- and second-generation immigrants need to be considered. Some of these have emerged, although their specific relationship to the stereotype threat effects has not been established. For example, second-generation West Indians were not as positive in their assessment of society's view of West Indians as were first-generation students. Thus, while both immigrant groups believed that people view West Indians more favorably than African Americans, the relative advantage of West Indians does not appear as great to second-generation immigrants. Further, when evaluating the positivity of their own ethnic identity as well as the perception of others' evaluation of that identity (assessed by the Private Regard and Public Regard subscales of the Luhtanen and Crocker [1992] Collective Self-Esteem measure), second-generation immigrants were less favorable toward their group than were first-generation immigrants. Additional research is needed to probe these connections further. As of now, however, it is clear that generalizations about West Indian immigrants, devoid of contextual analysis, are unwarranted.

Conclusions

What is the line on color and immigration in the United States today, as derived from the experience of immigrants from countries of the Caribbean? As Waters (2001) concluded, "Analysis of the experience of West Indians in the United States shows how rapidly structure affects culture" (p. 207). To this I would add, structure and culture rapidly affect individual beliefs and behaviors as well. The differences between first and second generation, here measured in terms of only a few years, provide a vivid illustration of how experiences with American racism can influence definitions and actions of self.

On a more optimistic note, one might hope that the increased Black immigration to the United States will provide the occasion for a rethinking of what Blackness (and indeed, what color more generally) might mean. Vickerman (2001) suggested that "the meeting of contending West Indian and American conceptions of race is helping to *slowly* erode the traditional monolithic conception of blackness" (p. 237). Increasing immigration from Africa as well as from the Caribbean may force a reconceptualization of what it means to be Black and what it means to be White—neither to be defined by "one drop of blood." The further hope is that this reconceptualization will not pit one Black group against another, vying for higher placement on the status hierarchy, but rather will change constructions of Black and White in ways that reflect more complexity and more justice for all.

References

Carter, S. B., & Sutch, R. (1999). Historical perspectives on the economic consequences of immigration into the United States. In C. Hirschman, P. Kasinitz, & J. DeWind (Eds.), *The handbook of international migration: The American experience* (pp. 319–341). New York: Russell Sage Foundation.

Chiswick, B. R. (1979). The economic progress of immigrants: Some apparently universal patterns. In W. Fellner (Ed.), *Contemporary economic problems* (pp. 357–399). Washington, DC: American Enterprise Institute.

Clark, K. B. (1976). *The reminiscences of Kenneth B. Clark* (Interviews conducted by Ed Edwin). New York: Columbia University Oral History Research Office.

Deaux, K., Steele, C., Eberhardt, J., Waters, M., & Thomas, E. (1999, September). *Ethnic identification and stereotype threat: The case of West Indians* (Proposal submitted to Russell Sage Foundation). New York: City University of New York, Graduate Center.

DeLaet, D. (2000). *U.S. immigration policy in an age of rights.* Westport, CT: Praeger.

Dubois, W. E. B. (1976*). The souls of Black folk.* New York: Knopf. (Original work published 1903)

Fairchild, H. P. (1926). *The melting-pot mistake.* Boston: Little, Brown.

Foner, N. (2000). *From Ellis Island to JFK: New York's two great waves of immigration.* New Haven, CT: Yale University Press.

Foner, N. (2001). Introduction: West Indian migration to New York: An overview. In N. Foner (Ed.), *Islands in the city: West Indian migration to New York* (pp. 1–22). Berkeley: University of California Press.

Glazer, N., & Moynihan, D. P. (1964). *Beyond the melting pot.* Cambridge, MA: MIT Press and Harvard University Press.

Gleason, P. (1964). The melting pot: Symbol of fusion or confusion? *American Quarterly, 16*(1), 20–46.

Grant, M. (1921). *The passing of the great race* (4th ed., Rev.). New York: Scribner's.

Herskovits, M. J. (1935). Social history of the Negro. In C. Murchison (Ed.), *A handbook of social psychology* (Vol. 1, pp. 207–267). New York: Russell & Russell.

Ignatiev, N. (1995). *How the Irish became White.* New York: Routledge.

Jacobson, M. F. (1998). *Whiteness of a different color: European immigrants and the alchemy of race.* Cambridge, MA: Harvard University Press.

Kalmijn, M. (1996). The socioeconomic assimilation of Caribbean American Blacks. *Social Forces, 74,* 911–930.

Kasinitz, P. (1992). *Caribbean New York: Black immigrants and the politics of race.* Ithaca, NY: Cornell University Press.

Kasinitz, P. (2001). Invisible no more? West Indian Americans in the social scientific imagination. In N. Foner (Ed.), *Islands in the city: West Indian migration to New York* (pp. 257–275). Berkeley: University of California Press.

Kasinitz, P., & Rosenberg, J. (1996). Missing the connection: Social isolation and employment on the Brooklyn waterfront. *Social Problems, 43,* 180–197.

Kennedy, J. F. (1964). *A nation of immigrants.* New York: Harper & Row.

Kevles, D. J. (1985). *In the name of eugenics: Genetics and the uses of human heredity.* New York: Alfred A. Knopf.

Loewen, J. W. (1971). *The Mississippi Chinese: Between Black and White.* Cambridge, MA: Harvard University Press.

Logan, J. R., & Deane, G. (2003). Black diversity in metropolitan America. Retrieved January 7, 2004 from http://mumford1.dyndns.org/cen2000/report.html

Luhtanen, R., & Crocker, J. (1992). A collective self-esteem scale: Self-evaluation of one's social identity. *Personality and Social Psychology Bulletin, 18,* 302–318.

Marshall, P. (1981). *Brown girl, brownstones.* New York: Feminist Press. (Original work published 1959)

Massey, D. S. (1995). The new immigration and ethnicity in the United States. *Population and Development Review, 21,* 631–652.

Model, S. (1995). West Indian prosperity: Fact or fiction? *Social Problems, 42,* 535–553.

Murchison, C. (Ed.). (1935). *A handbook of social psychology* (Vol. 1). New York: Russell & Russell.

Portes, A., & Rumbaut, R. (1992). *Immigrant America.* Berkeley: University of California Press.

Reid, I. D. A. (1939). *The Negro immigrant: His background, characteristics and social adjustment, 1899–1937.* New York: Columbia University Press.

Sanchez, G. J. (2000). Race and immigration history. In N. Foner, R. G. Rumbault, & S. J. Gold (Eds.), *Immigration research for a new century* (pp. 54–59). New York: Russell Sage Foundation.

Sidanius, J., & Pratto, F. (1999). *Social dominance: An intergroup theory of social hierarchy and oppression.* Cambridge, England: Cambridge University Press.

Steele, C. M. (1997). A threat in the air: How stereotypes shape intellectual identity and performance. *American Psychologist, 52,* 613–629.

Steele, C. M., & Aronson, J. (1995). Stereotype threat and the intellectual test performance of African-Americans. *Journal of Personality and Social Psychology, 69,* 797–811.

Udelson, J. H. (1990). *Dreamer of the ghetto: The life and works of Israel Zangwill.* Tuscaloosa: University of Alabama Press.

Vickerman, M. (2001). Tweaking a monolith: The West Indian immigrant encounter with "Blackness." In N. Foner (Ed.), *Islands in the city: West Indian migration to New York* (pp. 237–256). Berkeley: University of California Press.

Waters, M. C. (1994). Ethnic and racial identities of second-generation Black immigrants in New York City. *International Migration Review, 28,* 795–820.

Waters, M. C. (1999a). *Black identities: West Indian immigrant dreams and American realities.* Cambridge, MA and New York: Harvard University Press and Russell Sage Foundation.

Waters, M. C. (1999b). West Indians and African Americans at work: Structural differences and cultural stereotypes. In F. Bean & S. Bell-Rose (Eds.), *Immigration and opportunity* (pp. 194–227). New York: Russell Sage Foundation.

Waters, M. C. (2001). Growing up West Indian and African American: Gender and class differences in the second generation. In N. Foner (Ed.), *Islands in the city: West Indian migration to New York* (pp. 193–215). Berkeley: University of California Press.

Zangwill, I. (1994). *The melting pot: Drama in four acts.* New York: Ayer Co. (Original work published 1909)

Zhou, M. (1999). Segmented assimilation: Issues, controversies, and recent research on the new second generation. In C. Hirschman, P. Kasinitz, & J. DeWind (Eds.), *The handbook of international migration: The American experience* (pp. 196–211). New York: Russell Sage Foundation.

12

Interobjectivity and the Enigma of Third-Order Change

Fathali M. Moghaddam

Each generation of scholar-activists seeking to change society toward greater justice is confronted by the particular challenges inherent in their historical era. The type of societal change possible is circumscribed by the characteristics of the context, ranging from a context that fully supports equality of opportunities to a context that fully supports inequalities. Kenneth Clark and his generation of scholar-activists struggled to level the playing field in the context of *first-order change,* in which intergroup inequalities were justified by both formal law and the informal normative system. Their monumental efforts transformed the context to one allowing for *second-order change,* in which formal law has been reformed to ban inequality of opportunities on the basis of group membership, but the informal normative system still allows and in some cases even supports unequal treatment. The contemporary and future challenge is to create the context of *third-order change,* in which equal treatment is supported in both formal law and the informal normative system and a true meritocracy thrives (my classification of change builds on that of Watzlawick, Weakland, & Fisch, 1974). Thus, third-order change represents an ideal, not yet realized by major societies, in which both formal and informal law support equality of opportunity for all individuals.

Violent revolutions, massive collective movements, enormous educational programs—so far even seemingly monumental efforts to create the context for third-order change have failed. Twenty-five hundred years after Plato outlined a meritocratic society in *The Republic,* the enigma of third-order change still confronts scholar-activists (clearly, I see Plato's *Republic* as more open than do some of its critics, such as Popper, 1945/1966). Our actual situation is still far closer to the perpetual and universal inequalities postulated by Pareto (1935) than to fulfilling true meritocracy. Given that Clark and his generation helped to reform *black-letter law,* the formal laws of the land, why has it proved so difficult to also reform the normative system that regulates behavior in everyday life? Why is it so difficult to implement the law and put meritocracy into practice? My objective in this chapter is to take an albeit modest step toward addressing this issue and thus help to better understand the enigma of third-order change.

As part of my assessment, I introduce the concept of *interobjectivity,* the understandings that are shared within and between groups about social reality (Moghaddam, 2003), an example being understandings shared within and between African American and White American groups. Part of such understandings are stereotypes, values, and the like. Interobjectivity serves as a context for interpersonal relationships and the understandings individuals have of one another. Relations between individual African Americans and individual White Americans are shaped by interobjectivity, both what the groups share and how they differ in terms of objectifications of the world.

I begin by highlighting the continuing gap between formal black-letter law and the normative system, particularly in the treatment of minorities. Next, I distinguish between two fundamentally different types of psychology, and why traditional psychology has failed to address third-order change. Then, in the longest section, I argue that on the one hand, psychology is extremely well positioned to contribute to progress toward great justice and third-order change. This is because some fundamental human rights are psychological prior to being reflected in formal law. On the other hand, in practice psychology has not been able to contribute to progress toward third-order change because of the historic biases and limitations in psychological research. Finally, I refer to a new cultural theory of societal change to help better understand the enigma of third-order change.

Although Clark's work and this discussion are set in the context of North America, the enigma of third-order change confronts all human societies. The exportation of Western psychology to non-Western societies (Moghaddam, 1990), and the more recent growth of indigenous psychological research in non-Western societies (Carr & Schumaker, 1996), have raised expectations that psychology should contribute to national and international progress (Moghaddam, Bianchi, Daniels, & Harré, 1999), and particularly the equal treatment of minorities (Moghaddam, 1999; Moghaddam & Crystal, 1997). As with Clark's struggle, this discussion should be seen in the world context rather than just the U.S. context.

A note of caution is required at the outset. As part of their attempts to maintain the status quo and derail reform efforts, segregationists argued against Clark's position during the course of the *Brown* trial to the effect that it is useless to change formal law, because informal behaviors will remain the same (Jackson, 2001). This is obviously an excuse to prevent needed reforms. However, a central theme of my argument is that the reform of formal law is necessary but not sufficient, and that it is also essential to transform the informal ways of doing things and interobjectivity, the worldviews that people share within and across groups.

The Persisting Gap Between Black-Letter Law and Actual Behavior

Kenneth Clark and his generation of scholar-activists helped to reform black-letter law, so that legally, at least, all U.S. citizens now enjoy equality of opportunity in most domains. However, in many instances actual behavior has not been changed in line with black-letter law. Unfortunately, one does not have to look far to find examples of this gap in the United States. A few such cases, such as the Rodney King beating in Los Angeles and the Abner Louima torture in a Brooklyn police station, gain media attention and become widely known. But far less attention is given to more systematic institutionalized violations of black-letter law in the United States (Lott & Maluso, 1995), such as the use of the Astun belt, through which correctional officers can inflict a 50,000 volt shock to prisoners through remote activation from hundreds of feet away. Commenting on the increasing use of stun belts in the United States, the Executive Director of Amnesty International USA has argued, "Zapping a prisoner wearing a stun belt . . . is no less cruel, inhuman or degrading than sodomizing a suspect with a stick inside a police station" (Amnesty International USA, 1999). The stun belt is part of a new high-tech prison industry, holding about 2 million prisoners, disproportionally made up of ethnic minorities, which is becoming more privatized in some U.S. states. Private investors have found that the expanding U.S. prison system yields high returns, and a question comes to mind about conflicts of interest: Will the profit motive lead investors to push for a tougher "war on crime" so that the prisons they have invested in remain fully occupied? Even if we neglect such more subtle injustices, the more blatant ones stare us in the face in the U.S. justice system, such as the systematic abuse and execution of minorities (e.g., see Amnesty International, 1998; Bright, 1995).

As the only world superpower, the United States has more opportunities than any other country to influence intergroup relations and justice globally, whether it be by setting an example for others to follow or by directly applying political and economic pressure on other countries. More efforts need to be made to succeed using the first strategy, so that by improving its domestic justice record the United States can set a better example. Psychologists can contribute to this effort by examining and highlighting the experiences of those segments of U.S. society that experience violations of black-letter law. But a central characteristic of traditional psychology has limited the impact of psychological research in the justice arena. Next, I elaborate on this point by clarifying between two fundamentally different traditions in psychology, and the dominance of a research tradition that leads to the neglect of third-order change.

The Psychologies of Performance Capacity and Performance Style

From its beginning, scientific psychology has incorporated two fundamentally different traditions, each focused on two very different types of performance: *performance capacity,* how well isolated individuals do things based on their biological makeup, and *performance style,* the ways in which behavior is carried out through interactions with others and the meanings ascribed to phenomena. The dominant tradition in psychology has been concerned with performance capacity; performance style has received scant attention. This is in large part because of the model of science adopted in psychology, a positivist model that seeks to establish causal relations (Moghaddam & Harré, 1995). Indeed, behavior in the realm of performance capacity is best explained through a causal model: Biological characteristics causally determine aspects of behavior. For example, in the case of the patient H.M., neurosurgery removed parts of his hippocampus and associated regions, leading to an inability to add new information to his long-term store (see Milner, 1966). The lesion caused a change in memory functioning.

The tradition of research on performance capacity is strongly associated with the experimental laboratory; studies are conducted under controlled conditions, and independent variables (causes) are manipulated to test their impact on dependent variables (effects). The classic paradigm for such research was established in the 19th century (see Thorne & Henley, 2001), by Wundt (1832–1920) in thought and imagery, Fechner (1801–1887) in psychophysics, Ebbinghaus (1850–1908) in memory, among others, and focused on the performance of isolated individuals. For example, although Ebbinghaus used himself as the main participant in his research, creating more than 2,300 nonsense syllables to study his own remembering and forgetting, it was still his performance as an isolated person, and not in interactions with others, that remained his focus. Also, and very important, Ebbinghaus attempted to exclude meaning from his studies, and his use of nonsense syllables, rather than meaningful words, was one means of achieving this goal (subsequent research showed that people ascribe meaning to nonsense syllables, thus rendering them meaningful).

Research in the performance capacity tradition has given us valuable information about the range of abilities of individuals. For example, young adults can see light waves ranging from about 400 to 700 nanometers (nm) and have a short-term memory of about seven plus or minus two bits of information (Kalat, 2002). Information about performance capacity is particularly important in applied psychology, such as in the areas of education, health, and industry. However, performance capacity tells us nothing important about the meaning people ascribe to life experiences, such as those in the domain of justice.

Behavior in the realm of performance style, on the other hand, is best explained through a normative model and with reference to interobjectivity: Individuals behave appropriately according to one normative system rather than others. For example, in the domain of justice, it is performance style and interobjectivity that has primacy. Even when behavior in the realm of justice looks as if it is based on rigid cognitive mechanisms within isolated individuals, on closer examination the role of dynamic, socially constructed and collaboratively upheld meanings is revealed to be central. Consider, for example, Steele's research program on stereotype threat (Steele, 1997; see also chap. 4, this volume). The basic paradigm involves individuals being tested in the exam tradition under two conditions: In Condition 1 a detrimental stereotype is introduced pertaining to a particular group of participants (e.g., Women are not good at mathematics), but this stereotype is absent in Condition 2. The findings show that the presence of a stereotype detrimentally affects the performance of the participants belonging to the target threatened group (e.g., women) in Condition 1. How are we to explain this finding?

It is incorrect to interpret Steele's findings in terms of performance capacity and a causal model: Stereotype threats did not causally determine behavior, at least not in the sense of what Aristotle refers to as efficient causation, wherein the cause precedes the effect it produces. Participants in Steele's study, as in all studies in the realm of performance style, can and do sometimes behave differently, following alternative normative systems. Thus, not all of them are influenced by stereotype threat in the same manner.

Stereotypes are collaboratively constructed and collectively upheld; they are part of a shared meaning system "in the air," external to the individual. They are part of interobjectivity, based on collective processes. Stereotypes existed before the arrival of an individual and continue to exist after an individual has departed. Although stereotypes can and often are appropriated by individuals, their survival does not depend on particular individuals. They survive in discourse and communications generally, and that is in part why they are so powerful.

Like all aspects of performance style, stereotypes concern meaning and are integral to meaning systems in the larger society. Through such meaning systems, individuals may come to unconsciously hold negative views of ethnic minorities, and such negative evaluations could be correlated with higher activities in certain parts of the brain, such as the amygdala (see Phelps et al., 2000). However, it would obviously be a mistake to view the role of the brain in this case as causal, because stereotypes about groups are socially constructed and collectively sustained.

Similarly, human rights and duties are part of performance style, intricately interwoven in the way we do things and the meanings we give to different aspects of the world. I argue that some elementary human rights and duties are derived from universal features of human social relations. Such social relations are particularly important from a psychological perspective, because they suggest that at least some basic human rights and duties are psychological prior to being formalized in black-letter law.

Exploring the Psychological Roots of Human Rights

A major proposition of this chapter is that the political and legal concepts of some fundamental rights, as well as some fundamental duties, have their origins in certain psychological characteristics of human beings, and more specifically in *primitive social relations,* or the social relations that have to be present for even a rudimentary human society to function (Moghaddam, 2000). I elaborate on this proposition by discussing examples of primitive social relations, the cultural interpretation of such relations as rights and duties, the cultural transmission of normative rights and duties, and the evolution of legislated rights and duties.

Although I focus primarily on the psychological nature of primitive social relations, it is important to point out that they are both social and psychological. Primitive social relations are social in the sense that they are part of the normative system of norms, rules, values, and so on that inform individuals about how they should behave. Thus, for example, the norm in most societies is to generally behave in a trustworthy rather than an untrustworthy manner; this is taken to be the correct way of doing things. Primitive social relations are integral to interobjectivity and exist prior to the arrival of an individual, and they persist after an individual leaves the social scene. However, primitive social relations are psychological in that they become appropriated by individuals, accepted by most people in most situations as the way things should be done, and fundamentally influence thinking and action. For example, rules regulating trust are appropriated by individuals and come to influence thought and action in the details of daily life. In this way primitive social relations are psychological and integral to individual thought and action.

Primitive Social Relations

During the course of human evolution, biological and cultural factors have interacted to influence human survival. My focus here is on certain cultural factors, primitive social relations, which undoubtedly appeared early (Megany, 1995) and well before the beginnings of language about 150,000 years ago. Primitive social relations include styles of perceiving the world, such as the social categorization processes through which we group the social world, in ways such as "us and them," "young and old," "men and women," "Black and White," and so on. Experimental evidence suggests that there are certain continuities between how we categorize the nonsocial world and the social world, one such continuity being the tendency for between-groups differentiation and within-group homogeneity to follow categorization (see Moghaddam, 2002, chap. 4). That is, once a set of items are placed in two categories, X and Y, then there is a tendency for perceivers to exaggerate differences between X and Y and to minimize differences within X and Y. This occurs irrespective of whether the items categorized are social (people) or nonsocial (e.g., lines of different lengths). This implies that the act of categorization takes place, at least in some respects, at a superordinate level that embraces the relationships we have with both social and nonsocial phenomena.

Another example of primitive social relations is status hierarchies, which have been found to be inherent in most human societies, although the degree to which, and the basis of, status differentiation differs markedly across cultures. Although there are cultures in which the concept of group leader as it exists in modern societies does not exist (see Middleton & Tait, 1958), differential evaluation of group members and the ascription of unequal status on that basis, albeit in an informal manner, is found even in "communal" societies.

The objective of this chapter is not to conduct an exhaustive survey of possible primitive social relations but to explore in a more in-depth manner two specific examples of such phenomena: turn-taking and trust. The main reason for focusing on these two examples is that they have particularly central roles in all human social life, and it is difficult to conceive of any other primitive social relations that might be more important, either in contemporary societies or in the long evolution of human life. In what follows, I argue that trust and turn-taking have been absolutely essential to human survival. Of course, I am not equating survival with progress; just because some aspect of culture helps a group to survive does not imply improvement. Television evangelists, floaters of junk bonds, creators of violent video-games, and many others can thrive and multiply in given ecological conditions, but this does not necessarily represent progress.

Turn-Taking

Turn-taking is an integral feature of human social relations, not only verbal and nonverbal communications but also all forms of activities involving social interactions. Researchers from diverse scientific backgrounds have highlighted the pervasiveness of turn-taking and the transmission of appropriate cultural "rules of politeness" to infants and young children (e.g., DeLong, 1977; Eibl-Eibesfeldt, 1989). Nursing infants learn to take turns in sucking and resting, helped by the use mothers make of the infants' sensitivity to categories of speech to regulate behavior (Eimas, 1985). The centrality of turn-taking is not surprising, because without some basic level of turn-taking, communications would not be possible and group functioning would become less efficient.

One way to highlight the central role of turn-taking in social relations is to examine the rules, norms, and other aspects of informal normative systems that are central to interobjectivity and regulate social relationships, and rights and duties more specifically. An example is a practice that is pervasive in many traditional cultures, and known in China as *Guanxixue,* "the exchange of gifts, favors, and banquets; the cultivation of personal relationships and networks of mutual dependence; and the manufacturing of obligations and indebtedness" (Yang, 1994, p. 6). The centrality of Guanxixue practices derives from "the primacy and binding power of personal relationships and their importance in meeting the needs and desires of everyday life" (Yang, 1994, p. 6). For instance, a company employee learns that the son of his boss is ill and needs a certain hard-to-find medication. The employee scours the city and nearby areas and finally after 3 days he finds the needed medicine and takes it to his boss's house. The employee has now created an obligation that the boss must repay. The power of Guanxixue is in the necessity Chinese people feel to take turns in doing favors: Once an obligation has been created, it acts as a first step in a series of exchanges, with the network of those involved possibly becoming much larger.

Interobjectivity implies that those who become involved in Guanxixue relationships automatically acquire duties and rights, independent of their personal wishes. Yang (1994) and others have cited numerous examples of a person being tricked into accepting a favor or gift, but nevertheless having to meet their duties based on obligations associated with Guanxixue. The boss who is tricked into accepting a gift from an employee is duty-bound to approve a request for time off, just as the employee acquires a right to ask for the time off because of the obligations created. In this way, Guanxixue cuts through official ways of doing things and enmeshes people belonging to all status levels in a turn-taking process.

Of course, I am not suggesting that turn-taking is always or even often associated with democratic processes. We have known for some time that those who enjoy higher status tend to initiate and to end conversations (Brown, 1966). Inequalities of power characterize all major societies, and the more powerful typically are more in control of communications processes and outcomes. However, even when relationships are unequal, turn-taking has to be present at a basic level. Consider, for example, a teacher talking with a 6-year-old first-grader. The teacher will tend to initiate, direct, and end the conversation. However, the 6-year-old will still enjoy turns at saying things, otherwise the conversation would break down, and the child would typically be very quick to protest "It's my turn to speak!"

Although Guanxixue relationships are fairly malleable, in some societies systems of obligations are created that are far more stable, but still have turn-taking at their center. For example, Grinker's (1994) study of the Lese and the Efe (Pygmy) peoples in northeastern Zaire explores life-long partnerships between two people with seemingly very different characteristics, a "union of opposites." The Lese are farmers, the Efe are foragers and hunters; they speak distinct but mutually intelligible languages and have customs and rituals that are in major ways different. However, a sufficient level of interobjectivity allows for reciprocal relations. Through partnerships, which are for the most part hereditary ("a Lese man inherits the son of his father's Efe partner as his own," Grinker, 1994, p. 1), Lese and Efe men collaborate with one another in a wide range of activities: For example, the Lese give farm products and iron to the Efe, and the Efe give meat, honey, and other forest goods to the Lese. But exchanges go far beyond the material domain. Indeed, it would be a fundamental mistake to see turn-taking as simply the reciprocal exchange of material objects and services. For example, the Efe protect Lese villages from witchcraft; not to do so would be more than just abandoning "their turn" in doing things, it would be to step out of mutually upheld beliefs about how the world works. Constant across all the different domains of activities binding the Efe and the Lese are collaboratively upheld duties and rights, and socially enforced rules of turn-taking in activities.

Trust

Trust is another fundamental feature of primitive social relations. A characteristic of human societies that are functional is that members generally trust one another, although this trend is always broken by some individuals who others learn to distrust (Moghaddam, 1998, p. 9). Of course, there are fundamental cross-cultural differences in what we trust others with. For example, among a number of South American tribes, such as the Yanomamo (Chagnon, 1997, p. 20) and the Nambikwara (Lévi-Strauss, 1972, p. 270), the public use of proper names for people is insulting. Thus, for example, it would be an act of trust for a member of the Yanomamo to tell an outsider his real name, because it would mean the outsider has been placed in a position in which he now has the power to insult the Yanomamo individual by publicly using his name. But the fact remains that within the Yanomamo village, individuals do trust one another with such vital information, on faith that it will not be used against them.

The claim that trust is essential for the functioning of any human society is bolstered by studies that explore situations in which trust has broken down. One of the most exhaustive and best conducted of such studies is by Turnbull (1972), which focuses on the Ike, a traditionally nomadic group now forced to settle in northern Uganda, in a mountainous region bordering on Kenya to the east and Sudan to the north. The Ike were hunter-gatherers who lived a life that seems precarious from the outside but actually affords considerable security, as Turnbull pointed out, "For the farmer the results of a year's work may be destroyed overnight, whereas the most the hunter can lose is what he can replace tomorrow" (p. 21). The establishment of modern nation states, national boundaries, game reserves, national parks, and the like have forced many nomadic groups, including the Ike, to stay put in one location. The result for the Ike has been disastrous, because they have failed to adapt to a stationary life, farming proving virtually impossible in the land they now occupy, and their main sources of food have become cattle raids, prostitution, and such activities. The intense competition for survival has broken down all healthy social relationships and trust in particular, so that children do not trust parents, siblings lack trust for one another. The result is that all cooperative efforts have virtually ceased. Without trust, an extreme and maladaptive form of individualism has become pervasive in Ike society. But this is an extreme example, and for most societies people are socialized to trust one another.

The notion of trust as normative may appear strange from the perspective of an increasingly competitive capitalist world. However, without some level of trust, free-market capitalism could not survive because the everyday actions of participants in the marketplace would become impossible. Consider, for example, the following case of living without a norm of trust: John follows a stockbroker's advice and gives her his savings to buy shares in Company X, because she predicts prices will go up. A month later, John again follows her advice to sell all his shares in Company X, because she says prices will decrease. All this time John's mind is plagued by questions: Did his broker purposely mislead him? Did she really buy when he asked her to? Did she really sell? Perhaps she will wait until prices hit rock bottom and then sell, causing John's ruin? Will she walk away with his savings? Clearly, even though our minds may be plagued with such questions when dealing with some individuals, in most cases we do trust others and for good reason: Without doing so, life would become impossible. A minimum level of trust-based cooperation is essential for survival.

This idea matches extensions of Dawkins' (1976) "selfish gene" thesis into the social domain (e.g., Ridley, 1997). Optimum strategies for survival are proposed to involve a balance between cooperation and self-sacrifice on the one hand, and competitiveness and self-serving behavior on the other. Too much self-sacrifice will lead others to exploit an individual, but too much self-serving behavior will result in noncooperation on the part of others.

Primitive social relations such as turn-taking and trust evolved out of common practical challenges confronting human groups in their everyday lives and represent at least a functional level of interobjectivity. Primitive social relations evolved as public, as shared, and as part of collective life. Each newcomer to the group was taught the skills associated with primitive social relations and became integrated into the web of group life. Primitive social relations already existed in social practices before the arrival of a new infant, and such relations continued to rely on shared skills and accepted ways of doing things, and not just the private minds of individuals, after the infant developed, aged, and passed away.

Duty-Based and Rights-Based Tendencies in Societies

Primitive social relations, then, represent particular styles of functional behavior, constructed in the face of similar ecological challenges common to human societies. The evolution of primitive social relations took hundreds of thousands of years and began well before the appearance of language. But was it possible for primitive social relations to be transmitted across generations prior to human language skills? Research on chimpanzees supports the proposition that this is possible (Whiten et al., 1999), because chimpanzees living in different ecological conditions have been found to have different behavioral styles, indicating that some form of cultural transmission has been taking place across generations without human language skills. Even several million years ago, well before the appearance of language, humans were already far more advanced than chimps (bipedalism evolved among our ancestors about 4½ million years ago) and certainly capable of passing on behavioral styles, including primitive social relations. With the emergence of language, there was greater capacity for transmitting different interpretations of primitive social relations.

Primitive social relations can be interpreted in different ways with respect to rights and duties. Consider as an example the case of turn-taking in communications. During their conversation, Persons A and B can be said to have rights and duties. One interpretation is as follows: Person A has a right to speak and express her opinions, but she also has a duty to stop speaking so as to give Person B an opportunity to speak. While Person A is speaking, Person B has a duty to listen, but he also has a right to have his turn to speak. In interpreting this simple interaction, variations in cultural conditions and interobjectivity could lead to different levels of priority being given to the right of persons to speak, or not to speak, or the duty of persons to listen, or not to listen.

The interpretation of primitive social relations as rights and duties took place in different cultural conditions, associated with variations in interobjectivity, and is much more recent. Such interpretation was initially informal and tacit but acted as a first step toward the development of formal legal systems incorporating rights and duties. Across time and within cultures, the extent to which rights and duties were emphasized changed as societies went through historical transformations, such as a change experienced in Western societies from being duty-based in the Middle Ages to rights-based in the age of capitalism. At any given time, there emerged differences in interpretations of, and priority given to, rights and duties. For example, whereas individual rights are highlighted in the United States, duties to the collectivity are given greater emphasis in Islamic societies.

This is reflected particularly in legal procedures. For example, Rosen's (1989) study of procedures in Moroccan courtrooms highlights the role of normative systems at the community level in determining right and wrong. Truth and justice are not treated as abstract and detached, but as contextualized and arising from particular social relationships,

> unlike many complex legal systems that propel investigation and decision-making up to the higher reaches of the legal order, in Morocco the process of adjudication pushes matters down and away from the quadi [judge]— down to the level where local custom and circumstance can become more significant. (Rosen, 1989, p. 310)

Not only are local customs and standards given central place in the process of adjudication, but there is recognition that "shifts in the balance of obligations among people are indeed the normal course of things and that such alterations should be given judicial sanction" (Rosen, 1989, p. 311). Thus, the normative system shared by a collectivity and the duties binding people are not seen as static and abstract but as changing, concrete, and realized at the local level. This contrasts with Western legal traditions that place greater emphasis on general principles and the rights of individuals independent of local communities and contexts.

The Emergence of Legislated Rights and Duties

Whereas normative "informal" rights and duties evolved over hundreds of thousands of years, primarily as a means for the better functioning of small nomadic groups, formal rights and duties, as reflected in human rights declarations as well as formal written law, are relatively very recent and associated with large and complex societies. Among the factors leading to the emergence of formal rights and duties are the inadequacy of normative rights in large and more complex societies and a need felt to better defend people from increasingly powerful central authorities.

With the emergence of larger, more complex urban centers over the last few thousand years, and particularly since rapid industrialization from the 18th century onward, normative rights and duties proved inappropriate for the new social conditions. With industrialization came greater social and geographical mobility and more rapid change at all levels. Populations became increasingly concentrated in expanding urban centers, where most other people were strangers, and where a diversity of justice norms functioned side by side. Group differences and a low level of interobjectivity between groups posed potential problems. A need arose for a common set of rules for regulating rights and duties in relationships.

At the same time, central authorities became increasingly powerful, harnessing the capacities of new technologies and new professional middle classes to wield greater control over populations. Armies of specialists, including academic experts in multitudes of new fields, became available to central authorities. Ever-increasing specialization meant that central authorities and their agents have often been in advantageous positions for influencing and using the work of specialists scattered across hundreds of subspecialties often with little meaningful communication across subdisciplines (see Moghaddam, 1997). The enormous powers amassed by central authorities gave rise to new possibilities for violations of even minimal rights and duties, so that an elite few could control and abuse millions. Rights and duties enshrined in formal law was one means by which middle classes attempted to curb the abuse of power by elites, as evidenced by the actions of the middle classes in the French and subsequent revolutions (Schama, 1990).

In some respects modern formal law is fundamentally different from the informal systems of rights and duties present in premodern eras; for instance, it is written, and it is enforced by central authorities. But one should not see formal law as divorced from informal normative systems. Indeed, my argument is that the roots of formal law lie in the informal system. This becomes clear when one considers the history of common law:

> The rules of common law are social rules; never remote from life, they serve the rules of a society once feudal and agricultural but now industrial and urban. . . . Gradually, as social changes have occurred, the law has been adapted by judicial interpretation to meet new conditions. It continues as always to reflect the character of the social order. (Hogue, 1966, p. 3)

An important doctrine in modern law is *due process of law,* and one of the early foundations of this doctrine is taken to be the *Magna Carta,* specifically chapter 39, which states, "No free man shall be taken or imprisoned or dispossessed, or outlawed, or banished, or in any way destroyed, nor will we go upon him, nor send upon him, except by legal judgment of his peers or by the law of the land" (see Hogue, 1966, pp. 50–51). The *Magna Carta* was wrung from King John of England at Runnymede in 1215 by superior military power of the barons, who banded together to get back certain rights they had previously enjoyed. As Strong (1986) pointed out, the *Magna Carta* was preceded by a *Charter of Liberties,* granted by Henry I in 1100, and setting out in 14 clauses the rights and duties of the king in relation to "subjects." The *Charter of Liberties* and the *Magna Carta* formalize a ban on the invasion of "ancient" rights of personal freedoms and feudal property. The language of the *Magna Carta* reveals "the earlier existence of many customary services and payments which are assumed to be so well known and understood that they are given in the Charter without explanation" (Hogue, 1966, p. 183). In agreement with this thesis, Milsom (1985) asserted, referring to the barons who wrestled the *Magna Carta* from King John, "the due process that they used as their instrument, the judgment of peers, was not their creation: it was universally accepted in feudal custom" (p. 222).

Integral to the ancient roots of due process of the law, I argue, is turn-taking and associated rights and duties. The procedures followed in modern courts, particularly concerning the presentation of arguments and cross-examination of witnesses, follow turn-taking procedures that have their roots in the ancient informal system. Similarly, the assumption that individuals are innocent until proven guilty, and that the burden of proof is on the accuser rather than the accused, are founded on the primitive social relation of trust.

Just as human beings evolved to have trust in one another in their everyday activities and to take the trustworthiness of others as normative, the formal law courts proceed on the assumption that it is guilt rather than innocence that has to be proven.

One of the implications of this analysis is that orderly and fair behavior in large part arises from interobjectivity and the informal normative system, and is not solely dependent on formal law and the courts. Detailed studies of everyday behavior support this view. For example, Ellickson (1991) studied how neighbors settle ranching disputes in rural Shasta County, California. He discovered that, with very few exceptions, ranchers and farmers settled disputes, such as cattle going astray and property damage, by invoking norms of neighborliness rather than by "bringing in the law." The norms that people followed were well known by everyone, actually much better known than the formal law, and had evolved from an informal system that existed well before the establishment of formal law courts in that part of the world.

Interim Summary

Some fundamental rights and duties have their origins in certain primitive social relations that began to evolve as part of interobjectivity hundreds of thousands of years before the appearance of formal law. I discussed turn-taking and trust as two examples, but others are available (e.g., imitation is suggested by the research of Meltzoff & Moore, 1999). Given that certain fundamental rights and duties are integral to human social relations, a role for psychologists is to examine how in practice such psychological basis for justice could better serve the implementation of just procedures and outcomes. However, the reform of formal law is necessary but not sufficient because there is almost always a gap between formal law and actual behavior, and as one explanatory factor I next turn to differences in the maximum speeds of change possible at psychological and legal levels.

Bridging the Gap Between Formal Law and Actual Behavior

How can we move from a context supportive of second-order change, in which major gaps still persist between formal law and normative systems, to one supportive of third-order change, in which formal law and normative systems are in harmony, and justice is not just found "on the books" but is fully practiced in everyday life? This is a major challenge confronting the present generation of scholar-activists who endeavor to follow Kenneth Clark's path. Clark accurately saw the importance of reforming formal law, but the task of transforming interobjectivity and the informal normative system still confronts us. I argue that traditional psychology is not able to effectively tackle this challenge, because traditional psychology focuses on performance capacity, which is focused on causation and the biologically based abilities of isolated individuals, whereas the rift between second-order and third-order change can only be tackled effectively through a focus on performance style, on interobjectivity and the collaboratively constructed ways of doing things, and meaning systems "out there" in the social world.

One of the important features of performance style is that it is not capable of being controlled through a program that only adopts a "top down" approach, as various materialist and economic based theories might suggest (as an example of such theories, see Taylor & Moghaddam, 1994, chap. 3; Moghaddam, 2002, chap. 2). There are numerous examples of how even in societies in which the central authorities have dictatorial control, such authorities are unable to change everyday behavior according to official plans when they work mainly or exclusively in a "top-down" manner. As examples, consider so-called cultural revolutions in China in the late 1960s and in Iran in the early 1980s (Moghaddam, 2002; Yang, 1994). Both involved the most extreme measures, including the closing down of universities, forced "reeducation" of "antirevolutionary intellectuals," thousands of imprisonments and deaths, and massive propaganda campaigns, with no toleration for opposition voices. By any objective standards, both these top-down campaigns failed in their avowed goals: China has moved steadily away from Maoism and toward capitalism; and despite the rhetoric of fundamentalists, Iran has become even more economically dependent on Western capitalism and less like the "Islamic republic" originally outlined by Khomeini (e.g., Iranian banks and other institutions continue to charge interest for loans, even though this practice was supposed to be abandoned according to so-called "Islamic economics").

In exploring the ineffectiveness of purely top-down approaches to social change, a recent theory of social change has postulated a "micro/macro universal law," proposing that the maximum speed of change at the level of legal, political, and economic systems is faster than the maximum speed of change at the micro level of everyday behavior. Everyday behavior persists along the same lines in part through the influence of *carriers,* these being any means (e.g., a national flag, a stereotype, a speech code) through which cultural meanings and interobjectivity are sustained,

> This simple insight can help us understand why the normal trend for revolutions involves a paradox. On the one hand, a government is overthrown, and rapid and dramatic changes are made in the laws of the land and the economy. On the other hand, an invisible hand seems to pull things back to the way they were, so that soon people feel that nothing has changed. How people actually behave seems to remain the same. Like anchors that refuse to allow a ship to move far from a particular location, carriers sustain old ways of doing things, even though—by law—behavior should have changed. (Moghaddam, 2002, p. 33)

The power of carriers arises in large part through their flexibility; almost anything can be used as a carrier. For example, in much of the Islamic world, a veil is used as a carrier of traditional gender roles, and women are forced to wear the veil as a demonstration of the continuation of Islamic traditions. In the Western world, women are no longer limited by such blatant carriers, but they still face carriers that are perhaps even more subtle: stereotypes.

But carriers also give power to individuals. By ascribing meaning and value to particular things, individuals can help to sustain preferred interobjectivity and ways of life. For example, the Southerner who continues to fly the Confederate flag, the Islamic man who refuses to wear a beard or the Islamic woman who does not wear a traditional veil, the pacifist who displays a "peace" sign at a time of war, these are among countless examples of how individuals sometimes insist on using carriers to try to influence change in a direction that may be against the official policy of the government. This trend is clearly evident in minority movements, when relatively less powerful groups of individuals ascribe meaning to particular carriers as a means of solidifying and focusing their efforts. Examples range from early Christianity facing the enmity of the mighty Roman Empire and the use of the crucifix as a carrier, to modern feminist movements and the use of such carriers as titles (e.g., Ms. replacing Mrs. and Miss).

Carriers are used for convenience and will be retained or discarded depending on how useful they prove to be. For example, for a brief period in the 1960s the bra became a carrier of traditional gender roles, and "bra burning" was adopted among feminists (although in practice it is not clear if there were more than a few "bra burning" events). But this carrier did not prove to be useful and was very soon abandoned. Instead, a number of slogans (e.g., "glass ceiling") have proved to be far more useful carriers for the feminist cause, and persist today.

Implications for Psychology

In this final section I want to highlight a number of implications that my assessment has for psychology, and particularly the role of scholar-activists in tackling the challenge of third-order change. In particular, I point to implications for a need to pay closer attention to performance style and interobjectivity.

First, I have pointed out a fundamental gap between formal black-letter law and informal commonsense law and focused particularly on informal ways of doing things and interobjectivity. Reform of formal law is necessary but not sufficient; it is not possible to create justice in social relations through relying solely on a top-down approach that reforms black-letter law. On paper, all United States citizens are equal, but in practice fundamental inequalities in treatment persist. On paper, according to the Universal Declaration of Human Rights, all citizens of the world have equal rights, but in practice we are a very long way from that. According to a micro/macro universal law (Moghaddam, 2002), formal law can change faster than can actual behavior: A major challenge is to alter behavior to be in line with formal law.

Toward this goal, psychologists should pay closer attention to those human rights and duties that are already integral to human social relations. I discussed turn-taking and trust as examples of social behavior that have inherent within them the implementation of human rights and duties principles. Better understanding of rights and duties as practices in everyday life, and also the conditions in which their practice breaks down, can help us solve the enigma of third-order change.

A second major implication is that psychology should pay closer attention to performance style and a normative model for explaining human behavior.

This alternative or "second" psychology complements traditional psychology, which focuses on performance capacity and the causal model.

Informal or commonsense justice is part of performance style, as are the carriers, including stereotypes, that help sustain prevailing interobjectivity and particular ways of behaving in the justice arena. Psychological research has highlighted the end-product of the collective processes through which carriers are created and sustained. For example, Steele's research (see chap. 4, this volume) demonstrates how stereotypes can be a powerful and subtle force even in formal testing situations. This is the result of a collective process through which stereotypes are constructed and sustained. There is a need for psychologists to turn research attention to the process itself, and this requires a shift from looking at individuals to collectivities, and from looking at assumed causal mechanisms to normative meaning systems.

References

Amnesty International USA. (1998). *Rights for all.* New York: Author.

Amnesty International USA. (1999). Statement of William F. Schulz, Executive Director, Amnesty International USA. [Press Release, June 8, 1999, Washington DC].

Bright, S. B. (1995). Discrimination, death, and denial: The toleration of racial discrimination in infliction of the death penalty. *Santa Clara Law Review, 35,* 107–113.

Brown, R. (1966). *Social psychology.* New York: Free Press.

Carr, S. C., & Schumaker, J. F. (Eds.). (1996). *Psychology and the developing world.* New York: Praeger.

Chagnon, N. A. (1997). *Yanomamo* (5th ed.). New York: Harcourt Brace College.

Dawkins, R. (1976). *The selfish gene.* New York: Oxford University Press.

DeLong, A. J. (1977). Yielding the floor: The kinesic signals. *Journal of Communication, 27,* 98–103.

Eibl-Eibesfeldt, I. (1989). *Human ethology.* New York: Aldine de Gruyter.

Eimas, A. (1985). The perception of speech in early infancy. *Scientific American, 252,* 46–52.

Ellickson, R. C. (1991). *Order without law: How neighbors settle disputes.* Cambridge, MA: Harvard University Press.

Grinker, R. R. (1994). *Houses in the rainforest: Ethnicity and inequality among farmers and foragers in Central Africa.* Berkeley: University of California Press.

Hogue, A. R. (1966). *Origins of the common law.* Bloomingdale: Indiana University Press.

Jackson, J. P., Jr. (2001). *Social scientists for social justice: Making the case against segregation.* New York: New York University Press.

Kalat, J. W. (2002). *Introduction to psychology* (6th ed.). Pacific Grove, CA: Wadsworth.

Lévi-Strauss, C. (1972). *Tristes Tropiques: An anthropological study of primitive societies in Brazil* (J. Russell, Trans.). New York: Atheneum.

Lott, B., & Maluso, D. (Eds.). (1995). *The social psychology of interpersonal discrimination.* New York: Guilford Press.

Megany, T. (1995). *Society in prehistory: The origins of human culture.* New York: New York University Press.

Meltzoff, A. N., & Moore, M. K. (1999). Persons and representation: Why infant imitation is important for theories of human development. In J. Nadel & G. Butterworth (Eds.), *Imitation in infancy* (pp. 9–35). Cambridge, England: Cambridge University Press.

Middleton, J., & Tait, D. (1958). *Tribes without rulers: Studies in African segmentary systems.* London: Kegan Paul.

Milner, B. (1966). Amnesia following operation on the temporal lobes. In C. W. M. Whitty & O. L. Zangwill (Eds.), *Amnesia* (pp. 109–133). London: Butterworth.

Milsom, S. F. C. (1985). *Studies in the history of the common law.* London: Hambledon Press.

Moghaddam, F. M. (1990). Modulative and generative orientations in psychology: Implications for psychology in the third world. *Journal of Social Issues, 56,* 21–41.

Moghaddam, F. M. (1997). *The specialized society: The plight of the individual in an age of individualism.* Westport, CT: Praeger.

Moghaddam, F. M. (1998). *Social psychology: Exploring universals across cultures.* New York: Freeman.

Moghaddam, F. M. (1999). Carriers and change. *Cross Cultural Psychology Bulletin, 33,* 11–17, 31.

Moghaddam, F. M. (2000). Toward a cultural theory of human rights. *Theory & Psychology, 10,* 291–312.

Moghaddam, F. M. (2002). *The individual and society: A cultural integration.* New York: Worth.

Moghaddam, F. M. (2003). Interobjectivity and culture. *Culture & Psychology, 9,* 221–232.

Moghaddam, F. M., Bianchi, C., Daniels, K., & Harré, R. (1999). Psychology and national development. *Psychology and Developing Societies, 11,* 119–141.

Moghaddam, F. M., & Crystal, D. (1997). Reductons, samurai and revolutions: The paradoxes of change and continuity in Iran and Japan. *Journal of Political Psychology, 18,* 355–384.

Moghaddam, F. M., & Harré, R. (1995). But is it science? Traditional and alternative approaches to the study of social behavior. *World Psychology, 1,* 47–78.

Pareto, V. (1935). *The mind and society: A treatise in general sociology* (Vols. 1–4). New York: Dover.

Phelps, E. A., O'Connor, K. J., Cunningham, W. A., Funayama, E. S., Gatenby, J. C., Gore, J. C., & Banaji, M. R. (2000). Performance on indirect measures of race evaluation predicts amygdala activation. *Journal of Cognitive Neuroscience, 12,* 729–738.

Popper, K. R. (1966). *The open society and its enemies.* London: Routledge & Kegan Paul. (Original work published 1945)

Ridley, M. (1997). *The origins of virtue: Human instincts and the evolution of cooperation.* New York: Viking.

Rosen, L. (1989). Islamic "case law" and the logic of consequence. In J. Starr & J. F. Collier (Eds.), *History and power in the study of law* (pp. 302–319). Ithaca: Cornell University Press.

Schama, S. (1990). *Citizens: A chronicle of the French revolution.* New York: Vintage.

Steele, C. M. (1997). A threat in the air: How stereotypes shape intellectual identity and performance. *American Psychologist, 52,* 613–629.

Strong, F. R. (1986). *Substantive due process of law.* Durham, NC: Carolina Academic Press.

Taylor, D. M., & Moghaddam, F. M. (1994). *Theories of intergroup relations: International social psychological perspectives.* Westport, CT: Praeger.

Thorne, B. M., & Henley, T. B. (2001). *Connections in the history and systems of psychology* (2nd ed.). Boston: Houghton-Mifflin.

Turnbull, C. M. (1972). *The mountain people.* New York: Touchstone.

Watzlawick, P., Weakland, J. H., & Fisch, R. (1974). *Change: Principles of problem formation and problem resolution.* New York: Norton.

Whiten, A., Goodall, J., McGrew, W. C., Nishidas, T., Reynolds, V., Sugiyama, Y., et al. (1999). Cultures in chimpanzees. *Nature, 399,* 682–685.

Yang, M. M. (1994). *Gifts, favors, and banquets: The art of social relationships in China.* Ithaca, NY: Cornell University Press.

Part V _____

Conclusion

13

The American Psychological Association's Response to *Brown v. Board of Education*: The Case of Kenneth B. Clark

Ludy T. Benjamin Jr. and Ellen M. Crouse

If North American psychologists were asked to list the most important dates in the history of their field, certain events would likely be named: Gustav Fechner's mind–body insight on October 22, 1850; Wilhelm Wundt's establishment of his Leipzig laboratory in 1879; the publication of William James's *Principles of Psychology* in 1890; the founding of the American Psychological Association (APA) in 1892; John Watson's behaviorist manifesto published in 1913; the first state psychology licensure law in Connecticut in 1941; and the Boulder Conference of 1949 that established the scientist–practitioner model of professional training in psychology.

Not on this short list, and perhaps not even associated with the discipline by many psychologists, is a date certainly important in American psychology's history: May 17, 1954. This date marks the public validation of psychology as a science through the use of psychological data in a 1954 Supreme Court case that many have called the legal decision of the 20th century because it changed the fabric of American society. How was such a monumental event received by psychologists? More particularly, how did organized psychology, specifically APA, respond to this historic occasion in which psychologists and psychology had been so intimately involved? We offer some possible answers to these

We express our appreciation to George Albee, David B. Baker, Clifford L. Fawl, Leslie Hicks, Robert Perloff, John A. Popplestone, and Sherman Ross, and especially to Robert V. Guthrie, John P. Jackson, Jr., M. Brewster Smith, and Andrew Winston for their comments on earlier versions of this article, and to the Archives of the History of American Psychology, University of Akron; the Manuscript Division of the Library of Congress; and the American Psychological Association for permission to quote from materials in their archival collections. This chapter reprinted from "The American Psychological Association's Response to Brown v. Board of Education: The Case of Kenneth B. Clark," by L. T. Benjamin and E. M. Crouse, 2002, *American Psychologist, 57,* pp. 38–50. Copyright 2002 by the American Psychological Association. Reprinted with permission.

questions by focusing on the psychologist most involved in the court decision, Kenneth Bancroft Clark.

The Brown v. Board of Education Decision

On the morning of May 17, 1954, there was no indication of any unusual activity on the agenda of the United States Supreme Court. That Monday promised to be uneventful. Reporters covering the Court sat in the pressroom waiting for the decisions to arrive by means of pneumatic tubes, thereby allowing them to file their stories for their papers or news agencies. They could choose to be part of the audience in the Court's chambers, hearing the decisions read aloud, but it was easier and faster to work from the printed opinions (Kluger, 1975).

Shortly after noon, the press was notified that the Court would be rendering its decision on the school desegregation cases that had occupied the lower courts before reaching the Supreme Court in December 1952 as *Oliver Brown et al. v. Board of Education of Topeka*. Members of the press raced up the stairs to the courtroom to be part of the audience, many of them no doubt recognizing the historic significance of the moment. Chief Justice Earl Warren, who had been on the Court for only seven months and confirmed as Chief Justice only two months earlier, began reading the unanimous decision of the Court. He was two-thirds through the reading before he gave the first hint of what the Court's decision would be (Kluger, 1975).

The *Brown v. Board of Education* suit challenged the constitutionality of segregated public schools that had been sanctioned legally more than 130 years earlier and reinforced more recently by the Supreme Court decision *Plessy v. Ferguson* (1896) that had established the "separate but equal" doctrine. In recent challenges to *Plessy,* opponents had argued that government-sanctioned separation of the races created a strong sense of inferiority among African Americans. Proponents argued that no such position was inherent in the law and that if African Americans interpreted it that way, then the problem was with them and not the law. As he spoke, Warren addressed that claim:

Segregation of White and colored children in public school has a detrimental effect upon the colored children. The impact is greater when it has the sanction of the law, for the policy of separating the races is usually interpreted as denoting the inferiority of the Negro group. A sense of inferiority affects the motivation of the child to learn. Segregation with the sanction of law, therefore, has a tendency to retard the educational and mental development of Negro children and to deprive them of some of the benefits they would receive in a racially integrated school system. Whatever may have been the extent of psychological knowledge at the time of *Plessy v. Ferguson,* this finding is amply supported by modern authority. Any language in *Plessy v. Ferguson* contrary to this finding is rejected. We conclude that, in the field of public education, the doctrine of "separate but equal" has no place. (quoted in Kluger, 1975, p. 782).

That section of the decision and its footnote number 11—used to support the Court's references to inferiority, motivation to learn, and retarded mental development—generated a firestorm of protest among legal scholars and many other critics who felt that the Court had based its decision on psychological rather than legal grounds. They not only pointed out the inappropriateness of appealing to psychology for legal judgments but also attacked the scientific soundness of the psychological evidence considered by the Court (for arguments on both sides, see Cook, 1979, 1984; Gerard, 1983; Jackson, 2000a, 2000b). The Court asserted that the psychological evidence had been cited in the footnote only because it demonstrated the fallacy of the "cheap psychology of *Plessy*" and that it was not the foundation of the decision (Kluger, 1975, p. 706). As Richards (1997) has argued, however, "while, in point of fact, the Supreme Court . . . stressed that its decision was taken on purely legal and moral grounds, not scientific ones, the prominence given to the involvement in the case of psychologists and sociologists overshadowed this" (p. 245). Thus, the psychological evidence would become a lightning rod for critics of the decision in the years following *Brown v. Board of Education* (Tucker, 1994).

Kenneth B. Clark and the Desegregation Cases

Footnote 11 in the decision referred to the "psychological knowledge . . . supported by modern authority" (Kluger, 1975, p. 782). It listed seven social science publications. The first of these was "K. B. Clark, Effect of Prejudice and Discrimination on Personality Development (Midcentury White House Conference on Children and Youth, 1950)" (quoted in Kluger, 1975, p. 785). In his history of *Brown v. Board of Education,* Richard Kluger has suggested that the placement of Clark's (1950) work as first in the listing of seven sources was perhaps not arbitrary but a tribute to Clark for his considerable work in preparing the social science evidence for the case.

African American psychologist Kenneth B. Clark became involved with the litigation that would lead to *Brown v. Board of Education* in February 1951, when he was an assistant professor at City College in New York City. The call came from Robert Carter, an attorney with the Legal Defense Fund of the National Association for the Advancement of Colored People (NAACP), where he was Thurgood Marshall's deputy. Carter and Marshall were preparing to challenge the legality of segregated public schools. Carter had talked with Otto Klineberg, Columbia University psychologist and author of two critically important books, *Race Differences* (Klineberg, 1935b) and *Negro Intelligence and Selective Migration* (Klineberg, 1935a). Klineberg told Carter about the paper that Clark had prepared for the White House conference the previous year and suggested that Carter get in touch with Clark. Clark described his meeting with Carter as follows:

> So Bob Carter and I met for the first time. He told me the problem they faced; they had to prove to the Court that segregation, in itself, damaged the personality of the Negro child. They had come upon this question themselves. They had formulated their legal approach and the only thing they didn't know was whether they would get any support for it from the psychologists. They thought of Klineberg as the person who had done outstanding work in racial differences and he had worked with them before, giving testimony on the fact that there are no innate racial differences. So they went back

to Otto and he said your man is Kenneth Clark. I wasn't sure but I told Bob I would give him the manuscript to read, and if he felt it did fit into their legal structure then psychologists could help him. He took the manuscript and read it and called me about a week later, all excited. I'll never forget his words. He said, "This couldn't be better if it had been done for us." (Clark, n.d., pp. 132–133; see also Clark, 1986b, for a similar description)

Otto Klineberg (1986) has provided a supporting account and modestly claimed, "My own contribution to the case was the suggestion to ask Clark to work with the lawyers. The rest is history" (p. 55).

Marshall and Carter enlisted Clark's help almost immediately, asking him to testify in a segregation case in Charleston, South Carolina (*Briggs v. Elliott*) that was to come to trial in May 1951. Clark did so, taking to court his black and white dolls to explain how they had been used in the studies that he and his wife, Mamie Phipps Clark, had conducted on racial identification in African American children (see Clark & Clark, 1947; Lal, 2002). It was the beginning of a four-year involvement for Clark, including preparation for *Brown v. Board of Education* and assignments following the Court's 1954 decision. After South Carolina, he testified in cases in Delaware and Virginia, thus participating in three of the four desegregation cases that would be joined together as *Brown v. Board of Education*. Among the psychologists who testified for the plaintiffs in the lower courts were David Krech, Horace English, Louisa Holt, George Kelly, Helen Trager, Jerome Bruner, Otto Klineberg, Isidor Chein, M. Brewster Smith, and Mamie Phipps Clark.

Kenneth Clark joined Isidor Chein on a committee of the Society for the Psychological Study of Social Issues (SPSSI) chaired by Gerhart Saenger to prepare a social science appendix to the legal brief that the NAACP would submit to the Supreme Court. Stuart Cook later joined that committee, and he, Chein, and Clark wrote the initial draft of what would be called the social science statement ("Appendix to Appellants' Briefs," 1975). Their final product would be signed by 32 prominent social scientists including Floyd and Gordon Allport, Hadley Cantril, Allison Davis, Else Frenkel-Brunswik, Daniel Katz, Gardner Murphy, Nevitt Sanford, and Brewster Smith. The seven sources cited in *Brown's* footnote 11 were drawn from the reference list to the social science statement.

Although there were many psychologists, sociologists, and other social scientists involved in supporting the efforts of the NAACP in the school desegregation cases, it was generally agreed that no one was more instrumental in that effort than Kenneth Clark. At a Division 26 symposium organized by John A. Popplestone and honoring the 25th anniversary of *Brown v. Board of Education*, Brewster Smith (1979) said, "Kenneth Clark was the central figure in developing the social science support for the NAACP case" (p. 1). That opinion was echoed by Stuart Cook (1986) and, according to his biographer, by Thurgood Marshall (Williams, 1998). Clark used his passion, his energy, and his considerable work ethic to accumulate and organize the social science evidence needed for the trials. Subsequent to the May 1954 decision, he was heavily involved in gathering information and making recommendations about procedures to bring about school desegregation.

Psychology's Moment in the Spotlight

Since its beginnings in the last quarter of the 19th century, the "new" psychology had struggled to establish its identity as a legitimate science in America, separating itself from metaphysics, philosophy, and a popular psychology of the mind long in existence. In its early years, it sought to distance itself from phrenology, psychic research, and spiritualism, the pseudosciences that the public often confused with the new experimental psychology (Coon, 1992). In the 1920s, it battled psychoanalysis for the public's favor as the true science of the mind, a battle that psychologist–historian Gail Hornstein (1992) said was won by psychoanalysis.

In the 1930s, psychological science was attacked in books, magazine articles, and newspaper editorials as an art with misguided or unrealistic scientific aspirations (see Adams, 1931, 1934; "Page the Psychologists," 1934; Stolberg, 1930). The situation seemed bad enough that Walter Hunter, APA president in 1931, suggested changing the name of psychology to anthroponomy, a label that he believed was a more accurate description of the science and one that possessed fewer negative associations. In his autobiography, Hunter (1952) wrote, "I was never under any delusion that the designation of the science would be changed to anthroponomy, but the path of our science would have been much smoother in its public relations had some nonpsychic term designated it" (p. 172).

The success of psychologists' work for the military during World War II clearly helped the scientific and applied image of the field. Research opportunities for psychologists, largely through government contracts and grants, expanded the utility and visibility of psychological science after the war (Capshew, 1999). Moreover, the mental health needs of the returning veterans, along with the planning of the Veterans Administration, the United States Public Health Service, and APA, were largely responsible for launching the professions of clinical and counseling psychology and the concomitant growth of academic programs to train those professionals. In the 20 years following the war, American psychology underwent a rate of growth unlike anything in its history in terms of both the science and the profession of psychology. Still, it could be argued that psychology had not overcome its lack of respect or what Keith Stanovich (2001) has lamented is its standing as the "Rodney Dangerfield of the sciences" (p. 194).

It was the continued quest for respectability and recognition that made the *Brown v. Board of Education* decision so important for psychology as science. Probably for the first time in American history, psychological research was cited as crucial evidence in a court decision—and in perhaps the most important court decision in 20th-century America.

A Time for Congratulations

For many African Americans living in 1954 and certainly for all of those psychologists, lawyers, clerks, and others who worked on behalf of the NAACP's effort, May 17 must have provided a wealth of flashbulb memories. Otto Klineberg was working for the United Nations Educational, Scientific, and Cultural Organization in Paris, France, when he got the word by telegram. He promptly wrote to his former student Kenneth Clark:

> The great news has just reached me, and I am writing immediately because I know how you must be feeling, and because I want to take this occasion to congratulate you personally for the wonderful job that you have done. Although a number of social scientists did work with you, I have always felt that without your leadership and enthusiasm the task would not have been accomplished nearly so well. I noted with the very greatest of interest that there were a few references in the Supreme Court decision which indicated that what we collectively had to say did not go entirely unnoticed. . . . (Klineberg, 1954, p. 1)

Harvard University psychologist Gordon Allport, whose book *The Nature of Prejudice* (Allport, 1954b) had been published in January of that year, wrote to Clark the next day:

> You are probably receiving congratulations on all sides. Let me add my word of admiration for your Herculean labors and adroit handling of social science evidence for the Supreme Court. The happy outcome marks an epoch in the development of social science, in the history of the Negro race, and in the improvement of American foreign relations. Since you had a large part to play in all these achievements I congratulate you with all my heart. (Allport, 1954a, p. 1)

The letters and telegrams in the Kenneth Bancroft Clark Papers in the Library of Congress congratulating Clark are full of admiration and praise for his organizational skills, leadership, and persistence. They express exuberance, warmth, and a clear appreciation of the historic significance of the decision. Many acknowledge the inherent endorsement of the value of social science, as noted in the letters from Klineberg and Allport excerpted above. Many also indicate an awareness of the difficulties that lay ahead in making desegregated schools a reality and in eliminating other forms of segregation.

Buell Gallagher, president of the City College of New York, where Clark was a faculty member, wrote:

> With you, I am proud, deeply moved, and humbly grateful. That the real task is now before us is the sobering meaning of the hour. But I cannot let the moment of rejoicing pass without entering in the record my profound appreciation of your part in setting straight the course of American history. (Gallagher, 1954, p. 1)

What must it be like to have a part in "setting straight the course of American history"? What is it like to know, as one writer put it in her letter to Clark, that one has "assisted in the future development of the educational, cultural, and economic life of the Negro citizens of America" (Lewis, 1954, p.1) or, from another letter, that one has advanced "the equality of all men" (Bachrach, 1954, p. 1)? In Clark's case, he was ecstatic at the news of the decision: "My initial response was that of tremendous exhilaration. I just felt so enthusiastic. I felt joy at being an American. I was full of hope and optimism" (as quoted in Nyman, 1976, p. 112). In a few days, however, that feeling gave way to the grim realization of the many battles that lay ahead. Clark wrote to Klineberg:

> These three weeks since the Court's decision have been in many respects the most exciting period of my life. Starting from about 2:00 p.m. on May 17th, Mamie, Thurgood, Bob Carter and the entire staff of the Legal Defense and Educational Division of the NAACP and all of our friends have been celebrating. The first three or four days we were in the clouds and refused to be brought down to earth by a consideration of the really serious problems which we must now all face. There are so many things which I wanted to enjoy with you during this period. My only regret is that you were not here to celebrate with us the victory of which you were so much a part. The Court left no doubt that it was basing its decision as much upon contemporary social science knowledge and theory as it was basing it upon law. Anyone who knows this field knows that you have been in the forefront of providing the basic facts upon which we could move from the ideas about racial differences which were prevalent at the time of the *Plessy* decision to those which we now hold and which made the present decision possible and tenable. (Clark, 1954b, p. 1)

Clark's modesty was genuine and his feelings toward Klineberg ones of enormous respect and affection.

The Response of APA

While the NAACP team was celebrating its accomplishment and acknowledging the role of the social scientists in carrying the day for the lawsuit, what was happening within APA? To answer that question, we began by looking through the APA Papers and the Kenneth Bancroft Clark Papers, both housed at the Library of Congress, to see what correspondence existed between the two. We also looked at the minutes and correspondence associated with the APA Council of Representatives and Board of Directors. Furthermore, we examined all of the seemingly relevant correspondence folders from 1952 to 1956, for example, the correspondence of Fillmore Sanford, the executive secretary of APA at the time of the *Brown* decision. We then expanded our search to the Stuart Cook Papers, Brewster Smith Papers, and SPSSI Papers, all housed at the Archives of the History of American Psychology at the University of Akron, and to the Michael Amrine Papers at Georgetown University.

We were able to locate three letters from APA to Clark in 1954. One of those was dated four days prior to the Court's decision and, given the weekend, may have reached Clark on the Monday of the *Brown* decision. It was from Fillmore Sanford and informed Clark:

> Two facts have just been brought to my attention: (a) you have expressed a willingness to have your name appear on a slate of candidates for election to the Committee on Academic Freedom and Conditions of Employment; (b) you are just before being dropped from membership in the Association

for non-payment of dues. These two facts together constitute something of a problem. But only a technical one. . . . (Sanford, 1954a, p. 1)

These two events—news of the Supreme Court decision and news from APA that his dues were in arrears—make for an interesting juxtaposition! It seems a safe assumption that given the nature of the first event, the second one probably got no attention from Clark, at least not for some time. In fact, the evidence is clear on this point. Clark's secretary, Ruth Morton (1956), sent a check for $58 to APA in September 1956, more than two years later, for "payment of dues for the years, 1954, 1955, and 1956" (p. 1).

The second letter from APA came from Lorraine Bouthilet, managing editor of the *American Psychologist,* and was written two weeks after the *Brown* decision. It informed Clark that he was scheduled for two presentations at the upcoming APA meeting and that APA guidelines limited participants to only one (Bouthilet, 1954). Had Bouthilet known Clark, one might assume that her letter would have included a note of congratulation, perhaps even as a postscript. There was none.

The third letter in 1954 was from Michael Amrine, who worked for APA as a public information consultant. He wrote to Clark in November encouraging him to use a speech he had given recently as the basis for an article in *Scientific American.* Clark replied, sending him copies of two presentations that he had given and asking for his suggestions about how they might be combined into a single article (Amrine, 1954a; Clark, 1954a).

It appears that there was no resolution from the APA Board of Directors or Council of Representatives commending Clark and the other psychologists for their excellent work on the case. None could be found in our search. Indeed, there is no mention of the *Brown* decision anywhere in the minutes of the board or council in the period from 1952 to 1956. The only evidence that the desegregation cases might have been discussed by the board appears in a report of board discussions by Sanford (1954b). The relevant section of the report is labeled "Psychology and Public Affairs," and it acknowledged that psychologists were playing an increased role as expert witnesses in the courts and testifying before congressional committees, thus attempting to influence governmental decisions. Sanford commented that "such developments, pleasing to some and uncomfortable to others, appear to be inevitable concomitants of our maturation as science and profession" (Sanford, 1954b, p. 715). Perhaps paraphrasing some of the discussion at the board's September 1954 meeting, Sanford (1954b) noted that psychologists have

an increasing opportunity to contribute evidences, arguments, and points of view to the decision-making process of community, of government, and of society. Such an increasing opportunity brings with it an increasing responsibility and what to some represents an exhilarating challenge. How does psychology make its most effective contribution to its supporting society while maintaining its own sense of integrity? How does it play its increasingly influential role without doing insult to the traditions of science, scholarship, and democracy?

It is hard to imagine that in September 1954, with the *Brown* decision only a little more than three months old, the Supreme Court case and psychologists' participation in it were not part of the board's discussion of psychology and public affairs. Still, the report contains no such direct reference.

Perhaps there was an acknowledgment in "Across the Secretary's Desk," a monthly column in the *American Psychologist* that had been started by Dael Wolfle when the journal began publication in 1946 and continued by the subsequent executive secretaries of APA? That column typically reported Washington news related to psychology such as federal grants, legislation, Veterans Administration activities, and other items of interest to psychologists. Yet nowhere in those columns was any mention of *Brown* found, despite there being material where the *Brown* cases would have been relevant. For example, in a 1953 column, Sanford (1953a) included a section on "Psychology and the Law," yet no mention was made of the psychological testimony in the cases leading to *Brown* or the brief on social science research filed with the Supreme Court.

Were there any special acknowledgments for Clark and the others at the annual meeting of the association held in New York City, New York, in September 1954? No evidence could be found of a reception, social hour, or other session that recognized psychology's role in the *Brown* decision. Clark was involved in two symposia at that meeting (apparently he did not cancel one of those as requested by Bouthilet). One was a symposium on problems of desegregation sponsored by SPSSI. It was chaired by Isidor Chein and included presentations by Clark, John Dean (a sociologist from Cornell University), and Thurgood Marshall. It is not known for certain whether this symposium was organized before or after the court decision, but it seems likely, given the date of Bouthilet's letter, that it was before. The second symposium in which Clark participated was sponsored by APA's Division on Clinical Psychology and was on the subject of cultural approaches to psychotherapy.

At the 1955 APA meeting in San Francisco, California, there was another SPSSI-sponsored symposium on research on racial differences in which Clark participated. At the 1956 meeting in Chicago, Illinois, there were two SPSSI meetings, one a symposium and the other a workshop, both on desegregation, but Clark was not listed as a participant in either. In summary, nowhere in the APA programs for 1954–1956 is there any mention of *Brown*.

We also looked at the articles, comments, and notes and news sections in the *American Psychologist* between 1951 and 1956 to see if there were mentions of the lower court desegregation cases, *Brown*, or issues of segregation. There was a brief article written by Martin Grossack, a professor at Philander Smith College, that appeared in the May 1954 issue, the month of the court decision. This article reported the results of a survey of African Americans' perceptions of psychology and called for psychologists to do a better job of communicating the results of their research, especially as it would benefit minority group members (Grossack, 1954). In the following year, there was a single comment by Robert Perloff (1955) encouraging psychologists to use their science to aid the transition in schools that was mandated by the Court's desegregation decision. Two articles were published in 1956 on psychologists as expert witnesses in court. Both articles were received in the journal's editorial office after the *Brown* decision, yet neither mentioned psychologists' involvement in the cases leading up to that lawsuit (McCary, 1956; Schofield, 1956). Finally, there were two items in the "Psychological Notes and News" sections in 1955, the first appearing about a year after the *Brown* decision, that announced a grant program sponsored by SPSSI for research on desegregation. Isidor Chein chaired the grant awards committee, which included Kenneth Clark and Brewster Smith as well (see "Psychological Notes and News: Grants-in-Aid for Research on Desegregation," 1955, "Psychological Notes and News: Society for the Psychological Study of Social Issues," 1955).

In March 1955, almost a year after the *Brown* decision, Sanford wrote to Clark inviting him to do "a piece for the *American Psychologist* on psychological research and segregation" (Sanford, 1955, p. 1). The invitation was at the suggestion of Stuart Cook, a point Sanford acknowledged in his letter. Amrine was also encouraging of the article. Sanford (1955) added:

> Such an article would, I feel, be of real interest to many of our readers and the story should be recorded. I would hope, however, that you could write with relative brevity. We are facing pretty stringent space problems in the *American Psychologist.* (p. 1)

It is likely that the "story" to which Sanford referred was the involvement of psychologists in *Brown* and the cases leading up to that decision. For reasons unknown, Clark did not write such an article for the journal or, if he did, it was not published. The latter seems unlikely because the article had been invited by the journal's editor himself. Stuart Cook, however, did publish an article (Cook, 1957) on desegregation in the *American Psychologist* in 1957. Although Cook's article referred to the 1954 decision, it was not a recounting, in any way, of the story of psychologists' involvement in that case.

Michael Amrine had been hired by APA in 1952 to spearhead its public information efforts. Six weeks before the *Brown* decision, he issued a press release on behalf of APA entitled "Desegregation: An Appraisal of the Evidence" (Amrine, 1954b). The release was intended to publicize a recent issue of the *Journal of Social Issues* written by Clark (1953) that provided data on American communities that had undergone voluntary desegregation of schools. The press release noted that

> Dr. Clark's investigations are a direct result of the issue pending before the United States Supreme Court: whether segregation by law of facilities for Negro and White children in the public schools shall be ruled unconstitutional, regardless of purported "equality". The findings presented in this Journal, which has just been released, form part of the evidence under consideration by the Court. What, the Court asked in effect, is known about the social outcome of sudden or gradual segregation? (Amrine, 1954b, p. 1)

A search of relevant archival collections has not turned up any other APA press releases related to issues of desegregation or *Brown v. Board of Education* in the years 1952 through 1956.

In summary, following the 1954 Supreme Court decision, there was apparently no formal or official recognition from APA for any of the psychologists participating in *Brown.* There were no commendations from the APA board or APA council, no letters of congratulation or commendation from the office of the APA executive secretary. There was no official recognition of the work of the psychologists at subsequent APA meetings other than through the programs organized by SPSSI, and those do not appear to have been celebratory. There was no coverage of the subject in the *American Psychologist,* not even in the "Across the Secretary's Desk" column where such coverage would have been quite appropriate. Nor was there any coverage of *Brown* in the *American Psychologist* in the several articles on, for example, psychologists as expert witnesses, where not only would mention of the decision seem quite appropriate but its exclusion seems calculated. Only Robert Perloff's brief comment (Perloff, 1955) in the journal in 1955 made any mention of the court case in the years 1954 through 1956. How could it be that APA ignored such a visible accomplishment? Is it possible that the involvement of psychology in such a controversial case was not viewed as an accomplishment in 1954? Was racism a factor?

Why the Lack of Response From APA?

It is easy to slip into a presentist interpretation of the events of 1954 or what Butterfield (1931) called "Whig history," that is, an interpretation of the past in the context of the values, attitudes, beliefs, and practices of the present. Were psychological research to be cited in a Supreme Court decision today— especially one of the magnitude of *Brown v. Board of Education*—one can imagine a flurry of activity from APA that would include press releases, special symposia and celebratory events at the annual convention, and citations from the APA president for the individuals whose research was cited or who worked on the court case. In short, there would be incredible fanfare over what Klineberg (1986) described (with reference to the mention of psychology in the *Brown* decision) as "the greatest compliment ever paid to psychology by the powers-that-be in our own or any other country" (p. 54). Yet America is very different today, psychologists are different, and APA, too, is a very different organization. In discussing the possible reasons for a lack of response from APA to the *Brown* decision, we have sought to understand APA and psychology in the 1950s in terms of the perception of the significance of the court case, psychologists' beliefs about race, APA's position on issuance of public resolutions, the perception of SPSSI as a leftist organization, and the controversy over the scientific evidence presented in the desegregation trials.

The Perceived Magnitude of Brown v. Board of Education

Today, there seems little doubt about the significance of the 1954 Court decision as a defining event in American history. Editors at Oxford University Press have labeled it as such by making a book on *Brown* the initial title in a new series of books called "Pivotal Moments in American History" (see Patterson,

2001). Legal scholar Michael Klarman (1994) has written, "Constitutional lawyers and historians generally deem *Brown v. Board of Education* to be the most important United States Supreme Court decision of the twentieth century, and possibly of all time" (p. 81). Still, there is debate today about its role in the history of civil rights and racial equality in the second half of the 20th century and, of greater importance to our questions, about how important the decision was perceived to be when it was rendered in 1954.

Was the *Brown* decision viewed as an important decision in 1954? Could APA's lack of response have been because the association did not consider the decision to be of critical importance? The newspaper coverage of the decision suggests that the press viewed it as important. Of course, the issue of school desegregation was an ongoing one because the 1954 decision called for a further Supreme Court decision on a timetable and suggested procedures for the actual desegregation to begin. That second decision (*Brown v. Board of Education,* 1955, which also involved a brief prepared by Kenneth Clark and other social scientists recommending strongly against gradualness of desegregation), rendered on May 31, 1955, is usually referred to as *Brown II*; it ordered that the desegregation of public schools should proceed "with all deliberate speed" (quoted in Kluger, 1975, p. 745), a wording that had been adopted as a compromise between those who favored immediacy and those who argued for a more gradual transition. The wording, which Tucker (1994) labeled oxymoronic, proved to favor the gradualists as many school districts in the deep South did not begin to comply with the law until the 1970s.

The first *Brown* decision had been awaited for many months; thus, there was much anticipation built up in America's Black community. Patterson (2001) described how many African Americans vividly recalled their excitement over the news of 1954 in the way that their ancestors had recalled the events of the day on which they heard the news of President Abraham Lincoln's 1863 Emancipation Proclamation. Kluger (1975), on the other hand, described a more subdued response from African Americans, stating that they had witnessed the good intentions of the American government before and were taking a wait-and-see attitude regarding the ultimate impact of the decision. Legal scholars in 1954 recognized the case as one of the most important of all time, and some argued that the decision was the most important in the history of the Court (Kluger, 1975). *Time* magazine declared the decision to be the landmark decision of the Court; no other decision had "directly affected so many American families" (Kluger, 1975, p. 709).

Historian Ben Keppel (1995) has written, "From the moment of its announcement, the *Brown* decision became a sacred and redemptive chapter in the history of American democracy" (p. 115). In the 1950s, segregation in America had been used in Communist rhetoric to point to the hypocrisy of the nation. *Time* magazine called the Court decision a "timely reassertion of the basic American principle that 'all men are created equal' " (quoted in Keppel, 1995, p. 116). As Keppel (1995) noted, the message that the decision sent abroad was "that America was as good as its creed" (p. 116).

The comments offered here (and many more of similar vein could be included) suggest that the *Brown* decision's importance was recognized by various publics in 1954. Surely, psychologists would have been as aware as any other group of citizens of the meaning and significance of the Court's decision. More-over, APA leadership was aware of its members' work on behalf of the plaintiffs in the various lower court cases and in preparation of the social science brief for the Supreme Court. Thus, it seems unlikely that APA's lack of response was based on a view of the Court decision as being of marginal importance.

A Divided Psychology

In 1954, racially segregated schools existed by law in 17 states and the District of Columbia and were permitted in 4 other states at the discretion of local school districts. Other forms of racial segregation prevalent at the time could be found in churches, theaters, trains, buses, restaurants, housing, work settings, mental institutions, prisons, restrooms, and drinking fountains. In the 1950s, racism was visible in most American institutions, including polling booths, and it was no less present in psychology as an integral part of American society. Graham Richards (1997) has written, "Psychology is never separate from its host culture, the psychological concerns of which it shares, articulates, and reflects" (p. 153). Thus, for many psychologists, the *Brown* decision would not have been a cause for celebration, a point that Stuart Cook (1957) recognized in writing in the *American Psychologist* in 1957 about desegregation: "As *citizens* we may consider the Court's rulings wise or unwise, we may applaud or condemn specific actions taken in the South" (p. 1, emphasis in original). Cook was willing to concede differences of opinion as citizens, but regardless of those differences, he argued that as psychologists, there was an obligation to bring the objective methods of the field to bear on the questions dividing the country. Of course, many psychologists opposed to a social action agenda for their science would take strong issue with the claim for such an obligation.

The division within American psychology was evident in the lower court cases leading to *Brown*. In a 1952 Virginia case (*Davis v. County School Board of Prince Edward County*), the attorneys for the state of Virginia, who were aware of the psychological testimony from the earlier cases in South Carolina, Kansas, and Delaware, were determined to counteract that testimony. They brought in a Richmond, Virginia, child psychiatrist (William H. Kelly) and two psychologists (John Nelson Buck, a clinical psychologist, and Henry E. Garrett, chair of the Psychology Department at Columbia University and formerly president of APA in 1946) to testify as expert witnesses on behalf of the state.

Buck, who for more than 20 years had administered personality tests to patients entering the state mental hospital in Lynchburg, Virginia, was presented as an expert on psychological testing. He attacked the survey re-search of Isidor Chein and the doll studies and interviews of Kenneth and Mamie Clark as methodologically flawed and thus open to other interpretations. Garrett, the state of Virginia's star witness, had been the doctoral advisor for Mamie Clark and a member of the doctoral committees of Chein and Kenneth Clark. He viewed his assignment as "the role of teacher whose sad duty it was to report that his pupils had let their good intentions get in the way of objective science. . . . [They] were pushing their own political and moral agenda, dressed in scientific garb" (Jackson, 2000b, p. 241). In his testimony, Garrett characterized Brewster Smith's statements about the psychological damage of segregation as idealistic and lacking in common sense. He attacked Chein's surveys on segregation as yielding results that were dictated solely by the ways the questions were asked. He disparaged the work of the Clarks, arguing that their results were caused by disruptions in the schools that had preceded the student interviews (Kluger, 1975). Referring to Kenneth Clark's days as a student at Columbia University, Garrett said that he was "none too bright. . . . he was about a C student, but he'd rank pretty high for a Negro" (quoted in Kluger, 1975, p. 502).

Garrett argued that "the principle of separation in education . . . is long and well established in American life" (Kluger, 1975, p. 502); he supported separate schools for Whites and African Americans, he said, as long as the schools were truly equal. Indeed, Garrett advocated strongly for his segregationist beliefs, as described by historian of psychology Andrew Winston (1998): "In the 1950s Garrett helped organize an international group of scholars [the International Association for the Advancement of Ethnology and Eugenics (IAAEE)] dedicated to preventing race mixing, preserving segregation, and promoting the principles of early 20th century eugenics and 'race hygiene'" (p. 179). Clearly, in his court testimony, Garrett was pushing his own political agenda.

Undoubtedly, Garrett was not alone in his views on segregation, and at least one source has suggested that his views might have been commonplace among American psychologists in the 1950s. Richards (1997) wrote:

> Within American psychology's institutional structures, notably the APA, the anti-racist camp had relatively little power. . . . SPSSI could be little more than a specific lobby or interest group. With figures such as Garrett and [Stanley David] Porteus remaining eminent and respected within the APA, there was little hope of engineering any unambiguous, formal anti-racist commitment from the organisation on behalf of U.S. Psychology as a whole. (p. 254)

Although the antiracist group in psychology may have had little political power, its membership likely exceeded Richards' (1997) claim of "camp" size. Samelson (1978), in an article on the history of the psychology of race, documented the rather dramatic change of American psychological opinion from studies of the so-called race problem at the beginning of the 20th century to studies of prejudice by the 1930s. He noted that the Great Depression gave "many psychologists a powerful push toward the left" (Samelson, 1978, p. 273). Supporting Samelson's claim are two surveys: The first was of psychologist opinions taken from members attending the 1939 APA meeting and showed their responses to be "liberal, progressive, democratic" (Gundlach, 1940, p. 620), and the second was a survey of social psychologists (and other social scientists) that showed 90% believed that "segregation has detrimental psychological effects on members of racial and religious groups which are segregated, even if equal facilities are provided" (Deutscher & Chein, 1948, p. 261). It was this latter survey that Chein had presented in his Virginia court testimony and that Garrett had attacked based on the wording of the questions. In actuality, the questionnaire was a sound one, and the Deutscher and Chein (1948) survey was one of the studies the Supreme Court chose to list in footnote 11 of the *Brown* decision.

The experiences of World War II and Adolf Hitler's vision of a master race also made many Americans, psychologists included, reexamine their views on race. Made aware of the fact that African American members of APA were being discriminated against in convention hotels, APA's Council of Representatives adopted a policy in 1950 of not meeting at any hotels or other venues where minority members would face discrimination. That policy led to the cancellation of a planned meeting in Miami Beach, Florida, in 1957 when it was determined that some hotels and restaurants would not accommodate Black psychologists. The meeting was moved to New York City instead (Smith, 1992). Still, although both psychology and racial attitudes in America were undergoing change in the 1950s, racial questions continued to divide psychology's house. Such a division made it difficult for APA to speak on political and social issues without offending many members. (Note that a 1954 survey of "social attitudes of leading psychologists," avoided race altogether, focusing instead on attitudes about divorce, the death penalty, euthanasia, and religion; Keehn, 1955, p. 208.)

APA and Public Statements

Today, APA issues occasional resolutions that address social and political is- sues. These resolutions are approved by the Council of Representatives, APA's policy-making body. When the resolutions are approved by council, they are usually accompanied by a plan of dissemination. In its history of making such public statements by means of these resolutions, APA has typically come under attack each time from at least some members who resign because of the resolu- tion or threaten to do so if APA will not cease making such pronouncements. The varied concerns of these members include failing to put the issue to the vote of the entire membership, making claims that may not be well supported by psychological science, or just venturing into political domains where the aggrieved members believe APA has no business being.

Psychologists' aversions to political or social pronouncements have a long history in American psychology, grounded in part in the belief that science and application are separate activities and in the long-standing prejudices held against applied work. These forces were part of what stimulated the founding of SPSSI in the 1930s.

In the midst of the Depression and a host of social ills that had become more evident during America's economic crisis, a group of psychologists had the apparently radical idea of using psychology to solve some of the problems facing society. In 1936, they founded SPSSI to promote such social action. Whereas 333 of APA's nearly 2,000 members joined the new organization in its initial year, there were many other APA members who worried about its intent. George H. Estabrooks, a psychologist at Colgate University, wrote to Isadore Krechevsky (David Krech), expressing a complaint that was echoed by other psychologists who responded to Krech's invitation to join the new society:

With regard to your mimeographed sheets concerning the participation of psychologists in the contemporary political world, allow me to register my hearty dissent with approximately everything contained therein. If psychologists, as individuals, wish to make themselves politically vocal on any topic—white, red, or pink—it seems to me that is wholly up to them. . . . If any group of us wish to organize as a "Committee for the Propagation of Mild Pinkism", for goodness sakes let us organize ourselves as such and not in camouflage under the protecting skirts of the American Psychological Association. (Estabrooks, 1936, p. 1)

SPSSI, which joined a reorganized APA in 1945 as Division 9, was founded in part to use psychological science to address social and political issues. In the 1930s, SPSSI had issued policy statements as a scientific organization, but the society evidently changed its policy in the 1940s and 1950s (Jackson, 1998). Perhaps the change came because of its official ties to APA.

APA was reluctant to pursue such pronouncements as a regular part of its agenda, but it did approve and distribute occasional resolutions such as one in the 1920s on psychological testing and several in the 1930s on academic freedom. According to Richards (1997), within APA in the 1950s, "a policy of explicit avoidance of political issues was adopted and adhered to" (p. 254). However, no formal statement of such a policy could be found in the (incomplete) records of the APA Council of Representatives or Board of Directors. Evidence of this policy does exist in several letters in the APA Archives and other sources, for example, a letter from Roger Russell (APA's executive secretary, who succeeded Sanford in 1956) to Stuart Cook concerning requests for comments on a magazine article (McGurk, 1956) asserting the intellectual inferiority of African Americans: "We were approached by the Associated Press but in line with APA policy referred them to experts on matters of this kind, including yourself" (Russell, 1956).

Yet APA did take some political stands. In 1949, in the midst of McCarthyism, APA's Board of Directors sent a letter to President Harry Truman arguing that loyalty investigations should be made fairer by allowing accused persons knowledge of the charges and evidence against them (Wolfle, 1949). In that same year, APA founded a committee—the Committee of the Association on Academic Freedom and Civil Liberties—to deal with complaints about violations of academic freedom. Perhaps someone thought the committee name was too broad or too controversial. For unknown reasons, it was changed in 1951 to the Committee on Academic Freedom and Conditions of Employment, the committee that Kenneth Clark expressed interest in joining in 1954 (Smith, 1992). Moreover, APA approved resolutions in the 1950s, for example, notifying California Governor Earl Warren in 1950 that because of the loyalty oath required by the state, APA was encouraging its members not to accept teaching or research positions there until conditions of academic freedom improved (Sargent & Harris, 1986). That resolution brought objections from the membership, who wondered, "By what statistical formula does a sample of 10 (Board of Directors) represent a population of 8,500 (APA membership)" (Sell, 1951, p. 179)?

In 1952, APA wrote to the New York Convention and Visitors Bureau that because of the McCarran-Walter Act (which continued restrictions on immigration to the United States on the basis of country of origin), the association would not invite the International Congress of Psychology to meet in New York City in 1954 (Sanford, 1952). Moreover, in 1953, the APA Board of Directors passed a resolution opposed to "legislation restricting to any one profession the application of psychological techniques and knowledge" (Sanford, 1953b, p. 208).

In summary, it is difficult to argue that APA's lack of response to *Brown* was due to a policy of no official responses on political matters. Such a policy may have been in the official rules that governed APA operations, or the policy may have been only an unwritten, informal one. Clearly, APA endorsed resolutions in the 1950s. Did the organization do so inconsistently? It can be argued that the resolutions that were passed dealt principally with issues of academic freedom, freedom of scientific interchange, and the rights of psychologists in professional practice. APA did not respond officially to the claims in the 1950s about inferiority of intelligence in Blacks even when asked to do so. Perhaps APA avoided comment in the belief that the issue was political or social rather than scientific. The inferiority claims being made, however, were based on allegedly scientific evidence. It seems likely the topic was avoided largely because of its controversial nature. If so, then APA would have wanted to avoid noting psychology's involvement in *Brown v. Board of Education* as well. Moreover, if the left-leaning SPSSI was reluctant to issue official resolutions on issues such as race, it is not surprising that APA would show a similar reluctance.

SPSSI as a "Communist-Inspired" Organization

We have already indicated that when SPSSI was formed, there were psychologists who refused to join because they viewed the new society as pink, that is, as having Communist leanings or a Communist-inspired agenda (see the Estabrooks [1936] letter quoted earlier). In the SPSSI Papers at the University of Akron, there are several other letters expressing this concern. One of SPSSI's founders, Ross Stagner (1986), acknowledged that the initial membership of the society included "Norman Thomas socialists[,] some sympathizers with the Communist party, some disciples of Leon Trotsky" (p. 38). Also, as Ben Harris (1980) has reported, the FBI established a file on SPSSI in the 1930s because of its perceived leftist agenda. Andrew Winston (personal communication, March 4, 2001), in noting the juxtaposition of McCarthyism and the work of psychologists on the *Brown* cases, has suggested that because the psychologists who were involved in battling segregation were prominent in SPSSI, "the whole enterprise was viewed by some psychologists as politically suspect." Thus, APA's silence on the issues of *Brown* may have had to do with fears about the possible fallout from supporting the activities of what was perceived as a leftist organization or perhaps with the belief of some (many?) psychologists that desegregation efforts were Communist inspired.

Evaluations of the Scientific Evidence

The social science evidence presented in the lower court trials and included in the "Appendix to Appellants' Briefs" (1975) filed with the suit by the NAACP was attacked from its very beginnings. The inconsistencies in the Clarks' doll studies were particularly criticized by attorneys testifying for the defendants at the lower courts and before the Supreme Court (Newby, 1969; Tucker, 1994). Members of the Supreme Court shared some of the concerns about the status of psychology as an objective science. In a memorandum to his fellow justices dated three months before the *Brown* decision, Justice Robert Jackson wrote:

> I do not think we should import into the concept of equal protection of the law these elusive psychological and subjective factors. They are not determinable with satisfactory objectivity or measurable with reasonable certainty. If we adhere to objective criteria the judicial process will still be capricious enough. (quoted in Kluger, 1975, p. 689)

After the Court's decision was announced, Raymond Moley was one of scores of writers to denigrate psychology as a science. In his column in *Newsweek* magazine, he noted, "The assumption by the court that these psychological writings constitute firm and lasting facts determined by scientific methods is nonsense" (Moley, 1956, p. 104).

Many opponents of the *Brown* decision criticized the psychologists for acting as social reformers and not as dispassionate scientists (see Jackson, 1998, for a refutation of these charges). Garrett, in particular, had opened the door to attacks on the social science cited in *Brown,* and there was no shortage of such published accounts, particularly criticizing the doll studies of the Clarks that had actually begun as Mamie Clark's master's thesis research (see Clark, 1986a; Guthrie, 1990) at Howard University in the late 1930s (see Jackson, 2000b, for an excellent treatment of these arguments).

The decision started a new debate over race differences in intelligence (Guthrie, 1998), for example, an article by Villanova University psychologist and founding member of IAAEE Frank McGurk (1956), in the then prosegregationist magazine *U.S. News & World Report,* that asserted the intellectual inferiority of African Americans and their limited capacity for education. This article elicited many published replies, both pro and con, with respect to McGurk's data and his interpretations, but none of the replies carried an APA endorsement.

Perhaps the attacks on the specific sources cited in footnote 11 of *Brown* made APA reluctant to respond as an organization in defense of psychology. Instead, the strategy was to identify psychologists who seemed best suited as experts to respond and to ask them to write something for publication.

Summary and Conclusion

We began this article by arguing that the inclusion of citations to psychological publications and comments about psychological research in the *Brown v. Board of Education* Supreme Court decision of 1954 represented one of American psychology's greatest triumphs, arguably its greatest. That outcome was the result of individual psychologists working with the NAACP with the support of SPSSI. It was never an APA action.

We have described APA's response to the *Brown* decision and the psychologists involved or, more accurately, APA's lack of response. Finally, we have offered some explanations for why no official recognition was forthcoming.

In the years that followed the Court's decision, African American psychologists pressed APA for actions important to minority psychologists such as better training opportunities for minority graduate students, more involvement of minority psychologists on the boards and committees of APA, hiring of minority staffers to work in the APA central office, and greater attention to issues of concern for minority psychologists. When it was clear that APA would not provide the needed support, 200 Black psychologists met at the 1968 annual APA convention in San Francisco. By the end of that meeting, they had founded the Association of Black Psychologists, or ABPsi, as it came to be known (Guthrie, 1998).

The rise of the American civil rights movement in the 1960s gave new attention to Kenneth Clark's work. He had served as president of SPSSI in 1960. A new edition of his book (Clark, 1963) on raising children without prejudice appeared in 1963, and his *Dark Ghetto* (Clark, 1965) was published in 1965. The following year, he edited a book with Talcott Parsons entitled *The Negro American,* for which President Lyndon Johnson wrote a foreword (Clark & Parsons, 1966). These publications, plus his advocacy in the 1950s and 1960s and his prominent role in *Brown,* "launched him on a path that would culminate in his becoming the 'reigning academic' of the civil rights movement" (Keppel, 1995, p. 128).

In 1970, Kenneth Clark served as president of APA, the first ethnic minority psychologist to hold that position and the only African American to have held it to date. For APA, part of the legacy of his presidency was the establishment in 1971 of the Board of Social and Ethical Responsibility for Psychology (BSERP), which gave social and ethical concerns a major position for advocacy within APA (see Pickren & Tomes, 2002). Eventually, BSERP had oversight for APA's offices of women's programs, ethnic minority affairs, and ethics.

In 1994, at the 102nd annual meeting of APA and exactly 40 years after the *Brown* decision, Clark was presented with the APA Award for Outstanding Lifetime Contribution to Psychology. He was only the sixth psychologist to receive that prestigious award. The citation read in part:

> Your contributions to the Supreme Court case *Brown vs. Board of Education* were instrumental in having the Court find that racial segregation in the schools is psychologically damaging to children and, therefore, unconstitutional. Your contributions also marked the first time the Supreme Court considered social science research in its deliberations, blazing the trail for future contributions and further social action. . . . (quoted by Judy A. Strassburger, personal communication, September 1, 1999)

Kenneth Clark's life has been one of scientific advocacy on racial issues, especially prejudice and discrimination (see Keppel, 1995; Phillips, 2000, for descriptions of that work). Although he has written several books that have contributed importantly to the debates on civil rights and to an understanding of the Black experience in America, he is clearly best known—as Richard Kluger (1975) has named him—as "the doll man" for his pivotal role in *Brown v. Board of Education.* It was the defining moment of his life. The elation of that moment in 1954 eventually gave way to despair over the lack of progress in the subsequent decades. Thirty years later, a year after the death of his wife, Clark (1986a), speaking at a conference reflecting on the fate of the *Brown* decision, said:

> Thirty years after *Brown,* I must accept the fact that my wife left this earth despondent at seeing that damage to children is being knowingly and silently accepted by a nation that claims to be democratic. Thirty years after *Brown,* I feel a sense of hopelessness, rather than optimism, because the underlying theme of *Plessy* and the explicit statements of *Dred Scott* persist. The majority of Americans still believe in and vote on the assumption that Blacks are not worthy of the respect, and the acceptance of their humanity, which our democracy provides to others. (p. 21)

It is a sad fact that the legal decisions on race set in motion by *Brown v. Board of Education* did not bring about the equality dreamed of by many ethnic minorities (see Keppel, 2002). Yet, as a scientist, Kenneth Clark did his part to advance toward that hoped-for equality. In doing so, he has enjoyed a moment that few people will ever experience—the knowledge that his and Mamie's psychological research and work with the NAACP helped to change the course of American history.

There has been much debate among historians and other scholars in the past 30 years regarding the legacy of the *Brown* decision in affecting racial equality in America. Some have argued that the desegregation of the 1950s and 1960s was already underway before the Court decision and would have progressed better without the bitterness and backlash aroused by the federal mandate (Klarman, 1994). Others have acknowledged that, although the Court was not able to legislate social change with the *Brown* decision, the clear legal declaration against segregated schools was the watershed event stimulating the eventual collapse of many forms of discrimination (Patterson, 2001). That the task has yet to be completed almost 50 years later is still "the sobering meaning of the hour" (Gallagher, 1954, p. 1).

References

Adams, G. (1931). *Psychology: Science or superstition?* New York: Covici, Friede.

Adams, G. (1934, January). The rise and fall of psychology. *Atlantic Monthly, 153,* 82–92.

Allport, G. W. (1954a, May 19). [Letter to Kenneth B. Clark]. Kenneth Bancroft Clark Papers, Library of Congress, Washington, DC.

Allport, G. W. (1954b). *The nature of prejudice.* Cambridge, MA: Addison-Wesley.

Amrine, M.(1954a, November 2). [Letter to Kenneth B. Clark]. Kenneth Bancroft Clark Papers, Library of Congress, Washington, DC.

Amrine, M. (1954b). Desegregation: An appraisal of the evidence [Press release from the American Psychological Association, April 4, 1954]. Stuart Cook Papers, Archives of the History of American Psychology, University of Akron, OH.

Appendix to appellants' briefs: (1975). The effects of segregation and the consequences of desegregation—A social science statement. In P. B. Kurland & G. Casper (Eds.), *Landmark briefs and arguments of the Supreme Court of the United States: Constitutional law* (Vol. 49, pp. 43–61). Arlington, VA: University Publications of America.

Bachrach, J. (1954, May 17). [Telegram to Kenneth B. Clark]. Kenneth Bancroft Clark Papers, Library of Congress, Washington, DC.

Bouthilet, L. (1954, June 2) [Letter to Kenneth B. Clark]. Kenneth Bancroft Clark Papers, Library of Congress, Washington, DC.

Briggs v. Elliott 98 F. Supp. 529 (E.D.S.C. 1951).

Brown v. Board of Education 347 U.S. 483 (1954).

Brown v. Board of Education 349 U.S. 294 (1955).

Butterfield, H. (1931). *The Whig interpretation of history.* London: Bell.

Capshew, J. H. (1999). *Psychologists on the march: Science, practice, and professional identity in America, 1929–1969.* New York: Cambridge University Press.

Clark, K. B. (n.d.). [Untitled manuscript]. Kenneth Bancroft Clark Papers, Library of Congress, Washington, DC.

Clark, K. B. (1950). *The effects of prejudice and discrimination on personality development (Midcentury White House Conference on Children and Youth).* Washington, DC: Federal Security Agency, Children's Bureau.

Clark, K. B. (1953). Desegregation: An appraisal of the evidence. *Journal of Social Issues, 9*(4), 1–77.

Clark, K. B. (1954a, November 16). [Letter to Michael Amrine]. Kenneth Bancroft Clark Papers, Library of Congress, Washington, DC.

Clark, K. B. (1954b, June 7). [Letter to Otto Klineberg]. Kenneth Bancroft Clark Papers, Library of Congress, Washington, DC.

Clark, K. B. (1963). *Prejudice and your child* (2nd ed.). Boston: Beacon Press.

Clark, K. B. (1965). *Dark ghetto: Dilemmas of social power.* New York: Harper & Row.

Clark, K. B. (1986a). A personal view of the background and developments since the *Brown* decision. In L. P. Miller (Ed.), *Brown plus thirty: Perspectives on desegregation* (pp. 18–21). New York: Metropolitan Center for Educational Research, Development, and Training, New York University.

Clark, K. B. (1986b). The social sciences and the courts. *Social Policy, 17,* 33–38.

Clark, K. B., & Clark, M. P. (1947) Racial identification and preference in Negro children. In T. N. Newcomb & E. L. Hartley (Eds.), *Readings in social psychology* (pp. 169–178). New York: Holt.

Clark, K. B., & Parsons, T. (Eds.). (1966). *The Negro American.* Boston: Houghton Mifflin.

Cook, S. W. (1957). Desegregation: A psychological analysis. *American Psychologist, 12,* 1–13.

Cook, S. W. (1979). Social science and school desegregation: "Did we mislead the Supreme Court?" *Personality and Social Psychology Bulletin, 5,* 420–437.

Cook, S. W. (1984). The 1954 social science statement and school desegregation: A reply to Gerard. *American Psychologist, 39,* 819–832.

Cook, S. W. (1986). Participation by social scientists in litigation regarding school desegregation: Past contributions and future opportunities. In L. P. Miller (Ed.), *Brown plus thirty: Perspectives on desegregation* (pp. 92–98). New York: Metropolitan Center for Educational Research, Development, and Training, New York University.

Coon, D. J. (1992). Testing the limits of sense and science: American experimental psychologists combat spiritualism, 1880–1920. *American Psychologist, 47,* 43–151.

Davis v. County School Board of Prince Edward County 103 F. Supp. 337 (E.D. Va. 1952).

Deutscher, M., & Chein, I. (1948). The psychological effects of enforced segregation: A survey of social science opinion. *Journal of Psychology, 26,* 259–287.

Estabrooks, G. H. (1936, April 10). [Letter to Isadore Krechevsky]. SPSSI Papers, Archives of the History of American Psychology, University of Akron, OH.

Gallagher, B. (1954, May 30). [Letter to Kenneth B. Clark]. Kenneth Bancroft Clark Papers, Library of Congress, Washington, DC.

Gerard, H. B. (1983). School desegregation: The social science role. *American Psychologist, 38,* 869–877.

Grossack, M. (1954). Some Negro perceptions of psychologists: An observation on psychology's public relations. *American Psychologist, 9,* 188–189.

Gundlach, R. H. (1940). The psychologists' understanding of social issues. *Psychological Bulletin, 37,* 613–620.

Guthrie, R. V. (1990). Mamie Phipps Clark: 1917–1983. In A. N. O'Connell & N. F. Russo (Eds.), *Women in psychology: A bio-bibliographic sourcebook* (pp. 66–74). New York: Greenwood Press.

Guthrie, R. V. (1998). *Even the rat was white: A historical view of psychology* (2nd ed.). Needham Heights, MA: Allyn & Bacon.

Harris, B. (1980). The FBI's files on APA and SPSSI: Description and implications. *American Psychologist, 35,* 1141–1144.

Hornstein, G. A. (1992). The return of the repressed: Psychology's problematic relations with psychoanalysis, 1909–1960. *American Psychologist, 47,* 254–263.

Hunter, W. S. (1952). Walter S. Hunter. In E. G. Boring, H. S. Langfeld, H. Werner, & R. M. Yerkes (Eds.), *A history of psychology in autobiography* (Vol. 4, pp. 163–187). Worcester, MA: Clark University Press.

Jackson, J. P., Jr. (1998). Creating a consensus: Psychologists, the Supreme Court, and school desegregation, 1952–1955. *Journal of Social Issues, 54*(1), 143–177.

Jackson, J. P., Jr. (2000a). Blind law and powerless science: The American Jewish Congress, the NAACP, and the scientific case against discrimination, 1945–1950. *Isis, 91,* 89–116.

Jackson, J. P., Jr. (2000b). The triumph of the segregationists? A historiographical inquiry into psychology and the *Brown* litigation. *History of Psychology, 3,* 239–261.

Keehn, J. D. (1955). The expressed social attitudes of leading psychologists. *American Psychologist, 10,* 208–210.

Keppel, B. (1995). *The work of democracy: Ralph Bunche, Kenneth B. Clark, Lorraine Hansberry, and the cultural politics of race.* Cambridge, MA: Harvard University Press.

Keppel, B. (2002). Kenneth B. Clark in the patterns of American culture. *American Psychologist, 57,* 29–37.

Klarman, M. (1994). How *Brown* changed race relations: The backlash thesis. *Journal of American History, 81,* 81–118.

Klineberg, O. (1935a). *Negro intelligence and selective migration.* New York: Columbia University Press.

Klineberg, O. (1935b). *Race differences.* New York: Harper & Row.

Klineberg, O. (1954, May 18). [Letter to Kenneth B. Clark]. Kenneth Bancroft Clark Papers, Library of Congress, Washington, DC.

Klineberg, O. (1986). SPSSI and race relations in the 1950s and after. *Journal of Social Issues, 42*(4), 53–59.

Kluger, R. 1975. *Simple justice: The history of Brown v. Board of Education and Black America's struggle for equality.* New York: Random House.

Lal, S. (2002). Giving children security: Mamie Phipps Clark and the racialization of child psychology. *American Psychologist, 57,* 20–28.

Lewis, A. C. J. (1954, May 27). [Letter to Kenneth B. Clark]. Kenneth Bancroft Clark Papers, Library of Congress, Washington, DC.

McCary, J. L. (1956). The psychologist as an expert witness in court. *American Psychologist, 11,* 8–13.

McGurk, F. C. J. (1956, September 21). A scientist's report on race differences. *U.S. News & World Report, 41,* 92–96.

Moley, R. (1956, June 4). Psychosocial law. *Newsweek, 47,* 104.

Morton, R. A. (1956, September 17). [Letter to the American Psychological Association]. Kenneth Bancroft Clark Papers, Library of Congress, Washington, DC.

Newby, I. A. (1969). *Challenge to the court: Social scientists and the defense of segregation, 1954–1966* (rev. ed.). Baton Rouge: Louisiana State University Press.

Nyman, L. (1976). *Recollections: An oral history of the Psychology Department of the City College of the City University of New York.* New York: Author.

Page the psychologists [Editorial]. (1934, January 1). *The New York Times,* p. 22.

Patterson, J. T. (2001). *Brown v. Board of Education: A civil rights milestone and its troubled legacy*. New York: Oxford University Press.

Perloff, R. (1955). Desegregation and psychology. *American Psychologist, 10,* 42–43.

Phillips, L. (2000). Recontextualizing Kenneth B. Clark: An Afrocentric perspective on the paradoxical legacy of a model psychologist–activist. *History of Psychology, 3,* 142–167.

Pickren, W. E., & Tomes, H. (2002). The legacy of Kenneth B. Clark to the APA: The Board of Social and Ethical Responsibility for Psychology. *American Psychologist, 57,* 51–59.

Plessy v. Ferguson 163 U.S. 537 (1896).

Psychological notes and news: Grants-in-aid for research on desegregation. (1955). *American Psychologist, 10,* 801.

Psychological notes and news: Society for the Psychological Study of Social Issues. (1955). *American Psychologist, 10,* 183.

Richards, G. (1997). *Race, racism, and psychology: Towards a reflexive history*. New York: Routledge.

Russell, R. W. (1956, September 19). [Letter to Stuart W. Cook]. Stuart Cook Papers, Archives of the History of American Psychology, University of Akron, OH.

Samelson, F. (1978). From "race psychology" to "studies in prejudice": Some observations of the thematic reversal in social psychology. *Journal of the History of the Behavioral Sciences, 14,* 265–278.

Sanford, F. H. (1952). Across the secretary's desk. *American Psychologist, 7,* 162–166.

Sanford, F. H. (1953a). Across the secretary's desk. *American Psychologist, 8,* 54–55.

Sanford, F. H. (1953b). Across the secretary's desk. *American Psychologist, 8,* 208–212.

Sanford, F. H. (1954a, May 13). [Letter to Kenneth B. Clark]. Kenneth Bancroft Clark Papers, Library of Congress, Washington, DC.

Sanford, F. H. (1954b). Summary report on the 1954 Annual Meeting. *American Psychologist, 9,* 708–718.

Sanford, F. H. (1955, March 15). [Letter to Kenneth B. Clark]. Kenneth Bancroft Clark Papers, Library of Congress, Washington, DC.

Sargent, S. S., & Harris, B. (1986). Academic freedom, civil liberties, and SPSSI. *Journal of Social Issues, 42*(1), 43–67.

Schofield, W. (1956). Psychology, law, and the expert witness in court. *American Psychologist, 11,* 1–7.

Sell, D. E. (1951). How far left is the APA going? *American Psychologist, 6,* 179.

Smith, M. B. (1979, September). *The social scientists' role in Brown v. Board of Education: A non-revisionist appraisal*. Paper presented at the 87th Annual Convention of the American Psychological Association, New York, NY.

Smith, M. B. (1992). The American Psychological Association and social responsibility. In R. B. Evans, V. S. Sexton, & T. C. Cadwallader (Eds.), *The American Psychological Association: A historical perspective* (pp. 327–345). Washington, DC: American Psychological Association.

Stagner, R. (1986). Reminiscences about the founding of SPSSI. *Journal of Social Issues, 42*(1), 35–42.

Stanovich, K. E. (2001). *How to think straight about psychology* (6th ed.). Needham Heights, MA: Allyn & Bacon.

Stolberg, B. (1930, October 15). Degradation of American psychology. *The Nation, 131,* 395–398.

Tucker, W. H. (1994). *The science and politics of racial research*. Urbana: University of Illinois Press.

Williams, J. (1998). *Thurgood Marshall: American revolutionary*. New York: Times Books.

Winston, A. S. (1998). Science in the service of the far right: Henry E. Garrett, the IAAEE, and the Liberty Lobby. *Journal of Social Issues, 54*(1), 179–210.

Wolfle, H. M. (1949). Across the secretary's desk. *American Psychologist, 4,* 116–117.

Author Index

Numbers in italics refer to listings in the references.

Subject Index

263

266   SUBJECT INDEX

About the Editor

Gina Philogène, PhD, is a professor of psychology at Sarah Lawrence College, Bronxville, New York, where she teaches social psychology. She has published widely in both the United States and Europe. Among her most recent works are *From Black to African American: A New Social Representation* (1999) and *Representations of the Social: Bridging Theoretical Traditions* (2001), which she coedited with Kay Deaux.